Ethnic-Minorities
and
Evangelical Christian Colleges

Editor
D. John Lee

Assistant Editors
Alvaro L. Nieves
Henry L. Allen

UNIVERSITY
PRESS OF
AMERICA

LANHAM · NEW YORK · LONDON

CHRISTIAN
COLLEGE
COALITION

Copyright © 1991 by
University Press of America®, Inc.
4720 Boston Way
Lanham, Maryland 20706

3 Henrietta Street
London WC2E 8LU England

Co-published by arrangement with
The Christian College Coalition

Library of Congress Cataloging-in-Publication Data

Ethnic-minorities and evangelical Christian colleges / editor, D.
John Lee ; assistant editors, Alvaro L. Nieves, Henry L. Allen.
p. cm.
Includes bibliographical references and index.
Contents: Ethnic-minorities and evangelical Christian colleges /
D. John Lee — Ethnic-minorities and Christian higher education/
Alvaro L. Nieves — Ethnic identity and multiculturalism / D.
John Lee and Roger R. Rice — Racial minorities and evangelical
colleges / Donald N. Larson — Evangelical tribalism at Christian
Colleges / Donald N. Larson — An assessment of Christian
commitment and attitudinal prejudice among adults in various
academic and church settings / Michael J. Boivin and Harold W.
Darling —Ethnic-minority facility in evangelical Christian
colleges / Tony M. Wong and Kenneth Polite —Educating for
equity / Carol A. Jenkins and Deborah Bainer —
Multiculturalizing the curricula at evangelical Christian colleges /
Abraham Davis, Jr. — Berea College / Andrew Baskin.
1. Church colleges—United States.
2. Minorities—Education (Higher)—United States.
I. Lee, D. John.   II. Nieves, Alvaro L.
III. Allen, Henry L. (Henry Lee), 1955- .
LC621.E87   1991
378.1'9829—dc20   90–29148 CIP

ISBN 0–8191–8184–6 (alk. paper)
ISBN 0–8191–8185–4 (pbk.: alk. paper)

 The paper used in this publication meets the minimum requirements of
American National Standard for Information Sciences—Permanence
of Paper for Printed Library Materials, ANSI Z39.48–1984.

To

the member colleges

of the

Christian College Coalition

Acknowledgments

I would like to thank the Christian College Coalition for their willingness to co-publish this book. I also owe the staff of Calvin College's Publishing Services my thanks for their role in preparing the manuscript for its publication. This book was made possible, in part, by the support of Calvin College's Department of Psychology and a Calvin College Research Fellowship.

The Editor

Table of Contents

Table of Contents

Foreword

The Christian church is probably the most ethnically diverse grouping on earth; very few ethnic groups are not represented in Christ's body. Yet of almost all those ethnic groups it is true that if a member of the group attended one of the colleges belonging to the Christian College Coalition, he or she would feel alien—and worse, would typically experience discrimination. Nonetheless, to belong to the Coalition a college must identify itself as actively Christian in its teaching and practice. What accounts for this anomaly? One is tempted to say, What accounts for this *paradox*?, except that the situation has become so familiar that it no longer has the "feel" of a paradox. If you are not a white of West European stock who speaks English fluently, the chances are very high that you will not feel at home in these colleges.

This book is devoted to analyzing and trying to understand this situation—and to proposing steps toward improvement. The colleges which are members of the Coalition, and the Coalition itself, are to be applauded for finally facing up to this issue. Historically the Coalition has concerned itself intensely with what is taught in the colleges, specifically, it has assisted the colleges in their endeavor to teach "in Christian perspective". But it has said and done little about the fact that all the talk about Christian perspective is seriously undercut if in fact the colleges function as exclusive ethnic clubs of Euro-Americans.

I expect that some, after reading this book, will leave with the resentful feeling that a "load of guilt" has been laid on them. To feel that way would be to miss the point, however. The book's intent is not to point accusing fingers at some bad or slothful individuals. The book's intent is to discover the *structures* which have led to the present situation. To understand the book, one has to acknowledge that the fallenness and brokenness of our world is not exhibited solely in fallen and broken individuals but also in fallen and broken institutions and social practices. The endeavors of individuals of good will working within fallen institutions may have painfully damaging consequences. To understand the book one needs a theology of corporate sin and guilt.

Correspondingly, the path to healing requires not just personal repentance but some sort of corporate ritual of confession of sin and repentance and reconciliation. These colleges have caused one hundred years of wounds and cries in American Blacks, in American Indians, in Hispanic Americans, in Asian Americans, etc. The colleges must come to see these wounds and hear these cries; and then to empathize with them, to feel them as their own. Once they do that—and that will not come easily—they must seek reconciliation. But there can be no authentic reconciliation without confession and repentance—and yes, without forgiveness. It is my impression that we do not at present have any such corporate rituals; we shall have to work at developing them. And by "we" here, I mean the colleges *and* the wounded ones, together.

I have applauded the Coalition and its members for supporting this unflattering study of themselves. Let me close by applauding the writers—for their scholarship, but even more for their courage. A good many of those who speak here are themselves among the wounded ones of whom I spoke. It takes courage for one wounded to stand up and speak to the powers that wounded him or her. This courage in speech calls for its answer in action. If this book is the end of the matter it will have been in vain. The end must be in changed action, shaped in the context of corporate confession and repentance and forgiveness and reconciliation.

Nicholas Wolterstorff
Yale University

Ethnic-Minorities and Evangelical Christian Colleges: Basic Issues

D. John Lee

As the editor of this volume, I would like to take the privilege of stating what I believe are the central issues being addressed in this book. In no way should the arguments or positions presented below be considered the consensus of the assistant editors or the contributing authors.

Ethnic-Minorities

I begin my class in cross-cultural psychology with the following quotation:

> In some ways you are like everyone else, in other ways you are like some, and in some ways you are like no other.
> (after Kluckholn & Murray, 1953)

One of the major challenges of the social sciences is to describe the universal, the group, and the individual dimensions of human behavior and experience. In the past, this task has been divided up into "disciplines", but more recently it has become obvious that we cannot speak about universality without using a group's language, and we cannot discern uniqueness without making comparisons to others.

Thus, social scientific endeavors are necessarily bound to a particular context. Social scientists are not transcendent gods. They are a part of a historical and cultural context reflected in the language and methodology they use to pursue their disciplines. Myself and the rest of the contributors to this book are both influenced and influence the contexts of which we are a part. Our contexts serve as our vehicles to convey our purposes and proposals.

The primary focus of this book is on groups within North American culture, and in particular, ethnic-minority groups and evangelical Christians. These groups, however, are not mutually exclusive and they do not have firmly defined boundaries. For example, there are evangelicals who explicity identify with their ethnicity (e.g. Chinese Christian Mission), and there are Christians who are uncomfortable with the "evangelical" label (e.g. Reformed and Mennonite). Of course, some people argue that ethnicity is not a useful way to talk about sub-groups in North America, and that economic class would be much more representative and fruitful. Similarly, some argue that North American culture has become so secularized that any discussion about religious groups, especially Christian, is largely irrelevant. I respect these positions, and in some situations, I find these arguments to be sound and worthwhile. Professor Rice and I (Chp. 4) will outline what words have been used to describe North American groups and address the question of whether or not the ethnicity concept is historically and empirically supported. In our situation and for our purposes, the "ethnic" and "religious" groupings have proven to be helpful.

The ethnic-minority groups which I have in mind are Asian-Americans and Pacific Islanders, African-Americans, Hispanic Americans, and American Indians. Sometimes these groups are referred to as North America's "visible" ethnics or "people of color". I recognize the variety of labels available (e.g. Black, Chicano, Native American, etc.) and that each one can be sub-divided into smaller distinct groups (e.g. Asian-Americans include Chinese, Japanese, Korean, etc.). However, the labels are secondary to what all these groups share in common. All of them have experienced, and continue to confront, discrimination in North America because of their distinguishing physical features. Despite the immense diversity between and among these visible ethnics, the racism which pervades North American society is sufficient rationale for considering these groups together.

Evangelical Christian Colleges

We had originally planned this book to contain contributions from a variety of Protestant and Catholic traditions. However, as we progressed it became obvious that we would not have any Catholic representation. We sincerely apologize for this vacuum. With the exception of Professor Baskin (Chp. 9), all of the contributors are teaching, or have taught, at colleges who are members of the Christian College Coalition (CCC). The CCC is an association of over 75 colleges and universities throughout Canada and the United States. The criteria for membership in the Coalition are as follows:

1. An institutional mission based upon the centrality of Jesus Christ and an institutional commitment to achieving that mission;
2. The biblically-centered faith being clearly integrated with the college's academic and student life programs;
3. An institutional hiring policy which requires a personal Christian commitment from each full-time faculty member and administrator;
4. Primary orientation as a four-year liberal arts college and accreditation as such by the appropriate United States or Canadian regional accrediting body;
5. Institutional fund-raising activities which are consistent with the spirit and intent of standards such as those set forth by the Evangelical Council For Financial Accountability (ECFA);
6. A commitment to advancing the cause of Christian higher education through active participation in the programs of the Coalition;
7. Operations and practices which have been, are and will continue to be cooperative with and supportive of the other colleges in the Coalition;
8. Indication of responsible financial operation appropriate to support the above criteria.

Probably the criterion which most sets Coalition colleges apart from other Christian institutions of higher education is the policy of only hiring people with a "personal Christian commitment". How this policy is defined varies across the different colleges, but it usually takes the form of faculty members assenting to some doctrines held by the college and/or affiliated church.

The formation of the Coalition in 1976 is evidence for the emergence of public "evangelicalism" during the 1960s and 70s (cf. Marsden, 1984). Evangelicalism, as a social movement, is one reaction to the crisis of authority in conventional Protestantism. Some have described it as post-fundamentalist in its doctrinal distinctives. That is, most evangelicals have a conservative impulse which attempts to establish some sense of stability through appeals to the Bible. However, most do not go as far to the right as Jerry Falwell (Liberty Baptist University) or Bob Jones. Many evangelicals display what Marsden called the "paradox of revivalist fundamentalism" where separatist strategies co-exist with attempts to get America to "go back to the Bible" (Marsden, 1980). Certainly, not all the Coalition colleges would call themselves "evangelical", and many would deny being "fundamentalist", but their membership criteria reveals a concern for posturing themselves against the "liberal" trends in North American culture.

A review of the member colleges reveals both similarity and diversity. The majority are located in rural areas, but there are a few in large cities. Most of the colleges are affiliated in some way with a relatively small North American Protestant denomination. The following list gives a sampling of the denominational affiliations represented: e.g. Assemblies of God, American Baptist, Baptist (General Conference), Brethren in Christ, Christian Reformed, Church of God (Anderson), Church of the Nazarene, Evangelical Covenant, Evangelical Free, Free Methodist, Friends, Mennonite, Presbyterian Church (USA), Reformed Church in America, Reformed Presbyterian, Southern Baptist, and Wesleyan. In Chapter 5 of this volume, Don Larson argues that it is useful to conceive of evangelicals as an ethnic group. One piece of evidence which supports this argument is that 17 of the Coalition colleges, the largest sub-group, describe themselves as inter or nondenominational. It is almost an American truism that as an ethnic group emerges in America it builds its own colleges.

As stated earlier, all but one of the contributors to this book have experience with the Coalition colleges. Several of us have worked in more than one. If someone were to combine the number of years we have worked in these institutions the total would be over 125! There is no doubt in my mind that we have something valid to say about the character of these colleges. Our contributions are analyses which take human diversity seriously. Not all of us are visible ethnics, but we all have found the ethnic and cultural metaphors helpful in understanding ourselves and the contexts in which we work.

Perhaps the most salient issue in this book is plurality. Plurality within North American culture in general, and the Christian church in particular. Ethnic and cultural diversity seems to have always introduced theological and practical challenges to Christians. However, before I outline my response to the issues surrounding diversity it is necessary to make my philosophical presuppositions explicit.

Reality, Experience, and Revelation

Although it is popularly believed that the sciences "explain" and "establish facts", it is my position that theories are descriptions or metaphors which organize experience in such a way to achieve some purpose(s). This posture makes a distinction between four things: (1) reality, (2) people's experience or perception of reality, (3) the words or symbols people use to describe and organize their experiences, and (4) the values or purposes people hold which give their lives meaning and direction. These distinctions are made for the purpose of argument. They should not be taken as independent concepts, but rather as a set of ideas locked together into a inseparable web. That is, people's access to reality is through their experience, their perceptions are influenced by their language and values, their language reflects their values and can sometimes constrain the possibilities that they recognize, and finally, reality sets the parameters for what can be experienced and sought after. Having made these concessions, I will use these distinctions to outline my presuppositions.

Theory

All theories, regardless of their focus, are descriptions of some person or persons' experience. As people experience the world they sometimes choose to describe and organize their perceptions. Some theories address sensations which are only possible through the mediation of some lens or machine (e.g. electron microscope). Other theories are very broad in their scope and attempt to address ultimate questions like the purpose of human diversity. But the breadth of a theory is not my concern here. The critical point is that theories, models, concepts, or words describe and organize experience, they *may or may not* be accurate representations of reality. For centuries, European and American philosophers have tried to discern what criteria could be applied to distinguish whether a theory accurately represented reality. Or, stated plainly, they have looked for a way to discern truth.

There are at least three ways I can compare or evaluate theories. I can evaluate a theory for its logical consistency. But, simply because a theory follows the rules of some logic does not mean it accurately depicts reality. I can compare two theories on how well they predict some phenomenon, like the weather for example. But, simply because a theory is more predictive than another does not mean that it is the best representation of reality. For example, describing light as a wave is predictive in some situations, but in other situations the particle theory predicts better. Finally, I can evaluate how well a theory helps me achieve some purpose. But again, simply because a theory is useful does not mean it depicts reality. Logical consistency, predictive validity, and usefulness are all legitimate criteria to evaluate a theory. But, they fall short in addressing the question of which theories *match reality*.

To discern whether or not a theory matches reality, I would have to have access to reality before my experience of that reality (cf. Von Glaserfeld, 1984). In order to have access to reality before experience, I would have to precede or transcend reality: i.e. be a creator or transcendent being. And, as ridiculous as this statement sounds, it must be made: I am not a transcendent being. Reality, my experience of reality, and the words I use to describe my experience do not necessarily correspond. The empiricist philosophers (Locke, Hume, etc.) *assumed* a correspondence and offered *prediction* as the criterion to judge when a match had been found. But again, a predictive theory does not necessarily imply a match with reality. A predictive theory is useful for making predictions, nothing more and nothing less.

Skepticism and Relativism

The epistemological posture I have described is a form of skepticism. Due to the lack of access to reality before their experience of reality, human beings cannot judge whether or not their descriptions of reality are accurate or true. The skeptic's position often falls into solipsism, or "the theory that nothing really exists except me and my mental states" (Bullock and Stallybrass, 1977). However, I affirm the presence of a "real world", but also affirm my limitation in being able to discern true descriptions of this real world. (It should come as no surprise that I frequently make use of philosophers who argue that our descriptions of the world are essentially symbolic or metaphorical in nature: for example, Stephen Pepper's root metaphor theory [1942]).

My posture also resists relativism, or the stance that truth is relative to person, place, and time. This stance would apply to both scientific or descriptive *and* moral or prescriptive truth. I believe in the existence of absolute and universal truth (in both senses of the word), but also admit that I cannot describe this truth in any final or ultimate sense. When I lecture on these topics it is at this point that many of my students become uncomfortable with what I am saying. They have been conditioned to react against relativistic statements, and rightfully so. The traditional Christian argument against relativism proceeds in the following fashion:

1. A personal God exists who created the world, and therefore has access to reality before experience.
2. God's transcendent nature enables them to discern which words match reality.
3. God, the creator, has chosen to reveal themselves to people, the created.
4. The Bible, or "God's word" is a collection of uniquely inspired texts which reveal absolute and universal truth. The biblical writers were not using their own words, but God's words. The Bible, therefore, contains descriptions of reality (scientific and moral) which are accurate and true.

I agree with the first three propositions of this argument. The fourth could be criticized as an oversimplified doctrine of "inspiration", but I can point to several examples where the Bible is approached and used in exactly the way I have described (e.g. prooftexting with little or no regard to context). My challenge to this view of the Bible is that it incorrectly assumes that the language in which its texts were written is transcendent of human experience. This view implicitly argues that biblical Hebrew and Greek do not have an individual, cultural, and historical context. I firmly disagree.

Incarnational Revelation: Words and The Word

It is my belief that God's revelation to persons is through the interpersonal. That is, the transcendent Creator in order to reveal themselves enters the realm of the created. This is clearly a mystery, but it is a reason-able proposition. A creator could conceivably participate in what they are creating since he fully understands what she is making. (My mixing of pronouns is deliberate. I wish to emphasize the role of metaphors in talking about the transcendent). I believe that Abraham did hear God's voice, that Moses had a conversation with God on Mt. Sinai, and that an angel actually did speak to Mary, the mother of Jesus. I also believe that God and their angels spoke to these people in words that they could understand. The Creator spoke in a language; but, not in a language which has it origin outside of creation. God, the Creator, spoke through a cultural form developed by and for people, the created.

"For the Law was given through Moses". It is commonly argued that God's moral truth was made explicit in what Jews and Christians refer to as the Law. It is not my intent here to enter a discussion about the Law itself, but rather to simply emphasize that it was written in words not transcendent of human experience. The Law, like any other text, was written in words. And these "Law-words", like all words, do not have a single or definitive meaning. The Law had to be interpreted and an entire tribe was given this as their task. And as the Hebrew language changed, as all languages do, translations had to be made. The point is this: I believe that moral truth exists, but it cannot be grasped in any absolute sense. God's revelation was through a cultural form which is both ambiguous and dynamic. Thus, understanding and applying the Law would be a process, not a single event

frozen in time. A community of people would be necessary to interpret revelation. For a person to claim absolute understanding is to also claim a position of transcendence or equality with God.

"The Word became flesh...". The apostle John's metaphor--JESUS IS THE LOGOS--is very appropriate at this point in my argument. During John's time, the Greek word "logos" was used in at least two ways. The first was the common or everyday usage denoting word, symbol, speech, or that which is used to express, convey, or embody a message; the metaphor of logos being a "vehicle" seems to apply here. Thus, as John equated Jesus with logos he was forcing his readers to consider how Jesus was a statement, an expression, a word from God, but also a word who was God. Jesus was both God and a revelation of God.[1]

The second usage of logos was more specialized, but also more abstract and ambiguous. Greek and Roman philosophers, starting with Heraclitus and then the Stoics, had built elaborate metaphysical theories which utilized the word logos. It will suffice to say here that the philosophical use of logos referred to the essential truth, nature, and ordering principle of the universe. For example, logos is sometimes translated as "reason", both as an attribute of persons and the essence of natural law. The apostle John, therefore, wanted to address some philosophies of his day when he spoke of Jesus as the logos. He would also refer to Jesus as the "truth" and "light" in an attempt to communicate to the Greek mind that this man Jesus was what they were looking for and had identified to some extent in their philosophies.[2]

I certainly cannot unravel the paradox of a God-person, creator-created, transcendent-present, or logos-flesh. And, most attempts to resolve this contradiction end up emphasizing one side of the duality over the other. As an argument proceeds, Jesus either appears to be more God or more human. For the purposes of my argument, I will be emphasizing the human Jesus, but this does *not* mean that I am denying or downplaying the God-Jesus. I fully believe and acknowledge the importance of the dual-nature of Jesus. Given this qualification, let us explore what I call the "ethnic Jesus".

Jesus was a person, not a ghost. He was like all people in some ways, in other ways like some, and in some ways like no other. His group identification or his sub-culture was Jewish, which can be described as an ethnic-religious group. And within this group he could be further distinguished as a Nazarene. Jesus was a Jew. He ate Jewish food, observed Jewish holidays, dressed like a Jew, and followed the Jewish Law. *This God-Jesus was ethnic.* God chose to reveal themselves in a fashion with which people could relate, conceptually and literally.

Jesus lived within an ethnically and religiously pluralistic Roman-controlled society. He was probably trilingual–most scholars agree that he at least spoke Hebrew, Aramaic, and Greek. Jesus spoke in languages that people could comprehend. He spoke in languages which were both the product and shapers of cultural and ethnic communities. He spoke in languages which were both ambiguous and dynamic. Thus, understanding Jesus' words would be a process, not a single event frozen in time. A community of people would be necessary to interpret Jesus and His words as recorded by the apostles. The Creator meets people where they are at, and all people are in a particular cultural and historical context which is constantly changing. This incarnational view of revelation significantly challenges the traditional understanding of how Christians relate to culture *and* cultural diversity.

Christ and Culture Revisited

Richard Niebuhr's typology (1951) summarizes the traditional understandings of how Christians can relate to culture. Table 1 presents the five strategies which Niebuhr saw Christians adopting as they interacted with their culture.

Table 1

Niebuhr's Christ and Culture Typology   (1951)

TYPE	EXAMPLE
1. Christ against culture	Amish
2. The Christ of culture	Liberalism
3. Christ above culture	Thomistic
4. Christ and culture in paradox	Lutheran
5. Christ the transformer of culture	Calvinist

The first type sanctifies the "Christian" context and views "culture" as pagan. The strategy of Christians in this case is non-interaction or minimal contact with culture. The second strategy assumes a continuity between Christ and culture, with the latter naturally progressing towards the ethic of the former. The third type argues that some aspects of culture reflect the transcendent Christ and others do not. The fourth assumes that Christ and culture are irreconcilable, and therefore the two must be held in tension. The last position calls Christians to actively be involved in the transformation of culture.

From my perspective, Niebuhr's typology is built upon a faulty distinction and some very questionable presuppositions. This model assumes that in some way "Christ" is a separate conceptual category or distinct way of life which is above or transcendent of all cultures. The typology assumes that "Christ" or Christian community exists independent of a cultural context.[3] Given this assumption, the issue becomes one of "interaction" between a transcendent Christ and present culture. Thus, he organizes his analysis around the various ways two separate entities could relate to one another. For example, two ethnic groups could either avoid one another, assume they are the same or opposites, or one group could judge itself as better and pressure the other to conform to some set of standards. That is, Niebuhr's analysis was directed by how he conceived the issue.

Incarnation and Contextualization

A shift in metaphor reframes the issue and thus its analysis. Instead of Christ and culture being a problem of "interaction", it is possible to conceive of the issue as "incarnation". Again, I believe that God's revelation and presence is through the interpersonal. And, all persons exist within a cultural and historical context, including Moses and Jesus. Thus, the Christian challenge with regards to culture can be described as *contextualization*[4], not interaction (cf. Costa, 1988). There are numerous definitions for this concept, but I define contextualization as *the processes of discerning and creating cultural and ethnic forms (e.g. concepts, metaphors, symbols, practices, etc.) which can be useful in communicating and realizing some set of values within a particular time and place.* These processes assume a stance which is in constant dialogue with ethnic and cultural forms. That is, people who contextualize must continually evaluate their own context.

Contextualization must also recognize the relative and dynamic nature of language and praxis. For example, the concepts, metaphors, and practices that I am currently using to move closer to shalom may not be very helpful fifty years from now (in fact, I expect them not to be!).

Contextualization across cultures. Translating the Christian scriptures from Hebrew and Greek into another language is a long process of culture-learning, of which language is only one part. And, once a translation has been penned, it must be continuously revised to match the dynamic nature of cultures and their languages. Revisions are not only necessary because of the changes occurring in the "target" culture but also because of the changes which occur in the translator's culture. Translators are not gods. They do not begin with an interpretation transcendent of their own historical and cultural context. And, although rarely discussed, translators will often take what they have learned in their work and make alterations to the translations they use themselves. That is, translation can be a two-way street. As translators attempt to influence the faith of another culture, their own faith can be influenced as well.

Another example of contextualization is the apostle Paul's use of the Greek altar with the inscription, "TO AN UNKNOWN GOD" (cf. Acts 17:16-34). Paul uses this Greek symbol of uncertainty as a platform to speak of God's incarnation in the person of Jesus Christ and how Christ can fit within the metaphysical and religious context of his audience. Most of the Athenians sneered at the resurrection but Luke tells us that "a few men became followers of Paul and believed". (Acts 17:34).

An example of how a cultural practice can be used to contextualize Jesus is supplied by Don and Carol Richardson's story of the "peace child" (Richardson, 1974). The Richardsons were missionaries to the Sawi people of Irian Jaya Indonesia. They had learned some basics of the tribal language and began telling the gospel story to the people. Much to the Richardson's surprise, the people laughed and cheered at the point of Judas' betrayal. Within the Sawi culture, deceit and trickery were valued attributes and thus Judas was the hero of the story instead of Jesus. After searching for another vehicle to contextualize the gospel, the Richardsons became aware of a practice which secured peace between waring tribes. If a tribe wanted to "sprinkle cool water" on an enemy or establish peace with them, a tribal leader had to give up one of his children. This "peace child" was to be adopted into the enemy tribe and raised as one of their own. The child was a symbol of peace, a living sign of reconciliation through sacrifice. This act would then be reciprocated by the enemy tribe who would offer a peace child of their own. The Richardsons drew an analogy between Jesus, as God's son, being a peace child to all people. This rendering of the gospel story became the vehicle for the Holy Spirit to work in the hearts and minds of the Sawi.

However, the Richardsons' understanding of the gospel was also influenced. The practice of giving up a child to establish peace between two groups of people was *not* part of the Richardson's culture. As they witnessed this sacrificial event, their understanding of the gospel was changed at least as much as those Sawi who later acknowledged Jesus for the first time. Contextualization is a triangular relationship between concrete lives and two abstractions. It is a trilogue between people, texts, and contexts. The Richardsons brought a text with their context to the Sawi and discovered that the meaning of their text did not transfer into the Sawi context. They stumbled upon a cultural practice which served as a more appropriate vehicle, and this "peace child" sacrament created an opportunity for a text which could alter the context and lives of both the Sawi and the Richardsons.

Contextualization among ethnics. Thus far, the examples I have given describe Christians entering other cultures or language communities. In North America there are a variety of sub-cultures or ethnic groups who share elements of a common culture. What does contextualization look like in this situation? Paraphrases like Clarence Jordan's *Cotton Patch Version of Luke and Acts* (1969) and Kenneth Taylor's *Living Bible* (1971) are steps towards contextualizations of American sub-cultures. However, it would be exciting to see translations which were courageous in the ethnic language forms and symbols they employed. For example, an urban African-American version of the scriptures is well-overdue and a Chicano or "Spanglish" version would be a timely response to the changing demographics. In light of the growing multi-lingualism, it is inevitable that North American Christian colleges and seminaries will confront their reliance on English as the language of instruction and translation.

The diversity of worship styles in Protestant churches is unknown to many, but it is my impression that even the most traditional churches are loosening up what they consider acceptable expressions of praise. The use of dance, drama, poetry, and storytelling in their various ethnic styles are excellent ways to contextualize and create opportunities for fresh insights or revelations. It is my hope that a variety of liturgical forms will characterize the next generation of evangelicals.

For most Euro-American ethnic groups, Christianity is woven into the fabric of their ethnicity. However, Jesus is hard to find in these groups. Traditionalism, the dead faith of the living has replaced tradition, the living faith of the dead. The challenges of contextualization for Euro-American Christians is recognizing their context (cf. Wells, 1984) and finding fresh metaphors to represent the gospel. A perusal through an evangelical Christian book store will discover a variety of "psychotheologies" or attempts to understand and give direction to the Christian life through the use of psychological concepts and metaphors. This strategy seems to work best with the educated middle-class who can relate to verbal abstractions. Psychotheologies do not adequately represent corporate sin and the need for forgiveness and reconciliation between groups as well as individuals. After 15 years of studying psychology, I am aware of both the power and limitations of using psychological terms to contextualize Christ (cf. Lee, 1985).

Unfortunately, the contexts of most visible ethnic groups in North America are colored by oppression and injustice. For these groups, contextualizing Christ is a major challenge since Christianity was (and continues to be) used to sanction the slavery or slave-like labor, racism, and segregation. Williams (1988) points out that the context of slavery was hostile and sought to destroy the cultures and faiths of the African-Americans. In the face of almost insurmountable odds, they created a worldview which took some elements of their former cultures and wed them with "the secular and sacred symbol systems extant in their new land" (p. 131). In essence, African-Americans held other Americans accountable. They appealed to the nation's creed and its Christianity for equity and justice.

During the 1800s, people like T.G. Steward, a clergyman of the African Methodist Episcopal (AME) Church, envisioned an authentic Christianity which was "raceless, classless, and weaponless". Despite their participation in a civil war, nonviolent approaches to change were advocated by African-Americans as early as 1837 (even before

Ghandi!). Christ was realized in a way that not only offered hope but a means to move towards justice. A critical step for this contextualization was the establishment of independent congregations and denominations. The necessity of these institutions revealed the corruption within the Euro-American churches, but the AME and others provided room for African-American Christians to develop their own theologies and forms of worship. So, well before the 1960s, the seeds of a movement had been planted and were waiting for the right conditions to germinate. It was no surprise that the leaders and spokespersons for the U.S. Civil Rights movement came out of African-American churches. Martin Luther King Jr. and Jesse Jackson are two of the most salient examples. Today, the African-American church continues to strive towards equity and justice.[5] The legislation during the last 25 years has helped the situation immensely but laws do not change people's hearts. Racism, discrimination, and segregation are still running rampant across North America.

Costas (1988) argues that Hispanic churches have offered a place of survival and hope to their peoples. He describes three dimensions of survival which the parish can offer. The Hispanic church is a place where people can find personal meaning, it is a place where their language can stay alive, and it is a place where the poor can experience solidarity. Nevertheless, Costas criticizes Hispanic churches for truncating the gospel by "interiorizing" their Christian experience. He contends that they lack a theology which empowers them to confront the individuals and institutions which oppress them. They have contextualized the peace and hope of Jesus but have not discerned or created the forms (abstract and concrete) to realize Christ's justice. To support his argument, Costas tells the story of Piri Thomas (1978; 1982), an ex-offender, dope addict, and thief who turned to Christ and began a youth ministry in his New York city barrio. As Piri's ministry grew, so did his social consciousness and disillusionment with the institutional church. A church in the barrio can be an ethnic-religious oasis, but it will dry up if it does not confront structural oppression. Costas concludes:

> What the Hispanic church needs (and for that matter all minority churches) is nothing short of an ecclesiology of liberation. The Hispanic church needs to develop a vision

of itself and its mission beyond survival and hope. Indeed, it needs an ecclesiology which will free it from introversion, other-worldliness, and churchism, free it for mission, incarnation, and the kingdom of God. This is the enormous task that lies before the emerging generation of Hispanic pastors and theologians. (p. 144)

The Chinese churches in North America continue to wrestle with the inter-generational conflicts often referred to as the "ABC" (American-Born Chinese) and "OBC" (Overseas-Born Chinese) division (cf. Yew, 1986). I think Wong (1986) was correct when he warned the ABCs not to fall into the same provincialism or ethnocentrism that they rebel against in the OBCs. He urged them to "maintain the linkage between the drive toward contextualization as a church and its subsequent readiness for reaching the lost" (p. 170). Wong's sense of calling is to evangelize ABCs and I share this vision. But, I am quick to add that sharing the love of Jesus should not (cannot?) be separated from sharing the justice of Jesus. Saving souls must also involve changing lives. We need to offer alternatives to our materialistic and individualistic lives which rapes the environment and starves the majority of the world's population. It is time for non-conformity. We are response-able and it is time to develop alternative life standards which steward the earth and love others as Jesus loved us.

It is obvious to me that all Christians need to contextualize Jesus in a way which empowers us to confront corporate evil. We need metaphors which will re-present the cross of Jesus in its fullness. We need symbols which will re-mind us of who we are in Christ. We need rituals which will ignite our corporate consciousness. We need sacraments to re-member us when we sin against one another. Those of us who live in North America must listen carefully to our brothers and sisters in rest of the world. The hermeneutical methods of the base Christian communities throughout the Two Thirds World (e.g. Cardenal, 1976; Ferm, 1986) ought to be tried among the North American poor and illiterate *as well as* the educated middle class. The recent events in South Africa and Eastern Europe are an indication of what is happening globally–the oppressed are refusing to bow down. Christians must seize the opportunities to demonstrate the nonviolence and reconciliative strategies made possible by the death and resurrection of Jesus Christ. Reeves (1988) summarizes my sentiments well:

> Although it is true that God is love and that God loves all human beings, this divine love does not compromise divine justice. Justice is the result of divine love even as divine love compels just action. True love of God results in obedience (I John 4:8), sowing the seed that enables us to love others. This love then finds its expression in seeking justice for and behaving justly toward one another. This synthesis of God's justice, tempered with mercy and love, finds it ultimate expression on the cross--mercy, because God recognized humankind's inability to pay the penalty for sin; justice, because the price had to be paid, if not by the sinner then by another; and love because God sent the Son, Jesus Christ, to pay the price for our sins. Through him all people gained access to divine adoption and eternal life.
>
> The primary task of the church is missions, the making of disciples for Jesus Christ. Even today, the major obstacle of this commission has been the culture not of the disciple but the discipler. Contextualization must emphasize the inner struggle of the discipler to recognize cultural limitations in understanding and communicating the gospel. In addition, this process must acknowledge that cultures differ in their concepts of God and life, requiring other forms of expression and understanding. Through the Holy Spirit we are given the ability to be ministers to the nations--"becoming all things to all people." (p. 158-159)

Discerning Truth. At the heart of contextualization is the issue of discerning Jesus. How does a Bible translator know when a cultural metaphor points to the Truth? How did the apostles know which concepts to use to communicate Jesus? How did the Richardsons know that the "peace child" sacrament would convey the Truth? How do the base Christian communities know when Jesus is present? How will North American ethnic groups recognize the Truth as they begin to dialogue and enter relationships with one another? How will Christians discern incarnation? How will Christians discern which ethnic and cultural practices are consistent with the Truth? These questions are purposely phrased to emphasize that the task is to discern the presence of a person, *not* to discern the truth of a statement. Instead of equating Jesus with the Truth, there is a strong tendency to treat Jesus as a universal truth claim. Instead of equating Jesus with the Logos, it is easier to treat Jesus as a Christology. The gospel writers (John, in particular) employed several different metaphors when they spoke of Jesus. Perhaps they intended to thwart attempts to build conceptual idols and frustrate the tendency to worship words rather than the Word.

I believe Jesus Christ to be the Truth and Justice of God. Describing Jesus Christ, like describing any other person, demands the use of words and metaphors which only re-present and are not identical to the person. Most Christian scholars using the contextualization metaphor continue to treat Jesus as if he was an idea or concept. They fully recognize that the essence of Christianity must be distinguished from social, cultural, linguistic, and historical contexts, but they fall into the circle of hermeneutics by trying to describe this context-invariant "core". It is revealing that analogies are used when this dichotomy is presented. Some have spoken in agricultural metaphors like "seed and soil" or "kernel and husk". Kraft (1979) and I have used the anthropological terms of "content and form". Schreiter (1985) speaks of "gospel and cultural accoutrements" and the apostle Paul used the imagery of "treasure and earthen vessel". I fully agree with the distinction being made, but I resist the belief that the core, seed, gospel, or Jesus can be captured with words.

If Jesus is treated as a concept, then discerning Jesus becomes a conceptual task. And, the most likely group of people to do this task are the "logy" or word experts: historians, sociologists, anthropologists, psychologists, and those involved in comparative religious studies. One of these experts has suggested that the core can be discerned if more than one context converges on a text (cf. Lewis in Stackhouse, 1988). This is similar to the "converging operations" approach of the sciences which grants an abstraction validity if several empirical predictions are confirmed. However, an intercontextual view does not necessarily imply a transcontextual perspective. An intercontextual text is simply the product of another context. As Stackhouse (1988) points out the "here" and "now" of a context do not have clear boundaries. What defines a context?: regionality, nationality, cultural-linguistic history, ethnicity, political system, economic class, gender identity, social status or what?

When starting from the premise that Jesus is a concept, analyses end up with one of two possible conclusions. The first has been referred to as "Feuerbachian step". Stackhouse (1988) describes this nicely:

> "Feuerbach argued in 1841 that the 'essence of Christianity', and indeed of all religions, is a projection of context-derived interests, needs, hopes and dreams onto a cosmic screen... there is no identifiable core, kernel, text, essence, treasure, or gospel other than what specific groups project on the world as a reflection of their own context" (p. 7)

Feuerbach's conclusion is blatant skepticism and cannot avoid moral relativism. The second conclusion is not so much a resolution as it is a prescription. Even after admitting that all texts have a context, Stackhouse (1988) says "we must learn how to listen to contexts discerningly" but offers no criteria with which to do the task. Skepticism or hopeful prescriptions are the logical conclusions to approaching the Christ as a word.

My position does not mean that Jesus cannot be discerned.

Matthew and Luke both tell the story about John the Baptist who, in hearing about the activities of Jesus, sends two of his disciples to ask this miracle worker, "Are you the one who was to come, or should we expect someone else?". Luke's record of Jesus's response is worth quoting:

> At that very time Jesus cured many who had diseases, sicknesses and evil spirits, and gave sight to many who were blind. So he replied to the messengers, "Go back and report to John what you have seen and heard: The blind receive sight, and lame walk, those who have leprosy are cured, the deaf hear, the dead are raised, and the good news is preached to the poor. Blessed is the man who does not fall

away on account of me. (Luke 7:21-23, New International
Version [NIV])

John Perkins, of Voice of Calvary Ministries, framed this piece of the
gospel story as a passage which provides the criteria that Jesus suggested that people should use to evaluate His authenticity. Perkins argued that these things used to discern whether or not Jesus was the
Messiah, is the same criteria people should use today to discern
whether or not Christians are living in relationship to Jesus. I agree
with him. The authenticity of the Christian church can be evaluated
by what is happening or what the members are doing. Too often in
North America we define and measure faith by what people say, rather
than what they do. The apostle John was probably one of the first to
make this argument. I quote from his first epistle:

> This is how we know we are in him: Whoever claims to
> live in him must walk as Jesus did... Dear children, let us
> not love with words or tongue but with actions and in
> truth. (I John 2:5b-6; 3:18, NIV)

In my final analysis, Christianity is fundamentally relational, not
conceptual. The primary challenge for a Christ-follower is not discerning truth-statements or truth-words (which I have argued cannot be discerned), but living in relationship with the Truth-Person or
the Logos who became flesh, Jesus Christ. Being in the Truth is being
in relationship to Jesus. Therefore, the most important criteria for
evaluating theories, interpretations, translations, metaphors, symbols,
practices, etc. are their relational consequences. Al Dueck (1989) best
summarizes this posture:

> Ultimately the test of adequacy of a language is its effect on
> the quality of life for an individual or the human com-
> munity. A language system that inspires greater acts of
> justice, kindness, liberation, joy and forgiveness is a useful
> language or theory. Note that the criteria are derived from
> a point other than the language itself. In Athens the usual
> test of a language is its correspondence to physical reality.
> When there is an acceptable level of correspondence we say

the theory is true. The Hebrews tended to test the truth of a statement by its ability to inspire truthful actions. (p. 12)

Dueck's contrast of Greek and Hebrew understandings of truth supports my distinction between words and the Word. It is not unusual among evangelicals to find people teaching and preaching the truth, but not living in relationship to the Truth. We spend hours writing, reading, and discussing doctrine, but minutes learning how to love one another. We evangelicals should consider saving our "theology for the night" after we have spent the day learning how to be a neighbor. If we really take the incarnation of Jesus seriously, then knowing the Truth is relating to Jesus.

Relating to Truth. One guide for living in relationship with Jesus was defined or operationalized in Matthew's gospel. I quote:

> Then the King will say to those on his right, "Come, you who are blessed by my Father; take your inheritance, the kingdom prepared for you since the creation of the world. For I was hungry and you gave me something to eat, I was thirsty and you gave me something to drink, I was a stranger and you invited me in, I needed clothes and you clothed me, I was sick and you looked after me, I was in prison and you came to visit me".
>
> Then the righteous will answer him, "Lord, when did we see you hungry and feed you, or thirsty and give you something to drink? When did we see you a stranger and invite you in, or needing clothes and clothe you? When did we see you sick or in prison and go to visit you?"
>
> The King will reply "I tell you the truth, whatever you did for one of the least of these brothers of mine, you did for me." (Matthew 25:34-40, NIV)

Living in relationship with Jesus is living in relationship with the poor and needy (cf. Vanier, 1988). It is important to point out the plural nature of these processes. Healing, the preaching of the gospel, the responding to human need, love or *agape* are all acts of community, not of a single individual. Justice, liberation, and forgiveness are terms which only make sense if you are talking about more than one person; they are relational processes between individuals and/or groups.

Living in relationship with Jesus is living in relationship with Christians. The apostle Paul commonly referred to Christians as being the "body of Christ" (e.g. I Corinthians 12). This metaphor suggests that even after Christ's ascension, His presence or incarnation would continue, but in a different form. Matthew quotes Christ as saying "Where two or three are gathered together in My name, there am I in the midst of them" (Matthew 18:20, King James Version). John records a prayer of Jesus which points to a unity between God, Himself, and "those who believe in me through their message":

> ...that all of them may be one, Father, just as you are in me and I am in you. May they also be in us so that the world may believe that you have sent me. I have given them the glory that you gave me, that they may be one as we are one. I in them and you in me. May they be brought to complete unity to let the world know that you sent me and have loved them even as you have loved me. (John 17:21-23, NIV)

It is conceivable that these metaphors imply that Christ is in some way present or incarnate within a community of Christians, or more specifically within their relationships. This idea lies beneath "relational theology" which is characterized by an emphasis on people's relationships rather than on their beliefs or doctrines (cf. Larson, 1971). The role of beliefs and doctrines is to point people to relationships, particularly to a relationship with Jesus. That is, beliefs, doctrines, or words should not play the role of defining or authenticating truth; they can point to the Truth. There is an old Chinese proverb that captures this notion: "Don't mistake the moon for your finger pointing to it".

Summary. The presuppositions that I outlined earlier set the parameters of human experience and the role of theories and words. An incarnational view of revelation challenges the traditional understandings of how Christians relate to their culture. Niebuhr's typology sets up a false dichotomy between Christians and culture, failing to recognize that it is impossible to speak of the Law, Jesus, and Christians as if they were transcendent of a historical and cultural context. The metaphor of contextualization provides a way to conceptualize how Christians participate in the dynamic nature of language and culture, of God's creation.[6] This metaphor also provides a way to understand how the created can live *with* God's creative process rather than trying to define it.[7] From this set of presuppositions and arguments, cultural and ethnic diversity plays a critical role in God's continuing revelation to their creation. The next section reviews the argument against and for ethnic and cultural diversity within the Christian church.

Plurality

Arguments Against Diversity
It is my impression that the majority of evangelical Christians in North America do not value human diversity. There are at three arguments against valuing ethnic and cultural diversity that I commonly hear in churches and at Christian colleges. The first argues that differences between people should be ignored since we are all equal or "one in Christ".[8] The second interprets cultural diversity as a punishment from God, using the story of Babel for its support. And, the third equates diversification with compromise, or in the case of colleges, with the lowering of academic standards. There is a fourth stance against diversity which I will call "Christian segregation". This posture will admit that the Christian church should be culturally and ethnically diverse, but for one reason or another it is argued that any interaction between the groups should be minimal.

Equal means the same. It is a common mistake, particularly in the United States, to interpret the assertion that "we are all equal" to imply that we are all the *same*, or should be the same. But, it is one thing to say that everyone should be treated equally before the law. It is another thing to say that everyone should behave the same or share the same values and characteristics. To say the latter is to be "ethnocentric". *Being ethnic is doing what comes naturally, while being ethnocentric is believing that what you do naturally is Nature's or God's way.* Living with the belief that "equal" means the "same" assumes that one's own way of life is the best and should be the norm by which all others are judged.

Equating equality with sameness fails to recognize that people and groups of people differ from each other. Failing to recognize human differences results in defining "the same" as "like me". Treating everyone the same sounds laudable, but whenever I hear this slogan, I ask the question, "Whose definition of the 'same' are you using?". The group with the most power usually sets the standards, they define who is "equal", they define who is being "the same". The consequences of such a ploy are subtle. If someone emphasizes differences, he can be accused of pointing out how people are inferior and/or challenging the ideal of equality. If someone does not comply with the norms (what is considered "normal"), she can be accused of elitism or undermining an important premise of the American constitution (which originally had "free men" in mind and not women, slaves, or Indians when referring to all men as being equal). Maintaining the myth of "equal being the same" maintains a particular standard, discourages deviance, and refuses to consider the value and benefits of diversity.

Many evangelical Christians make a similar mistake when they equate being "one in Christ" to mean that we are all the same or should be the same. The support that is given for this posture is a quote from the apostle Paul: "There is neither Jew nor Greek, slave nor free, male nor female, for you are all one in Christ Jesus" (Galatians 3:28, NIV). Paul was addressing the divisions which often occurred within a body of believers, but he was not recommending that they deny or ignore their differences. Paul's willingness to adjust to ethnic norms in order to maintain peace among Christian Jews and Greeks (e.g. Acts 21:17-26 and I Corinthians 8-9) supports my interpretation. It is one thing to say that one's gender, ethnicity, or socio-political-economic position are not criteria for membership in Christ's body. It is quite another thing to say that every Christian should worship, serve, and love Christ in exactly the same way. To say the latter is ethnocentric and reflects a judgment which the apostles reserved for Christ, and Christ alone. Sanneh (1988) gives her interpretation of Paul's stance on culture:

Paul could with justice be seen as a cultural iconoclast in
his defiance of the absolutist tendencies in culture (i.e. he
challenged ethnocentrism--*mine*), but he cannot be regarded as a cultural cynic, for in his view God's purposes
are mediated (incarnated--*mine*) through particular cultural streams. (p. 26-27)

The Babel story. I grew up in a neighborhood where five different
languages were regularly spoken: English, French, Italian, Chinese,
and Japanese. After a day of English and French in the public schools,
many of us visible ethnics would attend our own language schools. It
was generally thought that we multi-linguals would suffer from cognitive confusion and not do as well as our monolingual colleagues in
school. Most of the research has suggested otherwise (cf. Lambert, 1977),
and indeed with our linguistic and cultural sensitivities, I would argue we were better prepared for the global village we now live in. My
positive view of linguistic plurality is not shared by some evangelical
Christians. These people interpret the multitude of languages (and by
extrapolation, ethnic and cultural diversity) among humanity to be
part of God's punishment for our ancestors' attempt to declare independence from their Creator. This, however, is only one possible interpretation of a very ambiguous story in the first book of the Bible.
The story of Babel occurs in Genesis in between the lineage of Noah
(Genesis 10) and Shem (Genesis 11:10-52). It is critical to point out that
ethnic plurality existed *before* the Babel story and immediately following it Yahweh selects an ethnic group to bless all the peoples of the
earth. I quote from the New International Version:

...These are the clans of Noah's sons, according to their
lines of descent, within their nations. From these the
nations spread out over the earth after the flood.

Now the whole world had one language and a common
speech. As people moved eastward, they found a plain in
Shinar and settled there.
They said to each other, "Come let's make bricks and bake
them thoroughly." They used brick instead of stone, and
tar instead of mortar. Then they said "Come, let us build

ourselves a city, with a tower that reaches to the heavens, so that we may make a name for ourselves and not be scattered over the face of the whole earth."

But the Lord came down to see the city and the tower the people were building. The Lord said, "If as one people speaking the same language they have begun to do this, then nothing they plan to do will be impossible for them. Come let us go down and confuse their language so they will not understand each other."

So the Lord scattered them from there over all the earth, and they stopped building the city. That is why it was called Babel–because there the Lord confused the language of the whole world. From there the Lord scattered them over the face of the whole earth.

The Lord had said to Abram, "Leave your country, your people and your father's household and go to the land I will show you. I will make you into a great nation and I will bless you; I will make your name great, and you will be a blessing. I will bless those who bless you, and whoever curses you I will curse; and all peoples on earth will be blessed through you." (Genesis 10:32-11:9; 12:1-3)

The Babel story contains what Anderson (1977) calls "a peculiar dialectic–Man strives to maintain unity, God's action effects diversity. Man seeks for a center, God counters with dispersion" (p.64). Anderson argues that the Babel story, instead of challenging, actually supports a theology of pluralism. His interpretation proceeds in two steps. The first considers the story itself and the second tries to place it within its context of the first eleven chapters of Genesis.

By itself, Anderson considers the Babel story to be "a masterpiece of narrative art". The story proceeds with a group of people settling down on a plain, developing a technology, and in an effort to make a name for themselves and perserve their language unity, begin building a tower. Yahweh's response to this is to come down and confuse the people's language, stop the building, and scatter them. The conclusion of the story is an ironic twist. Those who wanted to make a name for themselves received a memorial, but it was a comic name. In

Akkadian, a Babylonian language, Babel meant "gate of the god(s)" and referred to the temple center where heaven and earth met and where human beings could experience contact with the Divine. However, by a Hebrew word-play, Babel is to be understood as "confusion"--the Hebrew word for confuse or confound is *balal.*

The ambiguity of this story is around the motivations of the people and Yahweh. Were the people trying to storm the heavens and be like God? If this was their intent, Babel becomes an extension of the Fall story where the created are cast out from the garden for wanting to be like the Creator. The support for this reading is the statement by Yahweh that they see monolingualism as the prerequisite for omnipotence. Or, were the people gathering together into a central location using a tower to symbolize their unity, thus resisting God's dictum that they should multiply, fill the earth, and subdue it? From this latter perspective, the Babel story speaks to a tendency of humanity to work towards unity through its own devices and God's insistence that diversity remain the norm.

Anderson and I favor this second interpretation. We offer two observations as our support. First, there are the reoccurring themes of the people wanting a "name" and the fear of being "scattered". These themes can be viewed as representing a two-sided metaphor for human nature. On the one hand, people seek recognition or to make a name for themselves, but on the other hand they fear alienation, a loss of community, or being scattered. These two tendencies are expressed as the people attempt to establish fame and unity on their own terms. With this framework, an alternative reading of Yahweh's comment is possible. Instead of the Creator fearing omnipotence from the created, God recognizes the consequence of a human community without diversity, linguistic or otherwise. The consequence is not omnipotence but a community which cannot recognize its own limitations. Diversity invites a community to accept its created-ness. *Diversity challenges a community to evaluate its idols,* which in most cases, are artifacts of the community--things, practices, and concepts which they have created.

The second piece of evidence for our interpretation is the literary context in which the Babel story is found. The story comes immediately after what has been called the Table of Nations. This table is a listing of Noah's progeny, and it strongly suggests that this family had proliferated into a multitude of ethnic groups. Yet, the story of Babel begins with the assertion that the "whole world had one language and a common speech". How can this dissonance be resolved?

Anderson (1977) describes how Genesis 1-11 can be seen as a collection of epic stories and genealogies which run parallel to one another. If these chapters are read with a linear time frame there are several points of conflict. But, there is less tension if they are seen as a collection of parallel literary genre. Such an organization finds the Babel story existing as a narrative (vs. expository) footnote. Perhaps it provides an etiology of the ethnic pluralism which is found among Noah's descendents. That is, Babel does not occur after Noah's sons spread out over the earth, but offers a reason why the spreading occurred. In three different places *before* the Babel story the "scattering" motif is given (9:18-19, 10:18, and 10:32) which also supports our interpretation that ethnic diversity is to be seen as a divine blessing, not a condemnation. Anderson (1977) summarizes well:

> Viewed in this light, the Babel story has profound significance for a biblical theology of pluralism. First of all, God's will for his creation is diversity rather than homogeneity. Ethnic pluralism is to be welcomed as a divine blessing, just as we should rejoice in the rich variety of the non-human creation: trees, plants, birds, fish, animals, heavenly bodies. The whole creation bears witness to the extravagant generosity of the Creator. But something more must be added, and this the redactor has done by supplementing his work with the old epic story of the building of Babel. Human beings strive for unity and fear diversity. They want to be securely settled and are fearful of insecurity. Perhaps they do not pit themselves against God in Promethean defiance, at least consciously; but even in their secularity they are driven, like the builders of Babel, by a creative desire for material glory and fame and a corresponding fear of becoming restless, rootless wanderers. (p. 68-69)

It is revealing to note that the next story after Babel is Abram's. This story depicts a god that selects a particular people, a specific ethnic group, through whom all people will be blessed. Gregory Baum (1977) describes the balance between diversity and unity seen in the Bible:

> ... the Bible offers the powerful double message that God is at one and the same time the lover of humanity and the lover of a particular people. The Bible affirms both universality and particularity. God is inseparably the creator of pluriformity and the author of unity. This double message of the Bible reminds the church of that aspect of social life that is being forgotten or suppressed in the world to which it belongs. At times when a single race, people or tribe affirms itself as superior to others and adopts an aggressive stance toward humanity (we all remember such cases in recent history) the biblical message summon Christians to defend the unity of humankind as a family of brothers and sisters, but at times when particular races, peoples, or ethnic groups discover themselves as oppressed, the same scriptures call the church to a new appreciation of pluriformity and the defense of particular traditions. (p. 100-101)

Babel is often placed in juxtaposition to Pentecost, but maybe for the wrong reasons. It is appropriate to provide the Pentecost text to make the contrast:

> ... All of them were filled with the Holy Spirit and began to speak in other tongues as the Spirit enabled them. Now there were staying in Jerusalem God-fearing Jews from every nation under heaven. When they heard this sound, a crowd came together in bewilderment, because each one heard them speaking in his own language. Utterly amazed, they asked: "Are not all these men who are speaking Galileans? Then how is it that each of us hears them in his own native language?" (Acts 2:4-8, NIV)

I think the comparison is important, but I don't believe the contrast is between fall and redemption as it is usually presented in evangelical circles. Pentecost does not restore the linguistic unity that existed at

Babel before God came down and confused the language. Pentecost reveals the unity and solidarity that people can experience in the presence of the Holy Spirit. The yearning for security and oneness is not an evil human attribute. Living together in the same place, sharing a technology, and speaking the same language are human attempts to secure common-unity. The presence of the Holy Spirit is God's means of unification and God's presence does not imply the destruction of ethnic and cultural diversity.

Diversification is compromise. Some people perceive openness to diversity as being equivalent to compromising their standards. The implicit assumption is that in order to relate to people who are different from you, you must lower your moral or academic ideals. It is further assumed that in entering a relationship with a group with whom you have disagreements with, that you are endorsing their beliefs or behavior simply by relating to them. Both of these assumptions are based on the false belief that "being in relationship" means "being the same". In essence, people who adopt this stance are requiring that others conform to their standards before any relationships are initiated. They are saying, "You must be like me, before I will relate to you". Differences, of any type, are not valued but perceived as a threat to a particular way of life. This posture is another example of ethnocentrism where one group's way of life is judged to be superior to all others. Christians are called to a way of life but they are also warned to not sit in judgment of others.

The fear of lowering academic standards when admitting and educating ethnic-minority students stems from racist and discriminatory attitudes. For example, if I mark a student's paper less rigorously because they have dark skin, I am guilty of racial discrimination; which is differential treatment based solely on people's physical appearance. If a student, regardless of their skin color, needs remedial training, then it is my responsibility as a educator to see that he or she gets this assistance.

It is also a college's responsibility to periodically review its standards for hidden ethnocentric or racist assumptions. For example, it is not unusual to find a language requirement which can only be fulfilled by taking courses in an European language. I have spoken to several Asian-American students who were competent in their Asian language but were still required to take two years of a European language in order to graduate. In my own particular discipline, Rumpel (1988) has reviewed the contents of 35 contemporary introductory psychology textbooks and found that very little attention was given to cross-cultural and ethnic psychology. Abraham Davis (Chp. 9) argues in this volume that the curricula of most colleges and universities in North America reflect a Euro-American standard. For both ethical and practical reasons, serious attention must be given to curricular reform so that our educational standards show more respect for the multicultural and multi-ethnic world in which we live. In some disciplines, new courses need to be developed but in many cases existing courses need to be revised to be less ethnocentric. In my discipline, I suggest that the authors of introductory psychology texts and instructors read at least the following resources to acquaint themselves with the cultural context of Euro-American psychology (Bronstein & Quina, 1988; Guthrie, 1976; Pedersen et al., 1989; Segall et al., 1990; Triandis, 1980-81).

Christian segregation? Within North American missiology there is a strategy of church growth or evangelism which uses ethnicity to outline target populations. Unfortunately, this strategy has been interpreted as an endorsement of cultural and ethnic segregation in the Christian church. For example, people have argued that it is desirable to have separate Chinese, Korean, African-American, Puerto Rican, and Euro-American churches since these ethnicially homogenous congregations are the most successful at evangelism and discipleship. To bolster this stance people will often cite examples of how attempts at ethnically integrating congregations during the 1970s failed (e.g. Circle Church in Chicago). This posture will use the phrase that Christians are all "one in Christ" but advocate that ethnic groups maintain their own separate churches (i.e. an "equal but separate" doctrine). This is a distortion of contextualization and ends up being a form of "Christian segregation", which to me, is a contradiction in terms.

Respecting the ethnicity of people is a definite step forward for Christian missions. It was not too long ago that becoming a Christian in North America also meant becoming Euro-American middle-class. Now, there is much greater acceptance of there being different ethnic expressions of Christ. It is now conceivable that a person living in San Francisco or Vancouver can hear the gospel of Jesus Christ in

Mandarin from an evangelist using a Mandarin Bible who belongs to a Chinese church. This is an example of contextualization which I fully endorse as a means of evangelism. But, it only goes half way. Contexualization also involves relativization. Chinese churches, in order to continue to breathe, must discern the strengths and limitations of their context. And, as I have argued, this step is best taken through entering dialogues with other Christian ethnics. Inter-ethnic and cross-cultural dialogues must be more than occasional guest speakers or choir exchanges. They must be institutionalized programs or events which facilitate confession, reconcilitation, mutuality, and inter-action. Ethnocentrism and segregation are the results of churches not taking measures to contextualize themselves. Churches (and colleges) must build into their corporate life mechanisms which reveal the relative nature of their understandings and practices.

Arguments for Diversity

The Peter Syndrome. At the outset, people who argue for ethnic and cultural diversity within the Christian church must confront what I call the "Peter Syndrome". In Luke's account of the early Christian church, Peter refuses to believe that the gospel of Jesus Christ was for anyone else except Jews. It took an angel speaking to a God-fearing Italian and a reoccurring vision for a Jewish Christian for the latter to say, "I now realize how true it is that God does not show favoritism but accepts people from every nation who fear him and do what is right." (Acts 10:34). Luke continues the story:

> While Peter was still speaking these words, the Holy Spirit came on all who heard the message. The circumcised believers who had come with Peter were astonished that the gift of the Holy Spirit had been poured out even on the Gentiles. For they heard them speaking in tongues and praising God. (Acts 10:44-46, NIV)

Although it still hurts, it no longer surprises me to see Christians isolating themselves because they believe that the gospel only applies to them and no one else. The "Peter Syndrome" is alive and well within Christendom, although less prevalent among evangelicals.

Circumcision and compromise. Further on in Luke's history of the early church, he records a series of events which I interpret to be the first conference on Christianity and ethnicity. In response to the spread of the gospel among Gentiles at Antioch, some Jewish Christians from Judea went there and started teaching that "Unless you are circumcised, according to the custom taught by Moses, you cannot be saved" which some Christian Jews sharply disagreed with and opposed. The debate became so great that a contingent was sent to the home office, Jerusalem, where the issue became even more extreme and divisive.

> Then some of the believers who belonged to the party of the Pharisees stood up and said, "The Gentiles must be circumcised and required to obey the law of Moses".
> The apostles and elders met to consider this question. After much discussion, Peter got up and addressed them: "Brothers, you know that some time ago God made a choice among you that the Gentiles might hear from my lips the message of the gospel and believe. God, who knows the heart, showed that he accepted them by giving the Holy Spirit to them just as he did to us. He made no distinction between us and them, for he purified their hearts by faith. Now then, why do you try to test God by putting on the necks of the disciples a yoke that neither we nor our fathers have been able to bear? No! We believe it is through the grace of our Lord Jesus that we are saved, just as they are." (Acts 15: 5-11, NIV)

Despite Peter's speech, the results of the conference, like most debates, was a compromise. James the apostle said,

> ... we should not make it difficult for the Gentiles who are turning to God. Instead we should write to them, telling them to abstain from food polluted by idols, from sexual immorality, from the meat of strangled animals and from blood. (Acts 15:19-20)

His rationale for these requirements was a bold claim that Moses had been preached in every city from the earliest times. The apostle Paul later wrote to the church of Corinth not to get stuck on the food sacrificed to idols requirement (I Corinthians 8:1-8) and emphasized that ethnic and cultural idiosyncracies were not to be used to define the gospel.

Thus, very early in the history of the church we read accounts of ethnic or cultural conflict. An ethnic norm, having nothing to do with righteousness or justice, was being expected of Christian Gentiles by some Jewish Christians, who held most of the power. After much discussion, the leadership settled on a compromise that did not require the Christian Gentiles to endure a painful ritual, but did expect them to abstain from certain types of food and sexual immorality.

Singing a new song. Besides appealing to Luke's account of how the first Christians dealt with their ethnocentrism, the apostle John is often quoted where he hears the saints singing a new song to the Lamb:

> You are worthy to take the scroll and to open its seals, because you were slain, and with your blood you purchased people for God from every tribe and language and people and nation. You have made them to be a kingdom and priests to serve our God, and they will reign on the earth. (Revelation 5:9-10, NIV)

This passage is used by preachers to convince people that the gospel of Jesus Christ is for all people, regardless of what language they speak or what culture they are from. I am in agreement with this interpretation.

Camels, gold, and incense. Having established my position that God's revelation through the incarnation, death, and resurrection of Jesus Christ is for all people, we return to the issue of what purpose ethnic and cultural diversity has in the Church. A common argument for diversity within a church or college is that it brings a variety of gifts. Proponents of this view will often call upon the prophet of Isaiah. Isaiah's vision of Zion contains imagery of people from all nations bringing their riches to Israel. I quote selectively:

Nations will come to your light, and kings to the
brightness of your dawn... the wealth on the seas will be
brought to you, to you the riches of the nations will come...
young camels of Midian and Ephah... Sheba will come
bearing gold and incense... Kedar's flocks will be gathered
to you, the rams of Nebaioth will serve you... the ships of
Tarshish with their silver and gold... the glory of Lebanon
will come to you, the pine, the fir, and the cypress together.
(Isaiah 60:3-14, NIV)

Evangelical Christians often equate the City of the Lord with the ideal
church where people from many different cultures and ethnic groups
come bringing the best of all humanity to the feet of Christ. But, instead of each contributing some sort of material wealth, the nations
bring social psychological talents or gifts: e.g. Japanese discipline,
African expression, Indian piety, etc. The world's cultures are seen as
each having their strengths and weaknesses and, as they come together in Christ, their differences balance and complement one another. Sometimes "garden", "mosaic", or "fruit salad" metaphors are
used to describe this vision of a multi-ethnic or multicultural church.
These metaphors, which suggest diversity within a unity, are often
used to challenge the popular "melting pot" analogy.

I certainly share the vision of the Christian Church as being
multi-ethnic and multicultural, but I disagree with how this diversity is often described. The Isaiah imagery of each nation bringing a
special resource to Zion is fine, but to equate "trees of Lebanon" with
some social psychological trait is too simplistic. The immense complexity of the phenomena captured under the labels "ethnicity" or
"culture" cannot be reduced to a few interpersonal constructs.
Reducing a culture to a personality trait was the strategy of some early
anthropologists who were heavily influenced by Freudian theory.
This approach has very few followers today, some of which can be
found in Christian circles.

A more serious flaw in this kind of interpretation is that it assumes
a standard to which ethnic and cultural groups contribute. The
implicit assumption is that a group of people, a church or college for
example, *use* diversity to assist in achieving their objectives. That is,
the purpose of ethnic and cultural differences is to enrich some group;

some group who is defining what the differences are and what contributions need to be made. This posture is, in my judgment, ethnocentric and paternalistic. It assumes that one's own historical and cultural context is the privileged stance which can discern what is needed and who can meet those needs. At the root of this mistake is the assumption that one's own church is *the* Church. I believe that Zion, the City of the Lord, is a prophetic reality which no church has fully experienced or realized.

Ethnicity and culture: Vehicles of revelation and incarnation. Although I have made this position explicit earlier in the chapter, it seems appropriate to repeat it here: ethnicity and culture are vehicles of God's revelation and incarnation. Our understanding of the infinite is through the finite. Our understanding of the Creator is through the created. Our understanding of the transcendent is through the incarnate. Also, the mere presence of ethnic and cultural diversity relativizes our context. Diversity reminds us that the ethnic and cultural forms we use to understand God are not gods. That is, ethnic and cultural diversity disarms any attempts to idolize a single context. For example, Jesus was a Jew, but He did not allow Judaism to define God. He used Judaism to point people to their Creator and eventually to Himself. We are ethnic beings but we must not allow our ethnicity to define God. In sum, ethnicity can be used by God and ethnic diversity forces us to remember who is God.

Concluding Remarks

I have tried to make most of my presuppositions explicit. My friends who do philosophy will probably be uncomfortable with my metaphysics and epistemology. They might label my position as a "nominalistic instrumentalism" and express concern over my relativity. I invite them to respond to me with a serious playfulness and playful seriousness. The presuppositions which I have left implicit are those which would fall under the heading of axiology (values and ethics). Also, I have not made my social theory explicit. I recognize that my call for justice and liberation demands definitions. I know that one person's justice can be another person's injustice. I know my prescriptions need an explicit vision of social reality. To complete my arguments, I need to describe what I envision our world would look like if shalom was fully realized. However, the major purpose of this chapter was to provide a reason-able argument for cultural and ethnic diversity within Christianity. I hope my words have at least encouraged us to begin talking more about diversity.

To be consistent with my presuppositions, the final test of my arguments here and those of my colleagues will be what happens on our college campuses. If our words inspire greater acts of justice, liberation, and forgiveness, then our efforts have been worthwhile. This book and the words it contains are tools. They are instruments to help us achieve our objectives, to help us realize our values.

Book Summary

In the next chapter, Alvaro Nieves outlines the demographics of the Coalition colleges with regards to ethnic composition. Given where some of these colleges are located, the ethnic representation is embarrassing *and* sinful. Nieves speaks clearly to the issue of ethnic-minority representation: change is imperative. Chapter 3 addresses the terminological confusion which often pervades discussions addressing human diversity. Rice and I adopt an instrumentalist stance in our analysis. We focus on the *usage* of words and their *consequences* rather than trying to discern the "best" terms or definitions. We also review the research done in Canada on ethnic identity and multiculturalism. Finally, we offer a case study of how the Canadian experience can be applied to a Christian college attempting to become "a genuinely multicultural Christian academic community".

My colleague, Hank Allen (Chp. 4) uses a structural analysis to understand the situation at evangelical colleges. He distinguishes between formal and informal structures and reveals how both suffer from deeply ingrained ethnocentrism. Like Nieves, he offers rationale for change which are not simply in response to the demographic trends. Professor Allen states that "evangelicalism shapes the basic cultural milieu of the evangelical college". In support of Allen's claim, Larson (Chp. 5) applies the notion of ethnogenesis to argue that evangelicals are an ethnic group. Standard Evangelical Christians in America, or SECAs, are not defined by denominational affiliation but by a mixture of religious and cultural artifacts which have developed in North America by Northern European immigrants and their descendents. His distinction between *ethnic Christians* and *Christian ethnics* is critical and almost prophetic. Larson's argument is especially relevant to those Coalition colleges who describe themselves as nondenominational.

Boivin and Darling (Chp. 6) present some empirical data to support the claims that racism and prejudice exists among American evangelical Christians. Even with the limitations of pencil and paper tests the evidence is hard to refute. The authors analysis of the contradiction between racism and Christianity co-existing echos Larson's argument that evangelicals have not relativized their ethnicity or recognized their context. Part of American evangelical ethnicity is a theology which does not acknowledge corporate sin and response-ability. Thus, the concepts of racism and ethnocentrism, which imply group membership and perception, feel distant to most evangelicals; to them, sin is the result of corrupt individuals. Supporting this individualistic view of sin and redemption is an eschatology which discourages Christian social action. The argument is simple: if the second coming of Christ is imminent then efforts should be directed at "saving souls" rather than trying to change society. From this stance, the Christian life becomes one of personal piety and evangelism to the exclusion of social reform.

Five years ago, I took the initial steps necessary to make this collection of essays a reality. Taking this initiative was, in retrospect, a response to my own professional and social isolation as an ethnic-minority professor teaching at a Christian college. This book has its beginnings in a proposal that I made to the Christian College Coalition to develop a "survival guide" for ethnic-minority students attending its member colleges. I also suggested that the Coalition sponsor a national workshop which would address the needs and concerns of ethnic-minorities on our campuses. Again, in retrospect, these proposals were part of my own strategy of survival! That is, I was attempting to form a network of people who could understand what I was going through living in central Kansas! Professors Wong and Polite (Chp. 7) make use of three social psychological constructs to describe the situation and experience of ethnic-minority faculty working in Christian higher education. Their insights should prove to be extremely useful to ethnic-minority *and* ethnic-majority faculty as we attempt to realize our vision of ethnic and cultural diversity at Christian colleges.

Jenkins and Bainer (Chp. 8) offer several suggestions for educating for equity and justice. They challenge the assumptions that all students begin college with the same skills and learn in the same way. Pedagogy which is developmentally, ethnically, culturally, and gender sensitive is not only effective but moral. The college curriculum must also reflect a sensitivity to diversity and Abraham Davis Jr. (Chp. 9) shares some examples of what he has found useful over his 32 years of college teaching. He also argues that multiculturalizing the curriculum must be more than introducing separate courses which deal with diversity. He advocates the infusion of existing courses with "positive ethnic models". Certainly the contribution of ethnic-minorities and women to the disciplines has been neglected and needs to be remedied, but I also endorse the approach which continually reviews the presuppositions from which courses are taught. The basic assumptions about what it means to be "educated" and give birth to the curriculum requirements should also be scrutinized for ethno-centric elements. The Eurocentric nature of most curricula must be confronted for both practical and moral reasons. We now live in a "global village" which demands a re-value-ation of what it means to be "culturally literate".

Our concluding chapter is a case study of a college whose history is both inspiring and discouraging. Andrew Baskin (Chp. 10), the Director of Berea's Black Cultural Center and Interracial Education Program, tells the story of how a college founded as an "anti-slavery" institution fell away from its ideals and now is trying to reclaim its vision for justice and equality. Baskin addresses the issue of having separate ethnic courses and activities which can have both constructive and divisive consequences. There is no question in my mind that separate ethnic courses or centers are needed as evidenced by the impact the Asian American Studies Center at UCLA has had on Asian-American communities. Any divisiveness usually results from a perspective which adopts the "equal means the same" mythology and fails to recognize that most curricula is Euro-American.

As a final note I would like to apologize for not including a chapter which addresses the problems that student development personnel encounter when dealing with ethnic and cultural diversity. Three people were invited to contribute chapters but they were unable to break away from their schedules to meet our writing deadlines. This is perhaps an indication of the work overload that exists among these type of positions. It is my hope that in the future there will be an entire book devoted to multicultural student development. Fortunately, George Jackson III has been organizing the *National Christian Multicultural Student Leadership Conference* which has met annually since 1988 at Messiah College. This conference has mushroomed from 30 to 150 participants in three years and will probably continue to grow, both in numbers and influence. I encourage the organizers to use their conference to generate publications and policy statements.

References

Anderson, B. (1977). The Babel story: Paradigm of human unity and diversity. In A.M. Greeley & G. Baum (Eds.), *Ethnicity*. New York: Seabury Press.

Baum, G. (1977). Editorial summary. In A.M. Greeley & G. Baum (Eds.), *Ethnicity*. New York: Seabury Press.

Bronstein, P. & Quina, K. (Eds.). *Teaching a psychology of people: Resources for gender and sociocultural awareness*. Washington, D.C.: American Psychological Association.

Bullock, A. & Stallybrass, O. (Eds.). (1977). *The Fontana dictionary of modern thought*. London: Fontana Books.

Cardenal, E. (1976). *The gospel of Solentiname*. Marknoll, NY: Orbis Books.

Costa, R.O. (1988). Inculturation, indigenization, and contextualization. In R.O. Costa (Ed.) *One faith, many cultures*. Maryknoll, NY: Orbis Books.

Costas, O.E. (1988). Survival, hope, and liberation in the other American church: An Hispanic case study. In R.O. Costa (Ed.) *One faith, many cultures*. Maryknoll, NY: Orbis Books.

Dueck, A. (1989). On living in Athens: Models of relating psychology, church, and culture. *Journal of Psychology and Christianity, 8*, 5-18.

Ferm, D.W. (1986). *Third World Liberation Theologies: A Reader*. Maryknoll, NY: Orbis Books.

Frame, R. (1988). For Black evangelicals, a silver anniversary. *Christianity Today*, May 13, 43-44.

Jordan, C. (1969). *The cotton patch version of Luke and Acts.* New York: Association Press.

Kluckholn C. & Murray, H. (1953). Personality formation: The determinants. In C. Kluckhohn, H.A. Murray, & D.M. Schneider (Eds.), *Personality in nature, society and culture.* New York: Random House.

Kraft, C.H. (1979). *Christianity in culture: A study in dynamic biblical theologizing in cross-cultural perspective.* Maryknoll, NH: Orbis Books.

Guthrie, R.V. (1976). *Even the rat was white: A historical view of psychology.* New York: Harper and Row.

Lambert, W.E. (1977). The effects of bilingualism on the individual: Cognitive and sociocultural consequences. In P.A. Hornby (Ed.), *Bilingualism: Psychological, social, and educational implications.* New York: Academic Press.

Larson, B. (1971). *No longer strangers: An introduction to relational theology.* Waco, TX: Word Books.

Lee, D.J. (1978). *The Logos concept: First century philosophy and modern psychology.* Unpublished bachelor's thesis, University of British Columbia, Vancouver, B.C.

Lee, D.J. (1985). *Storytelling for the integration of Christianity and psychology.* Unpublished manuscript.

Marsden, G. (Ed.) (1984). *Evangelicalism and modern America.* Grand Rapids, MI: W.B. Eerdmans.

Marsden, G. (1980). *Fundamentalism and American culture.* New York: Oxford University Press.

Niebuhr, H.R. (1951). *Christ and culture.* New York: Harper and Row.

Pedersen, P.B., Draguns, J.G., Lonner, W.J., & Trimble, J.E. (Eds.) (1989). *Counseling across cultures*. Third Edition. Honolulu: University of Hawaii Press.

Pepper, S.C. (1942). *World hypotheses: A study in evidence*. Berkeley: University of California Press.

Reeves, T. (1988). A prophetic reconception of God for our times. In R. Costa (Ed.), *One faith, many cultures*. Maryknoll, NY: Orbis Books.

Richardson, D. (1974). *The peace child*. Glendale, CA: Regal Books.

Rumpel, E. (1988). *A systematic analysis of the cultural content of introductory psychology textbooks*. Unpublished masters thesis, Western Washington University, Bellingham, WA.

Sanneh, L. (1988). Pluralism and Christian commitment. *Theology Today, 45*(1), 21-33.

Schreiter, R.J. (1985). *Constructing local theologies*. Maryknoll, NY: Orbis Books.

Segall, M.H., Dasen, P.R., Berry, J.W., & Poortinga, Y.H. (1990). *Human behavior in global perspective: An introduction to cross-cultural psychology*. New York: Pergamon Press.

Stackhouse, M.L. (1988). Contextualization, contextuality, and contextualism. In R. Costa (Ed.), *One faith, many cultures*. Maryknoll, NY: Orbis Books.

Taylor, K.N. (1971). *The living Bible, Paraphrased*. Wheaton, IL: Tyndale House.

Thomas, P. (1978). *Down these mean streets*. New York: Knopf.

Thomas, P. (1982). *Savior, Savior, hold my hand*. New York: Bantam Books.

Triandis, H.C. (Ed.) (1980-81). *Handbook of cross-cultural psychology.* In Six Volumes. Boston: Allyn and Bacon.

Vanier, J. (1988). *The broken body.* New York: Paulist Press.

Von Glaserfeld, E. (1984). An introduction to radical constructivism. In P. Watzlawick (Ed.), *The invented reality: How do we know what we believe we know? Contributions of constructivism.* New York: Norton.

Wells, D.F., (1984). An American evangelical theology: The painful transition from *Theoria* to *Praxis.* In G. Marsden (Ed.), *Evangelicalism and modern America.* Grand Rapids, MI: W.B. Eerdmans.

Williams, P.N. (1988). Contextualizing the faith: The African-American tradition and Martin Luther King, Jr. In R. Costa (Ed.), *One faith, many cultures.* Maryknoll, NY: Orbis Books.

Wong, H. (1986). Contextual or evangelical? In W. Yew (Ed.), *ABC and OBC: Understanding the cultural tensions in Chinese churches.* Petaluma, CA: Chinese Christian Mission.

Yew, W. (Ed.) (1986). *ABC and OBC: Understanding the cultural tensions in Chinese churches.* Petaluma, CA: Chinese Christian Mission.

Footnotes

1. My colleague in philosophy, John E. Hare, shared the following observation with me concerning the incarnation. One possible translation of John 1:14 is "The Word became flesh and *tabernacled* among us". The King James Version uses the word "dwelt" and the New International Version uses "lived" for what is literally the Greek word for "tabernacle" (used in the form of a verb). The apostle John is playing with Greek and Hebrew semantics in this verse. The Greek word for tabernacle sounds the same (shares similar consonants) as the Hebrew word for "glory". Thus, John completes the verse by saying, "We have seen his glory, the glory of the one and only Son who came from the Father, full of grace and truth" (NIV). Perhaps the imagery John was trying to convey was that God was present in the Word-Jesus in the same way that Glory (Yahweh) was present in the tabernacle. That is, in one phrase John drew upon two cultures to communicate the nature of Jesus Christ. Furthermore, the use of "Son" and "Father" metaphors appeal to a pan-cultural dimension of human experience which conveys a "same but different" relationship.

2. I have reviewed the logos concept as it was used in the first century in another paper (see Lee, 1978).

3. It is interesting that Niebuhr wished to challenge the argument that a particular culture could claim some special status and equate itself with what God intended (i.e. the Christ *of* culture model). But, when his model frames Christ and Christians as if they exist independent of culture, he ends up sanctifying a cultural context, be it Moses', Jesus', or his own.

4. My historian friend, Joel Carpenter, encouraged me to find a word which did not find it roots in a Latin abstraction. I was ready to employ an Asian concept, but decided against this shift in metaphor and opted to remain within the current scholarly jargon. The words "integr*ation*", "incultur*ation*", "indigeniz-*ation*", "incarn*ation*", and "contextualiz*ation*" all share the

"*atio*" suffix which forms an abstraction from a concrete noun or verb. The Latin noun "contextus" implies of state of being closely joined or interwoven; the verb "contexto" describes a uniting, connecting, or weaving together in a coherent fashion. The implied analogy is that just as a piece of thread maintains its identity while being woven into a piece of cloth, Christians are entwined within their culture but can remain discernible.

5. In 1988, the National Black Evangelical Association (NBEA) celebrated its 25th anniversary and introduced the Institute on Black Evangelical Thought and Action. The Institute's purpose was to develop an evangelical theology in the context of the Black American experience. Clarence Hilliard, argued that "all theologies come out of a cultural context, although not all theologies admit it... Black theology is committed to the victimized and the marginalized". The NBEA is sometimes accused of being "racist towards racists". However, NBEA membership is not determined by skin color and the use of the word "black" is not intended to be divisive (Frame, 1988).

6. I am indebted to Charles H. Kraft (1979), Robert J. Schreiter (1985), and Max L. Stackhouse (1988) for the words, metaphors, and models which guide this position. Also, my thanks to Randall and Rebekah Basinger at Messiah College for providing a safe but challenging environment in which to air some of my ideas.

7. Our desire to have God's revelations or presence stand still is reflected in the story of Jesus' transfiguration (Luke 9:28-36; Matthew 17:1-13; Mark 9:2-13). After this incredible event of transformation, Peter's first response is to want to build an altar which would capture the moment. I believe that the "altars" North Americans build are words which attempt to define and control the presence of God.

8. Some people have argued that individual and group differences are minor and do not deserve much attention. It is revealing, however, that most conflicts between individuals and groups occur over their differences and not their similarities.

The Minority Experience in Evangelical Colleges

Alvaro L. Nieves

During my first year of teaching in an evangelical Christian college several experiences dramatized the plight of minorities (especially underrepresented minorities) on our campuses. First, soon after arriving I was asked to serve on a team reviewing the Office of Multicultural Student Affairs. Second, I was also asked to serve on the Multicultural Student Affairs Committee. These first two appointments might ordinarily seem unremarkable or even positive except that I was the only underrepresented minority faculty member on campus.

Another event had greater impact. We had taken our family to a campus event where various musical groups were performing. My thirteen year old daughter leaned toward me and whispered, "Dad, how come there are no dark people up there?" I remember mumbling something about discussing it later. Throughout the remainder of the concert I was preoccupied with the question. I knew the answer would not be easy. That simple question, posed by a thirteen year old, was to become the focus of much of my research over the subsequent years.

Preliminary Research

The first part of my work involved identifying the minority presence in the member schools of the Christian College Coalition (CCC). An earlier article summarized what I discovered (Nieves, 1987). Statistics for Fall 1983 showed that, on average, minority students (African-American, Hispanic-American, Asian-American and Native-American), represented 7.2% of total enrollment in CCC schools. If Asians are excluded we have a figure for the remaining (underrepresented) minorities which totaled a mere 6.1% in 1983. This was a time when, nationally, underrepresented minorities approached 13% of enrollments at private four year colleges and universities.

Work by a colleague at another evangelical college pointed to a similar absence of minorities on the boards of trustees of these institutions (Collette, 1985). Since these boards are responsible for fiscal and administrative policies at the schools, the absence of minorities was tantamount to an absence of diversity in campus and institutional leadership.

My preliminary research included sending a short survey to the chief academic officer of Coalition colleges. Over ninety percent of those responding indicated that they were *somewhat* or *very dissatisfied* with the number of full time minority faculty employed at their institution. This earlier research also suggested problems in budgeting for minority related programs, an absence of recruitment/ retention strategies and a paucity of minority administrators and staff.

Purpose of the Present Chapter

The purpose of the present chapter is twofold. First, I wish to convey and reaffirm the continuing importance of diversity in higher education in general and evangelical higher education in particular. This calls, of course, for a consideration of the meaning of diversity. Second, I will bring my earlier work up to date in a number of areas, including describing changes which have occurred since 1983 in the status of minorities in evangelical colleges. I will also report on some aspects of a survey of minority faculty at CCC institutions, a phone survey of CCC schools, and some new programmatic efforts which were attempted or are under way. I will conclude with recommendations for changes in policy and for further research suggested by the present work.

Diversity

Diversity, pluralism, multiracial, multicultural, multiethnic; these are terms which are presently in vogue. A search of the literature quickly turns up articles, manuals and books dealing with the topics of enhancing diversity, living in a multicultural world, etc. The fact of changing demographics--one estimate puts non-whites as one third of the American population by the year 2000 (Bjork, 1989)--have given rise to concerns about managing diversity in the work place. The shrinking globe and increasing demand for a technologically skilled work force have convinced employers of the need for greater sensitivity to racial and ethnic minorities.

Similarly, colleges and universities have been forced to the realization that we must begin to educate students differently if we are to prepare them for a world in which contact among people of diverse groups is increasing. For many schools, part of this process of education involves changing the composition of the campus community to reflect the new demographics. For other, usually larger state universities, it is changing the climate of the campus to reduce the potential for interracial conflict.

In the past, the goal of diversity has been defined in terms of numerical pluralism; i.e., increasing the number of minority group members in the campus community. While this would appear to be a logical starting point, major universities like Stanford University have discovered that without deeper changes intergroup conflict is virtually inevitable. This has led Stanford to call for "...a new commitment: ...the transition from numerical diversity to interactive pluralism."(Standford University, 1989)

With similar motivation, the American Council on Education (ACE) recently published *Minorities on Campus: A Handbook for Enhancing Diversity* (Green, no date). In this handbook reference is made to both diversity and pluralism. For the handbook editor "pluralism has a much more positive and active connotation." Citing a Brown University report, she explains further that it "asks of the members of all groups to explore, understand and try to appreciate one another's cultural experiences and heritage." She sees pluralism, further as a "dynamic atmosphere of collaboration."

This is consistent with Stanford's conceptualization of *interactive pluralism* which calls for a "process of mutual enrichment." These formulations are consistent with what Triandis (1988) refers to as "additive multiculturalism." By his definition, majority persons who learn appreciation for a minority culture are benefitting from additive multiculturalism. Blacks or Hispanics who give up their culture to become culturally white or anglo have experienced "subtractive multiculturalism." We can conclude, therefore, that multiculturalism can be represented by either positive or negative pluralism. Triandis states further that, "Desirable pluralism permits everyone to have additive multiculturalist experiences. Ideally, pluralism involves enjoyment of our ability to switch from one cultural system to another. There is a real sense of accomplishment associated with having the skill to shift cultures. The balanced bilingual-bicultural person--or even more, the multicultural person-- gets kicks out of life that are simply not available to the monolingual-monocultural person." He further states that "the majority culture can be enriched by considering the viewpoints of the several minority cultures that exist in America rather than trying to force these minorities to adopt a monocultural, impoverished, provincial view-point that may, in the long run, reduce creativity and the chances of effective adjustment in a fast-changing world." (pages 42-43)

It should be clear from these brief comments that it is important to consider not only increasing numerical diversity, but altering the climate within which such diversity exists. Enhancing diversity, promoting pluralism or enriching the multicultural experiences of our students is imperative if we are to equip students for participation in the modern world. The choices we make in implementation will obviously effect whether the experience is a positive or negative (read additive or subtractive) and for whom. Recommendations for enhancing positive outcomes will be discussed subsequently.

Minority Student Enrollment in Coalition Schools

In examining annual enrollment patterns since 1983 one might expect an improvement in the percentage of minority students enrolled in institutions which have indicated a desire for greater diversity. Unfortunately, member schools of the Christian College Coalition have not succeeded in significantly increasing the percentage of minority students enrolled in their schools. Figure 1 is a stacked bar chart presenting average minority enrollment as a percentage of total enrollment in all CCC schools. Total minority enrollment includes Asian-, Hispanic-, Native- and African-American students. The average percentage rose from 7.24% in 1983 to a high of 8.63% in 1989, the last year for which published statistics are available. While Figure 1 gives a good indication of total variability it is more difficult to see what is happening separately in each minority group.

Figure 1

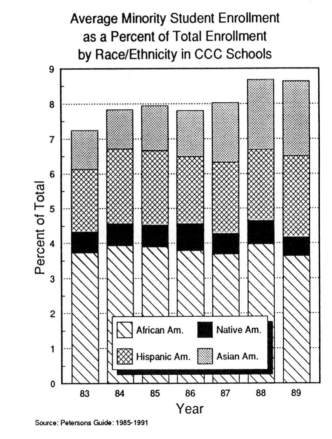

Average Minority Student Enrollment
as a Percent of Total Enrollment
by Race/Ethnicity in CCC Schools

Source: Petersons Guide: 1985-1991

Figure 2 represents the data for each minority group, a sub-total for underrepresented minorities and total minorities in a scatter plot with a linear regression line fitted to the seven annual data points. Underrepresented (sometimes referred to as targeted minorities) consisting of African-, Native- and Hispanic-American students appear to have fitted lines which are almost flat. The only upwardly sloping lines are for the Asian-American and the total minority data. These representations are consistent with regression equations for each group in which the beta coefficients associated with year as a predictor of the percentage of underrepresented minorities and its constituent groups do not differ significantly from zero.

Figure 2

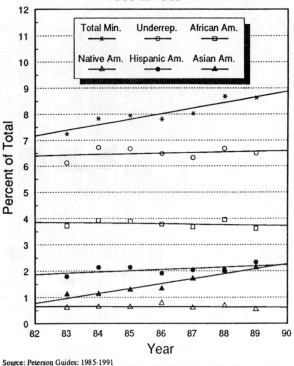

Minority Student Enrollments
in Christian College Coalition Schools
1983 to 1989

Source: Peterson Guides: 1985-1991

The coefficients for year in those equations predicting Asian-American and total minority enrollments, on the other hand, are highly significant. These relationships are also reflected in the correlation (Pearson product moment *r*) between year and minority enrollments by group, sub-total and total. Table 1 provides these correlation coefficients and the associated *t* statistic as well as an indication of the level of significance for a two tailed test of significance of the form H_0: rho = 0. The t statistic is calculated as

$$t=\sqrt{N\text{-}2/1\text{-}r^2}$$

where *r* is the Pearson product moment correlation, *N* is the number of paired observations and r^2 is a measure of the variation in the percentage enrollment explained by the year.

If one were to examine only the total number of minority students as an average percentage of the total, one might conclude that progress was occurring. An examination of the components of the total gives a more accurate picture and demonstrates the significant increase in the total is a result of significant growth in the Asian-American student population. The figures for underrepresented minorities, on the other hand, show no statistically significant growth.

Table 1
Correlation Coefficients for Minority and Year

Group	*r*	r^2	student's *t*
African-American	-0.264	.0696	-0.612
Native-American	-0.138	.0910	-0.312
Hispanic-American	0.585	.3422	1.613
Asian-American	0.964	.9293	8.107*
Underrep. Minority	0.257	.0660	0.623
Total Minority	0.919	.8446	5.210**

* p<.001   ** p<.01

Minority Faculty in CCC Schools

In my earlier work I lacked data on minority representation among the faculty of CCC schools. As a result, I employed the self report of key academic leaders of their satisfaction with minority representation. This was, clearly, a measure of last resort. It pointed to the need for more information than anyone seemed to have at that time.

To correct the situation I undertook a phone survey of academic deans or the equivalent in each of the CCC schools. At each school we asked for the number of minority faculty, the department in which each taught and their faculty rank and whether or not they taught full or part time. In addition, we sought to ascertain the number of full and part time faculty in each of the four major ethnic-minority categories. We also asked for the names of minority faculty to allow for a subsequent mail survey to minority faculty. Of the 77 schools contacted we were able to get useable information for most data items from 59. While most schools were very cooperative, a few were uncooperative or chose not to participate. In one case, for example, an administrator stated that the survey ought to come through the mail and directly from the CCC office in Washington, D. C. This, in spite of the fact, that I had coordinated with and had agreement from the appropriate person at the CCC to proceed. In another instance, when asked whether his/her school employed any Native-American faculty one administrator responded that all the faculty were native American since, to the best of his/her knowledge none were foreign born.

Table 2 provides the average number of minority faculty in CCC schools by ethnic-minority status and full time versus part time status. The column labeled N gives the number of schools (N) providing valid (useable) information in arriving at the average.

Table 2
Average Number of Full and Part Time Faculty at CCC Schools

Faculty Group	Full Time	N	Part Time	N
All Faculty	55.579	57	16.288	59
African-American	0.390	59	0.276	58
Native-American	0.017	59	0.000	59
Hispanic-American	0.271	59	0.259	58
Asian-American	0.492	59	0.241	58

Since the presence of minority faculty is important to the diversity and pluralism of a campus community it is instructive to go beyond the averages reported above. Table 3 presents information on the number of full time minority faculty at Coalition colleges. The column heading indicates the number of minority faculty of a particular group employed. The cell frequency indicates the number of CCC schools employing that number. A cursory examination of the data in Table 3 reveals the modal category for all targeted groups to be zero. Clearly, a challenge faces CCC schools if diversity is to become a reality.

One way to increase ethnic and racial diversity is to employ minority persons from nearby communities on a part time basis. To what degree are CCC schools using this approach? Table 4 answers this question by showing the number of part time faculty employed by group membership. Results are based on 58 schools which responded to this question. Once again, the interior cell frequencies represent the number of schools employing the number of faculty indicated in the column headings.

Table 3
Number of Schools Reporting Minority Faculty by Number of Full Time Faculty and Minority Group Membership

Minority Group	0 Fac.	1 Fac.	2 Fac.	3 Fac.	4 Fac.	7 Fac.
African-American	43	12	2	1	1	
Native-American	58	1				
Hispanic-American	47	8	4			
Asian-American	41	12	5			1

Table 4
Number of Schools Reporting Minority Faculty by Number of Part Time Faculty and Minority Group Membership

Minority Group	0 Fac.	1 Fac.	2 Fac.	3 Fac.	4 Fac.	7 Fac.
African-American	44	12	2			
Native-American	58					
Hispanic-American	45	11	2			
Asian-American	48	7	2	1		

The information reported by the deans or their representatives is both interesting and useful. Some additional information concerning country of birth and citizenship would have allowed us to judge whether we were seeing American minorities or internationals identified as minorities.

The follow-up questionnaire which was sent to minority faculty asked both for birth country and country of present citizenship. Interestingly, of 56 faculty who returned questionnaires (out of approximately 100 sent) 36 or 64.3% were born in Puerto Rico or countries other than the U.S. When it came to citizenship, however, 44 or 78.6% are presently citizens of the U.S.

In order to ascertain whether faculty defined themselves as minority group members we asked, "Do you consider yourself a minority group member?" Of the 53 who responded to this question, 38 (71.7%) said "Definitely," and an additional 10 (18.9%) said "Somewhat." Of the 53 responding to questions concerning how they thought they were by perceived by colleagues and students over 80% felt that colleagues considered them a minority and that students related to them as a minority faculty person.

Respondents to the mailed questionnaire were very willing to answer questions identifying their race/ethnicity, age and gender: 26.4% identified themselves as Black (Non-Hispanic), 30.2% as Hispanic (Non-Black), 41.5% as Asian/Pacific Islander and 1.9% as American Indian/Alaskan Native. In age, respondents ranged from 26 to 65 years with an mean of 41.4 and a standard deviation of 10.557. Males made up 67.3% of the respondent group and females 32.7%. Approximately 65% did not respond to questions about marital status and number of children.

The length of time minority faculty served on the faculty at their institution ranged from 4 months to 33 years with a mean of 7.02 years and a standard deviation of 7.65. Nearly 60% of minority faculty responding indicated they were in possession of an earned doctorate. Of the remainder only four did not have at least a Masters degree and 13 indicated they were working on an advanced degree and intended on staying in their present position after completing it. Interestingly, more than half of respondents indicated they had earned their highest degree after 1982.

In terms of work responsibilities on their campuses minority faculty teach, on the average, 17.67 credit hours per semester, officially advise an average of 13.98 students and serve on 1.33 committees.

Concerning tenure, 65% of minority faculty have not been granted tenure at their institution. Nevertheless, slightly more than 50% of minority faculty consider the tenure and promotion process to be fair and equitable. In a related area only 11% of responding minority faculty felt there was "a great deal of pressure" to publish at their institution.

In spite of an overall willingness to remain at their institutions, and a perception of equitable promotion and tenure policies all was not seen as positive. In order to give respondent's greater flexibility without guiding their response the following item was included:

"Please relate any incidents (positive or negative) in your teaching experience at this or any other Coalition College which you feel resulted from your minority status. Use additional paper if necessary."

There was a recurring sense of alienation and loneliness on the part of minority faculty. The sense of alienation appeared to be tied to the perception of prejudice on the part of both colleagues, students, and others, with little corresponding support. In addition, there was a sense of pressure to perform at exceptional professional levels and, at the same time, be the ideal minority professional. This latter often manifested itself through the expectations of others that minority persons should be prepared to serve as minority representative "for all seasons."

Among words and descriptors which seemed to indicate the sense of alienation were: harassment, burn-out, lack of respect from white students, hostility, discrimination, tokenism, singled out. In addition, some minority faculty indicated they felt they were "not taken seriously," or had to continually "prove themselves" and felt their expertise was constantly challenged--even in their own specialty area. One respondent wrote, "Sometimes I get the feeling that important positions are not given to me due to my ethnic background or my ideas are not taken seriously." This was consistent with others reporting their perception of an absence of opportunity for minorities to advance within the institutional structure.

Although there were also some positive aspects to the open-ended item, its responses conveyed a sense that the climate for minority faculty was something less than ideal. There was a consistent sense of loneliness, dismay, and alienation. Through it all, however, one does not get an impression of cynicism, but a realistic appraisal of the situation and a willingness to be a part of the solution to the problem as long as there appears to be some sense of hope.

These observations are consistent with ideas in another chapter in this volume which suggest that the choice for minority faculty is often between assimilation and isolation. I question, albeit on the basis of admittedly limited research, whether real assimilation is even possible. Were it possible, however, it is doubtful that it is desirable, either from an individual or societal perspective.

Minority Student Attitudes and Experience

At the present time I have done very little direct contact research with minority students on our campuses. More is planned for the near future. I have had several opportunities, however, to conduct group discussions with minority students on a number of campuses across the country. My contact with these students suggests that the issue of campus climate continues to be a relevant and serious concern.

At one campus students of color have reported classroom experiences in which professors have openly ridiculed suggestions that Black and Hispanic literature and theology be taught. A Hispanic student told about a professor who had been discussing the drug trade and wealthy distributors. "Who knows," the professor continued, "it could be one of _____'s relatives supplying the kilos" (mentioning the name of the only Hispanic student in the class). The class roared with laughter. The targeted student was not amused.

Minority students, faced with evidence of individual and institutional racism on campus, sometimes struggle with bitterness. A comment I hear repeatedly involves the difficult social climate, especially in the sphere of dating. It must be understood that the difficulty stems from the very small pool of minority students which make it difficult to establish relationships within one's own group.

Students of color, however, are tired of being told that Scripture proscribes inter-racial dating and marriage. They often interpret such advice as further subordinating them to the white majority. In reality, this may occur even when students have little or no interest in intergroup dating and marriage. That this is an area of concern for both majority and minority students was recently demonstrated at one CCC school, when a forum on interracial dating and marriage attracted over 300 students on a mid-week evening.

In addition to the stressful personal experiences, students of color are very conscious that they are called on to be bilingual and bicultural. Concerts and performances on campus seldom reflect their culture. Curriculum is seen as lacking in courses which reflect or accurately portray subjects of interest to them. The paucity of minority faculty is a further burden. They see many of the attempts to modify structure as tokenism. Everywhere I have visited I have seen these students struggling with decisions to stay or transfer to a secular or historically Black college or university.

Their sense of alienation and isolation is similar to the minority faculty experience. There must be an increasing awareness of and sensitivity to these and related concerns if recruiting efforts are going to succeed and if retention of minority students is to reach an acceptable level.

Strategies for Positive Change

Fortunately, there is a growing recognition of the need to improve the racial climate on college campuses. This is true in all sectors of higher education. That need has been dramatically emphasized by recent incidents on campuses across the nation. A number of books have recently been published which reflect these concerns (e.g. Hidalgo, et al., 1990; Hively, 1990). Along with the recognition of need programs are being developed to foster positive social change.

The Colleges of the Christian College Consortium (a sub-group of the coalition) are among those seeking positive change. Over the last 5 years I have seen an increase in the efforts being made to recruit minority students, faculty and staff. Along these lines, some schools have hired minority recruiters, developed minority scholarship funds, and are establishing linkages with high schools with minority student populations as well as with churches in the minority community.

In addition to recruiting minority faculty who are already credentialed, a number of CCC institutions are seeking ways to support and encourage students at various stages of graduate education. Some are establishing teaching fellowships, others are providing for campus visits with a view to linking minority fellows to active faculty mentors in their areas of study. This is an encouraging development since the alternative is to promote the rotation of a limited number of faculty through the practice of inter-institutional raiding.

At the same time that recruiting at student, faculty and staff levels is targeting minority candidates an attempt is being made to sensitize majority faculty to critical related issues. Among these are concerns relating to minority participation in decision making including board, administrative and staff composition. Of special interest to faculty are changes in the curriculum to reflect a more culturally diverse and pluralistic environment.

Recommendations

For persons and institutions desirous of change a closer reading of the above section coupled with an understanding of a specific campus situation will suggest ways in which these strategies may be applied.

If little has been done in this area then an assessment of the campus climate is in order. Among questions which must be addressed are:

1. How do you rate the friendliness of the racial environment on and around campus?
2. How much sensitivity to racial issues is there among faculty and staff?
3. Is there an anglo-centric, eurocentric focus that is antagonistic to other worldviews?
4. Is there evidence of differential treatment of minorities on your campus?
5. Have there been racist incidents and, if so, how have they been dealt with?
6. Is there an established policy to deal with such incidents when they occur and is there strong leadership to indicate that such acts will not be tolerated?

After these and related questions are addressed each institution must develop a set of objectives which reflect the outcome associated with amelioration of problems in each area of concern. When Stanford was confronted with the problems the committee charged with addressing them identified major areas relating to undergraduate curriculum, faculty, students, student life and staff. In each area they undertook a detailed assessment and followed up with recommendations.

In the area of undergraduate curriculum their preliminary objectives may prove instructive (Stanford University, 1989) :

1. To increase the scope of course offerings on racial minorities in the U.S.;
2. To integrate more content on racial minorities into the existing undergraduate curriculum;
3. To develop and enhance ethnic studies programs;
4. To promote the hiring of faculty to teach courses on ethnic and racial minorities; and

5. To examine how ethnic studies curriculum can be included in University course distribution requirements.

Examination of these objectives reveals that there are a number of facets to the curriculum strategy which could be useful in smaller schools which do not possess Stanford's great resources. For the smaller school the integrative nature of numbers 2 and 5 above may be the logical first line of attack. We should note, here, that these are consistent with the concepts of additive multiculturalism and interactive pluralism discussed earlier in this chapter.

Creativity in the pursuit of the goal is clearly the watchword. Each institution will have to begin from its strength. Has a school had a particularly strong English department promoting writing across the curriculum? A small modification to require multicultural topics might begin the integration process of the second objective. Has there been an emphasis on experiential learning components? Changing the locus of such experiences may go far toward meeting a goal of interactive pluralism.

Anyone considering policy implications related to the issues discussed here must certainly be cognizant of limited resources available for the magnitude of change necessary. This does not, however, relieve us of the responsibility to move in appropriate directions. We have too often been willing to spend in traditional areas, especially capital improvements. We must alter priorities and divert some of those scarce resources to this important area of change.

A failure to meet the educational demands of the twenty-first century and to prepare our students for a world of which they are ignorant will have dire long term consequences. The survival of Christian higher education may well depend on how we meet the challenge of pluralism today and in the near future.

References

Bjork, L.G., (1989). Introduction, *Education and Urban Society, 21*(3), 243.

Collette, M.E., (1985). Comparison of Boards of Trustees of Member Institutions of the Christian College Coalition with Other Institutions of Higher Learning. Unpublished doctoral dissertation, Indiana University.

Green, M.F. (Ed.), (no date). *Minorities on Campus: A Handbook for Enhancing Diversity.* Washington, D.C.: American Council on Education.

Hidalgo, N.M., C.L. McDowell and E.V. Siddle (Eds.), (1990). *Facing Racism in Education*, Cambridge, MA: Harvard College.

Hively, R. (Ed.) (1990). *The Lurking Evil: Racial and Ethnic Conflict on the College Campus*, Wahington D.C.: American Association of State Colleges and Universities.

Nieves, A.L., (1987). Minorities in Evangelical Higher Education. In Carpenter, J.A.. & K.W. Shipps, *Making Higher Education Christian.* Grand Rapids, MI: Christian University Press.

Triandis, H.C., (1988). The Future of Pluralism Revisited. In Katz, P.A., & D.A. Taylor, *Eliminating Racism: Profiles in Controversy.* New York, N.Y.: Plenum Press.

Stanford University Committee on Minority Issues (1989). Building a Multi-racial, Multicultural University Committee: Final Report on the University Committee on Minority Issues. Stanford University.

Ethnic Identity and Multiculturalism: Concepts, History, Research, and Policy

D. John Lee and Rodger R. Rice

This chapter is divided into four parts. The first part considers the concepts that have been used to describe and explain human diversity. The second provides a historical context for understanding the notions of identity and ethnicity in America. Part III reviews the empirical research which asks people to identify their ethnicity. The final part presents a case study of ethnic identity and multiculturalism at a Christian college.

Part I

Describing Human Diversity

Any attempt to understand humanity must confront the diversity which exists between people. Some have argued, however, that the similarities between people far outweigh the differences. Nevertheless, even the most fervent advocates of our commonalities would not deny that differences still exist. Others have argued that humanity is in a process of homogenization, or that differences between people are shrinking and will eventually disappear altogether. This is a possibility, of course, but our concern is the present and immediate future where diversity exists and is not vanished through prophecy or pleas for cooperation. This is not to say that we are against cooperation among differing peoples or believe that it is impossible to attain. We simply disagree with the view that homogenization is inevitable, necessary, or an appropriate strategy for global peace. Regardless of strategy or ethic, we affirm the presence of human diversity to which this chapter is generally addressed.

At the outset it is appropriate to carefully consider the words, concepts, or tools we will be using for our task. Some of the more recent Euro-American English constructs used to categorize human diversity are *race, culture*, and *ethnicity*. The now fashionable term to simultaneously describe diversity itself and an ideal of maintaining some form of ethnic or cultural plurality is *multiculturalism*. In this section, each of these abstractions will be reviewed.

1. Race

Initially, anthropologists divided homo sapiens into subspecies which they called 'races' (derived from 'ratio', which in medieval Latin was used to designate species). A race was characterized by a common gene pool which was arbitrarily defined by some physical marker such as color of skin. Race, intended only to be descriptive, quickly became an explanatory concept. That is, differences between people—for example, intelligence—were also accounted for by racial membership. Out of this perspective grew racially-based hierarchies which, when combined with a social Darwinism, provided the justification for white supremacy and racial discrimination.

Today, most scientists have abandoned the racial classification because it is poorly supported. There are three arguments commonly made against race theory. First of all, genetic variation within so-called races is as great as that of between racial groups. Second, the only difference between people which can be attributed to biological heredity with any degree of confidence is blood type; but populations sharing the same blood type do *not* coincide with racial groups. Third, human characteristics, both physical and social, are not inherited in any simple fashion but are the result of an interaction between dynamic biological organisms and dynamic environments (Berger, 1983).[1]

Racism, discrimination, and nativism. Racism is the belief that socially relevant abilities or characteristics are purely a function of genetic transmission or/and intrinsically associated with physical attributes. *Discrimination* is a legal term describing a situation where some person or persons have been denied requests and/or rights because of conditions unrelated to the phenomena being requested or granted. For example, denying women the right to vote because they were women was a case of gender discrimination. Given these definitions and evidence to date, we consider racial classification to be untenable, racist, and oftentimes discriminatory (cf. Montague, 1964; Boas in Stocking, 1968)

Closely related, but not identical to racism is *nativism*. John Higham (1955) defined it as the "intense opposition to an internal minority on the ground of its foreign...connections" (p. 4). Later in the chapter we will use the word to describe the attitudes and actions of some American Protestants towards immigrant Catholics. It should be made clear that Protestants were not indigenous to America, but were members of the most powerful immigrant group in the United States. Only a small number of people in America can make claim to be the original natives of the land, and this does mean that they are automatically nativists.

2. Culture

Anthropologists do not agree on the definition of culture, but a look at its etymology gives us a sense for what the word is trying to describe. The noun 'culture' has its roots in the Latin word 'cultura' which also gives birth to our word 'cultivate'. That is, some anthropologists had gardening or farming metaphors in mind when they began developing concepts to describe their observations. Differences among human beings could be accounted for by the "soil" or environment in which people were cultivated. All of the forces and processes which contributed to a discernible group of people were objectified into an abstract word. Culture represented all those activities which contributed to the cultivation of a group of people. For example, people who shared the same language were often described as belonging to the same culture. Thus, another way in which anthropologists began categorizing human diversity was rooted in a culture metaphor.

Like race, the support for cultural classification is weak. Again, variation within so-called cultures is as great as the variation between them. In addition, human characteristics are not purely the result of environmental pressures or contingencies. The concept is frequently criticized for being ill-defined and circular if used as an explanatory construct; that is, it makes no sense to explain differences between cultural groups by saying they are a result of culture. Despite these problems, the concept of culture is still frequently used by social scientists.

3. Ethnicity

Formally, 'ethnicity' is a noun recently derived from the adjective 'ethnic'. In the same way beauty is the quality of a beautiful flower, ethnicity represents the character or quality of an ethnic group. David Reisman is attributed to have coined the term in 1953. Glazer and Moynihan (1975) note that the word did not appear in an English dictionary (*Webster's Third New International*) until 1961 and did not make the Oxford (*Supplement*) until 1972. Although there is no agreement over the definition of ethnicity it is now widely used in the sociological and anthropological literature (Yinger, 1985). From our vantage point, we see ethnicity being used in three distinct ways. Each usage will be reviewed separately.

Ethnicity as otherness. As before, some etymology offers us insight into the usage of the ethnicity concept. Petersen (1980) continues:

> The word 'ethnic' derives via Latin from the Greek 'ethnikos', the adjectival form of 'ethnos', or nation. As originally used in English, ethnic signified "not Christian or Jewish, pagan, or heathen"; for example, in *The Leviathan* Thomas Hobbes exhorted Christian converts to continue obeying their 'ethnic' rulers. (p. 234)

That is, it was strange for an English person to refer to him or herself as being 'ethnic' since that term was reserved for those people who were different from themselves in some significant way. Ethnicity was something other people possessed. That is, foreigners or minorities have ethnicity, whereas the English or majority do not. This use or dimension of the term is still popular today as will be evidenced later in the chapter.

Ethnicity as subculture. In a review of 27 definitions of ethnicity, Isajiw (1985) found that ethnic groups were most frequently defined as one type of subgroup in North American culture. Thus, in the *Modern Dictionary of Sociology,* an ethnic group is defined as "a group with a common cultural tradition and a sense of identity which exists as a subgroup of a larger society. The members of an ethnic group differ with regard to certain cultural characteristics from the other members of their society" (as quoted in Isajiw, 1985; p. 7). In addition, the *Harvard Encyclopedia of American Ethnic Groups* (Thernstrom, 1980) states the following:

> Ethnicity is an immensely complex phenomenon. All groups are characterized by some of the following, although in combinations that may vary considerably: (1) common geographical origin, (2) migratory status, (3) race (4) language or dialect, (5) religious faith or faiths, (6) ties that transcend kinship, neighborhood, and community boundaries, (7) shared traditions, values, and symbols, (8) literature, folklore, music, (9) food preferences, (10) settlement and employment patterns, (11) special interest in regard to politics in the homeland and in America, (12) institutions that specifically serve and maintain the group, (13) internal sense of distinctiveness, and (14) an external perception of distinctiveness. The degree to which these features characterize any group varies considerably with the size, history, and length of time it has been in the United States. Ethnic groups persist over long periods. But they also change, merge, and dissolve. New ones come into being through the process known as ethnogenesis; others disappear. (p. vi)

In these definitions, ethnicity is almost equivalent with culture, but is distinquished by its migratory and subgroup status. Thus, despite all the problems of defining what comprises 'culture', ethnicity has been defined as a subculture. The popular term *ethnic-minority* reveals the notion of a subgroup defined by ethnicity. The word 'minority', however, can be misleading. Louis Wirth introduced the term *minority group* to refer to victims of subordination but pointed out that "the people whom we regard as a minority may actually, from a numerical standpoint, be a majority" (as quoted in Petersen, 1980; p. 234).

As Wirth emphasized, a minority group may be a numerical majority but at the same time lack *power*. There are at least four dimensions of power. (1) Military power or the ability to threaten or take another person's life. Those in power can kill those without power. (2) Governance power or the ability to establish laws and policies. Those in power decide what is right and wrong for those without power. Those in power decide who and what gets rewarded and punished. (3) Monetary power, or the ability to buy and control goods. Those in power control the resources and how they are used or distributed. Finally, (4) educational power, or the ability to define what is "normal, natural, healthy, and mature". A minority group, as Wirth used the term, does not have military, governance, monetary, or educational power. Minority groups may vary with regards to the extent or degree of power they may possess, but they all share the experience of some form of oppression.[2]

The defining features of an ethnic group can be divided into two types: (1) objective features such as language and (2) subjective features such as an internal sense of peoplehood (or belongingness). This distinction reflects two theoretical perspectives, the structural and the phenomenological. The former sees ethnicity as a phenomenon existing 'out there' capable of being precisely and directly measured. The latter views ethnicity as existing 'in the minds' of people; thus capable of being measured by inference only. Most definitions will try to find some middle ground, including both objective and subjective features. Such attempts, however, must struggle with the situation where a person has objectively been defined as a member of an ethnic group but does not identify him or herself as a member. The converse may also be true. A person may identify her or himself as an ethnic group member but s/he may not fit any of the objective characteristics. Isajiw (1985) resolves this difficulty by arguing that there are "involuntary" and "voluntary" dimensions of ethnicity. Since a person rarely chooses what group controls his or her basic processes of socialization, there is usually an element of ethnic identification which a person cannot shed easily, if at all. Also, other people can attribute an ethnicity to a person regardless of that person's awareness or consent. In contrast to these involuntary aspects, a person can resurrect, adopt, or create an ethnic identity voluntarily. This 'willed' dimension involves remembering, recapturing, and reinterpreting cultural symbols and institutions.

In popular usage, ethnicity is static. It is something from the past which does not change—like some family heirloom (e.g. wooden shoes). This usage emphasizes the involuntary nature of ethnicity. The fact that the heirloom may mean different things at different times to different members of the family emphasizes the symbolic and dynamic, or voluntary nature of ethnicity. Regardless of whether one views ethnicity as involuntary, voluntary, or both, it inevitably has policy implications.

Over eighty years ago, William Graham Sumner (1906) analyzed the "folkways" of the American populace. In his analysis, Sumner introduced the term *ethnocentrism* to describe the processes which a group uses to create and affirm its sense of communal identity. The term would take on negative connotations as later writers would use it to criticize ethnic groups for their inclusive behaviors. Unfortunately, this criticism would be generalized to all behaviors which distinguished a group or affirmed their sense of peoplehood. That is, being ethnic was equated with being ethnocentric. Certainly, there is a very strong tendency for members of the "in-group" (another Sumner term) to make evaluative contrasts with "out-groups". For example, a language, a set of words (jargon), or a style (dialect) is usually used to define a community and bond its members together. This bond, however, can very easily become a barrier. Mimicking and making fun of other languages or dialects is a common in-group behavior that reflects the judgment that other groups are inferior. However, the defining characteristics of an ethnic group do not necessarily have to be evaluated and compared against other groups. What is meant to act as a bond between people does not necessarily have to be a barrier to keep others out. A preference does not necessarily have to be a standard. What is relative does not have to be treated as an absolute. *What is ethnic does not have to be ethnocentric.*

Some social psychologists argue that human beings not only naturally form groups but also naturally display an "ingroup bias" (cf. Myers, 1987). This perspective would probably view ethnocentrism as a necessary attribute of all ethnic groups. We disagree. Treating one's ethnic characteristics as being the best is not a natural and unavoidable thing to do. If it was, any form of cooperation between groups, ethnic or otherwise, would be impossible. Clearly, constructive inter-ethnic relationships are difficult, but they are not impossible.

Ethnicity as ideology. Similar to the culture concept, ethnicity has been criticized as being ill-defined and circular if used as an explanatory construct. To explain the variations between ethnic groups by saying they are the result of ethnicity is redundant. What exactly is responsible for cultural and ethnic differences has been a matter of debate among sociologists for a long time. On one side of the debate are the idealists who argue that an ethnic groups' religious and political beliefs, values, or 'ideals' are primarily responsible for its distinctives. On the other side are the materialists who emphasize the historical, economic, or 'material' conditions of a group as the causal factors in determining ethnic characteristics. For example, the idealists might point to an immigrant groups' strong 'work-ethic' as an explanation for their prosperity. The materialists, however, might argue that it was the economic resources and opportunities available to the group when they immigrated that was responsible for their wealth. Of course, some sociologists take a middle-of-the-road position and argue that 'ideals' or values interact with 'material' or economic conditions to determine a groups' characteristics at any particular time in history.

The religious and political ideals of a group have been called its *ideology.* To the idealists, a groups' ideology helps explain the groups' characteristics, development, and can predict its future direction. The materialists, however, are suspicious of the idealists' arguments because they view religion and politics simply as tools the rich property owners use to maintain their positions of power and wealth. To the materialists, an ideology is a belief system which distorts reality or masks some specific set of interests. For example, the belief that hard work is a service to God is interpreted to be part of an ideology which assisted the rich to get richer by keeping their labor costs low during the growth of industrial capitalism in Europe and North America.

Sometimes the concept of ethnicity is accused of being part of an ideology which only serves the economic and power interests of certain groups. For example, Stephen Steinberg in his book *The Ethnic Myth: Race, Ethnicity, and Class in America* (1981) has said:

> ...just as ethnic groups have class (or economic—*ours*) reasons for tearing down ethnic barriers ahead of them, they also have class reasons for raising ethnic barriers

behind them. Thus, it is not uncommon for ethnic groups to invoke democratic principles to combat the ethnic exclusivity of more privileged groups, but to turn around and cite pluralistic principles in defense of their own discriminatory practices. (p. 258)

Steinberg believes that the concept of ethnicity which divides the North American population into ethnic groups disguises the 'real' divisions which are based on wealth and power, or *class*. In this argument *both* the lower and upper classes use ethnicity to further or protect their economic interests. The lower classes will point to ethnic discrimination and call on the ideals of equality and cultural pluralism to move up the socio-economic ladder. The upper classes will explain an ethnic groups' poverty by the low priority the group places on work and education. If a groups' poverty is a result of an ethnic characteristic, there is no need to change the status quo and it would be useless to provide opportunities for the group to improve their conditions.

In summary, ethnicity is a relatively recent concept used to interpret North American society. Probably to most, an ethnic group is a group besides ones own—"it is those *other people* who live over there". To social scientists, ethnicity is used to describe *sub-groups* delineated by a mixture of ideological, historical, and economic factors. A debate continues as to which factors are the most salient in determining a groups' boundaries. An extreme position exists which sees ethnicity or ethnic classification as part of a deceptive *ideology*.

4. Multiculturalism

At the turn of the century, Canadian Prime Minister Wilfrid Laurier made the following analogy:

I have visited in England one of those models of Gothic architecture which the hand of genius, guided by an unerring Faith, has molded into a harmonious whole. The cathedral is made of marble, oak, and granite. It is the image of the nation I would like to see Canada become. For here, I want the marble to remain marble; the granite to remain granite; the oak to remain oak; and out of all these

> elements I would build a nation great among the nations
> of the world. (as quoted in Wienfeld, 1981; p.82)[3]

Almost seventy years later, Prime Minister Pierre Trudeau would
express a similar sentiment:

> Canadian identity will not be undermined by multi-
> culturalism. Indeed we believe that cultural pluralism is
> the very essence of Canadian identity. Every ethnic group
> has the right to preserve and develop its own culture and
> values within the Canadian context. (House of Commons
> Debates, 1971)

Applying the prefix 'multi' and the suffix 'ism' to culture was made
popular by Trudeau during the 1960s. The term was used and could be
interpreted in three ways: (1) a description of Canada's social
structure, (2) a social policy, and (3) an ideology (cf. Burnet, 1978;
Kallen, 1982). First of all, what is implied when Canada is referred to
as multicultural nation?

Multiculturalism as descriptor. Most sociologists would agree that
Canada is a pluralistic society, but how this pluralism is most
accurately described (by class, ethnicity, region, etc.) is met with much
disagreement. Obviously, advocates of multiculturalism view
Canada's diversity as one of cultural pluralism. However, using our
definitions given above, Canada would be more appropriately
described as bilingual (officially, at least) and multi-ethnic.[4] So why
was the term multicultural used instead of multi-ethnic to describe
the heterogeneity of the Canadian population? Multi-ethnic was not
appropriate since members of the two Canadian "charter groups" (as
they are fond of calling themselves), the British and French, do not
think of themselves as being ethnic (Anderson & Frideres, 1981).
Ethnics were the 'other' immigrant groups. And since the policy-
makers in Canada were (and still are) mostly British and French, the
term multicultural was applied.

Multiculturalism as policy. Multiculturalism, when presented as a
policy, refers to two related intentions. The first intent is that the
multi-ethnic nature of Canada be maintained, and the second, that
equity be achieved among all Canadians. Multiculturalism was first
accepted as an official policy in Canada in 1971 and took on the status of
an Act in 1988. The Canadian Multiculturalism Act of July, 1988 states:

...the Government of Canada recognizes the diversity of
Canadians as regards race, national or ethnic origin,
colour and religion as a fundamental characteristic of
Canadian society and is committed to a policy of
multiculturalism designed to preserve and enhance the
multicultural heritage of Canadians while working to
achieve the equality of all Canadians in the economic,
social, cultural, and political life of Canada. (p. 2)

Despite the unsupported notion of diversity based on "race", this quote
captures the rhetoric of multiculturalism when used as a descriptor
and social policy. As Parts II and III will reveal, the ideal of cultural or
ethnic pluralism can be easily stated, but what it exactly implies or
means is much more difficult to describe.

Multiculturalism as ideology. When multiculturalism is described
as an ideology, a critique is being made of the Canadian government.
The critics argue that the political apparatus created to implement the
multiculturalism policy is a 'lame duck'. The Office and Minister of
Multiculturalism can help support ethnic festivals and alike, but they
have little or no power to confront the inequities which exist between
Canadian ethnic groups (cf. Li & Bolaria, 1983). Thus, as an ideology,
multiculturalism represents and encourages the belief that equity
among the peoples of Canada can be achieved by fostering ethnic pride.
The inequities remain difficult to challenge and the interests of those
ethnic groups in power are protected. As an example, one of the
purposes of the multiculturalism office is to deal with charges of
racism or ethnic discrimination. However, in most cases the office
lacks the power and resources to adequately solve the problems.
Meanwhile, it is difficult to be critical of the multicultural office
because it legitimates the ethnic-minority voices and usually provides
them financial assistance. This situation effectively neutralizes the
complaints and protects the status quo from any serious
confrontations and revisions.

The fiercest attack on Canada's multiculturalism policy has come
from a Ukrainian-Canadian historian who served on the citizens
advisory committee to the Multiculturalism Directorate for seven
years. Manoly Lupul (1982a) provides several reasons why the policy
failed. He begins his argument by assuming that the intent of

multiculturalism is the "sharing of power and opportunity" and that "ethnic groups are a valuable force with legitimate political claims" (p. 93). One reason for the policy's impotence is that the Royal Commission on Bilingualism and Biculturalism (1963-66) did not adequately define multiculturalism and the issues related to it (e.g. ethnicity, assimilation, national identity, etc.). The Commission, however, was clear about bilingualism and this became the framework for how multiculturalism was presented. When Prime Minister Trudeau introduced the policy he said that "although there are two official languages, there is no official culture, nor does any ethnic group take precedence over any other" (House of Commons Debates, 1971). This effectively removed language as a defining criterion for all ethnic groups except the French and English. Rejecting the notion that multiculturalism necessitates multilingualism, the federal government took the position that ethnicity was primarily *voluntary* and *private*.

Another reason the policy failed is that the Multiculturalism Directorate and its minister were buried deep in the bureaucracy of the Canadian government. For example, the minister was one of 47 executive officers responsible to one of 5 assistants to the secretary in charge of Citizenship and Official Languages (COL). French Canadians have held the positions of power in the COL and they have usually been indifferent towards multiculturalism or seen it as a threat to bilingualism. The Directorate did not have direct access to, nor the cooperation of, the most powerful offices and people in the government (e.g. the Prime Minister and his Office, the Treasury Board, the Priority and Planning Committee, etc.). With this political structure the Multiculturalism Directorate was crippled. Lupul continues:

> In this situation it was unrealistic to expect a weak, junior minister to effect any horizontal coordination among such governmental cultural agencies as the Public Archives, the National Library, the National Museum, the Canada Council, the National Film Board or the Canadian Broadcasting Corporation, or between such government departments as Manpower and Immigration or External Affairs, whose policies and programmes often affect ethnic groups in special ways. (p. 95)

Two proposals were made to bridge the agencies and review the impact of all federal department programs on various ethnic groups but both neither materialized. In a similar vein, the citizen's advisory council to the Directorate, the Canadian Consultative Council on Multiculturalism (CCCM), was never taken seriously. Prime Minister Trudeau was invited to address the biennial conference of the CCCM in 1974, 1976, 1978, and 1980, but he refused to appear before the body he had himself created. Also, the CCCM's first annual report given in 1975 made the recommendation to set long and short term priorities for implementation, but the Directorate tried to move out in all directions at the same time. Confronting racism and discrimination, strengthening ethnic organizations, French language training, reviewing the portrayal of ethnic-minorities in media and school curricula were all attempted by an office crippled by its position and lack of support.

Finally, Canada's multiculturalism policy has had very little money. In comparison to the $190 million spent on bilingualism, $7.7 million was spent on multiculturalism during the 1979-80 fiscal year. During the 1988-89 fiscal year $336 million was spent on Official Languages and $25.9 million on Multiculturalism. French immersion and English as Second Language programs have grown significantly and are firmly established. Programs to maintain or facilitate "non-official" language and cultures are scattered, disconnected, and vulnerable to cuts in federal spending annually. To some, the multiculturalism policy of Canada is more rhetoric than reality. The 1988 Act is no different. It does not solve any of the problems that the Policy had nor does it provide the financial and political support it needs for effective implementation. The label and some names have changed (e.g. CCCM is now called the Canadian Multiculturalism Advisory Committee or CMAC) but its meaning and power (or lack of it) has not.

The word multiculturalism has been used as a *description* of and *policy* for Canadian society. Some critics argue that multiculturalism is best seen as an *ideology*. Both multiculturalism and ethnicity are recent abstractions whose usefulness continues to be debated. The next two parts evaluate the historical and social scientific evidence that ethnicity is a useful construct to understand American and Canadian society.

Part II

Ethnic Identity: A Historical Context

In a country which has been described as 'multicultural', what does it mean to be a 'Canadian'? In a country which has been described as 'culturally pluralistic' and 'ethnically diverse', what does it mean to be an 'American'? Is there really any sense of unity among the peoples of Canada or the United States? What is the unity that is expressed in the American motto "E Pluribus Unum"? Philip Gleason has addressed these questions for Americans in an essay he wrote for the *Harvard Encyclopedia of American Ethnic Groups* (1980).

Gleason begins by arguing that the issues of identity and ethnicity in America are interrelated. The concepts share a common origin, having been developed to deal with the same issues. Erik Erikson (1950), the psychoanalyst largely responsible for introducing the identity concept into the minds of North Americans, said:

> We begin to conceptualize matters of identity at the very time in history when they become a problem. For we do so in a country which attempts to make a super-identity out of all the identities imported by its constituent immigrants (p. 242).

Twenty-five years later, in an autobiographical account, Erikson (1975), himself an immigrant, continued:

> It would seem almost self-evident now how the concepts of 'identity' and 'identity crisis' emerged from my personal, clinical, and anthropological observations in the thirties and forties. I do not remember when I started to use these terms; they seems naturally grounded in the experience of emigration, immigration, and Americanization (p. 43).

From these quotations we can conclude that identity and ethnicity are recent inventions to assist North American immigrants interpret themselves and their society (cf. Gleason, 1983).

The intention of Gleason's essay was "to ascertain the relative salience that issues we now think of as ethnic have had when Americans have debated among themselves about what is means to be an American" (p. 31). Gleason divides American history into 4 phases, each representing a "period of intense concern" over American identity. During the first period (1776-1815), the American identity was largely ideological. Religion became the focus for the second period (1815-1860), ethnicity for the third (1860-1924), and during the fourth period (1924-1979) ethnicity goes through recession and resurgence. It is worth reviewing Gleason's arguments closely since they provide a historical argument for the multi-ethnic nature of American society and a context for interpreting empirical ethnic-identification.[5]

American Identity as Ideological (1776-1815)

Gleason repeats Han Kohn's argument that America could have only been founded on ideas since

> ...the great majority of Americans shared language, literature, religion, and other cultural traditions with the nation against which they had successfully rebelled, and from which they were most determined to establish their spiritual as well as political independence (p. 31).

What were these ideas? The founders of the United States combined their experience of self-government and protection of individual liberties with the abstract ideals of liberty and equality for all men. However, "all men" did not include women, the natives, the slaves, and later, the Asian immigrants. Fortunately, the founding documents remained sufficiently vague to allow for more inclusive interpretations several years later.

Despite the contradictions, the mark of an 'American' during this time was *his* social and political ideals. To be or to become an American, a person did not have to be of any particular national, linguistic, or religious background. A classic statement written during the 1760s by Michel-Guillaume Jean de Crevecoeur captures some essential elements of this American identity:

> What then is the American, this new man? He is either a European or the descendant of a European, hence that strange mixture of blood, which you will find in no other country. I could point out to you a family whose

grandfather was an Englishman, whose wife was Dutch, whose son married a French woman, and whose present four sons have four wives of different nations. He is an American, who, leaving behind him all his ancient prejudices and manners, receive new ones from the new mode of life he has embraced, the new government he obeys, and the new rank he holds. He becomes an American by being received into the broad lap of our great Alma Mater. Here individuals are melted into a new race of men, whose labours and posterity will one day cause great changes in the world. (as quoted in Gleason, p. 33)

The emphasis is clearly on what an American is becoming, not what he has been. Ethnic diversity was only to be temporary. America was in the business of melting, of transforming its people (Europeans, to be exact) into a new nationality.

In a review of the naturalization laws of this period, Gleason finds support for this part of his analysis. In 1802, "any free white immigrant could become a U.S. citizen simply by swearing that he had lived in the U.S. for five years, that he renounced all hereditary titles and political allegiances to any other states, and that he would support the U.S. constitution" (p. 34). These naturalization requirements would remain until 1906, enabling massive immigration for more than a century.

Religion in American Identity (1815-1860)

After the War of 1812, immigration began to increase steadily until 1830 when, for the next 25 years, 4 million people would flood the country. The important point for Gleason's analysis is that one-third to one-half of these immigrants were Catholics. Catholicism was the largest religious denomination in the country, and by 1852 there were 30 bishops (only 8 of whom were American-born), more than 1,400 priests, and a growing number of colleges, seminaries, parochial schools, newspapers, and Catholic societies. The response to this influx of Catholicism was explicit Protestant nativism, evidenced by Catholic church and convent burnings and the formation of an anti-Catholic political party in 1850. Officially known as the American Party, but referred to as the Know-Nothings, this party was dedicated to minimizing, if not ceasing, Catholic immigration and participation in American politics. The Know-Nothings were a British-American

Protestant reaction to the vast influx of Irish and German Catholics who appeared to be challenging the American ideology, the political process, and the educational system. By 1855, the Know-Nothings controlled six states and sent some 75 representatives to Congress.

Gleason identifies six factors which contributed to this anti-Catholicism. First, there was a long history of Protestant-Catholic hostilities. Second, Protestant revivalists were linking America's destiny to the millennial promise and saw Catholicism as a barrier. Third, newspapers constantly accused Catholics of political wrong-doings such as bloc voting and swearing in of citizens before they met the resident requirement. Fourth, Irish immigrants openly supporting the political causes of their homeland raised doubts about their true allegiances. Fifth, coming from a famine-stricken homeland, many Irish lived in poverty conditions. This made them perfect targets for stereotyping and being blamed for all forms of immorality. And sixth, the establishment of separate Catholic schools and attempts to get public funds enraged the Protestant majority. In fact, the 'common or public' school movement was, in part, developed to overcome the Catholic bid and serve the Americanizing function from a nondenominational Protestant outlook.[6]

The Catholic response was to encourage the separation of nationality and religion. The implicit assumption that Irish and Catholic were interchangeable terms troubled Catholic leaders, particularly those who were not Irish! Gleason interprets the writings of Orestes A. Brownson:

> Catholicism should not be identified with any nationality... Catholicism in the U.S. must cut itself free from identification with the Old World and be brought into line with American norms and values wherever that could be done without threat to the faith. If the church were to be true to its universal mission, it had to be at home in all cultures (p. 37-38).

Brownson, who is credited for coining the term "Americanization", was affirming the separation of church and state and of government noninterference in religious affairs. This strategy of trying to separate ethnicity from religion still exists today and continues to create contradictions in the American identity.

Certainly anti-Catholicism would flare up again after this period, but it would never be the focus of a nativist movement again. The Know-Nothings lost their battle, partly because of the Catholic response but also because after 1856 the issue of slavery started to overshadow all others.

Ethnicity in American Identity (1860-1924)

At least for the Union States, the Civil War reawakened nationalism and solidified the identification with liberty. (It would still take another hundred years, however, before equality would be reinterpreted to include African-Americans). The decades surrounding the turn of the century saw unprecedented immigration which would strain and eventually alter the nation's historic policy of free immigration. The Chinese Exclusion Act of 1882 again proved that "all men" still meant European. And, in the aftermath of World War I, a series of restrictionist laws were enacted culminating in the national-origins quota system of 1924. Race and nationality became the focus of debates concerning what is meant to be an American. Four perspectives on ethnicity and American identity can be identified from this period and several terms which are still used today find their origin there.

(1) *The melting pot.* Some lines from a play written in 1908 by Israel Zangwill (1917) contains the most popular symbol of diversity in America.

> ...America is God's crucible, the great Melting Pot where all the races of Europe are melting and re-forming! Here you stand, good folk, think I, when I see them at Ellis Island, here you stand in your fifty groups, with your fifty languages and histories, and your fifty blood hatreds and rivalries. But you won't be long like that, brothers, for these are the fires of God you've come to. A fig for your feuds and vendettas! Germans and Frenchmen, Irishmen and Englishmen, Jews and Russians—into the Crucible with you all! God is making the American. (p. 33).

Zangwill resurrects Crevecoeur's metaphor of 'melting' to describe what happens to European immigrants. With the help of the "great equalizer" (i.e. public education), the conditions of American life were supposed to automatically transform foreigners into Americans. A new identity or culture would be created with the ingredient cultures making contributions but essentially disappearing as separate entities. In the 1920s, Zangwill's drama was turned into a social theory by Robert E. Park who argued that all immigrant groups go through an invariable and irreversible process of contact, competition, accomodation, and assimilation. Some factors may temporarily interfere with the progression, but full assimilation eventually would be attained. Despite its popularity, there was very little evidence that the melting pot was doing its job. Thus, a movement developed that tried to turn-up the heat, or 'force' assimilation.

(2) *Americanization*. From the turn of the century to the post World War I years, several agencies and organizations, private and public, began programs to make American citizens. In the public schools, restrictions on the use of language other than English and compulsory attendance were introduced. For adult immigrants, courses in English and citizenship were offered in churches and factories to inculcate American English and ideals. Gleason points out that during the war anti-German sentiment gave rise to,

> ...a formidable campaign against 'hyphenation'. The hyphen in such compounds such as German-American was regarded as symbolizing divided loyalties and '100 percent Americanism' became the goal of the Americanization programs (p. 40).

Because of its close links to Anglo-Saxon racialism, Americanization would slow down in the late 1920s when race theory started to be challenged by the intellectuals.

(3) *Anglo-Saxonism*. By the mid-19th century in England, race theory combined with romantic histories such as Sharon Turner's *History of the Anglo-Saxons* and Walter Scott's *Ivanhoe* had developed into a national racist theory—Anglo-Saxonism (Gleason uses the phrase "Anglo-Saxon racialism"). The Anglo-Saxon race was characterized as being freedom-loving and independent-thinking. The natural political and religious preferences were democracy and Protestant, respectively. These qualities were not a matter of heritage, but of "native genius"; i.e. one's blood determined one's political and religious beliefs. These overtures matched the ideology on which America was founded and it was quickly adopted by Americans. Soon

after the publication of an American edition of Sharon Turner's history in 1841 a writer observed that "of late years, we have come to call ourselves Anglo-Saxons in common parlance".

The American version of this racist theory was represented by Madison Grant's *The Passing of the Great Race* published in 1916. Gleason summarizes Grant:

> He flatly denied the traditional American premise of equality, characterized the idea of melting pot as 'folly', and warned Americans that this generation must completely repudiate the proud boast of our fathers that they acknowledge no distinction in 'race, creed, or color'(p. 42)

Such racism, with the support of the scientific community, led to the 1924 national-origins quota system of immigration which would remain in force until 1965. In the introduction to the fourth edition of his book, Grant states that one of his main purposes was "to adopt discriminatory and restrictive measures against the immigration of undesirable races and peoples" (as quoted in Gleason, p. 42).

(4) *Cultural pluralism*. At the same time Anglo-Saxonism was brewing, a German-American Jew tried to challenge the assimilationist viewpoint. Horace M. Kallen, in 1915, introduced the term cultural pluralism to not only describe what he saw in America but what should remain the case. Kallen saw America as a political state comprised of a number of different nationalities. Instead of forcing conformity which he argued violated America's ideal, he recommended the goal of harmony, holding out the following vision:

> Its form would be that of the federal republic; its substance a democracy of nationalities, cooperating voluntarily and autonomously through common institutions in the enterprise of self-realization through the perfection of men according to their kind. The common language of the commonwealth, the language of its great tradition, would be English, but each nationality would have for its emotional and involuntary life, its own peculiar dialect or speech, its own individual and inevitable esthetic and intellectual forms. The political and economic life of the commonwealth is a single unit and serves as the

foundation and background for the realization of the distinctive individuality of each 'natio' that composes it and of the pooling of these in a harmony above them all. Thus 'American civilization' may come to mean the perfection of the cooperative harmonies of 'European civilization'—the waste, the squalor and the distress of Europe being eliminated—a multiplicity in a unity, an orchestration of mankind (as quoted in Gleason, p. 43).

Kallen was certainly against forced assimilation, but his vision suffered from two major problems. First, there was the fact that the different nationalities in America did not stand on equal grounds. The political, economic, and military power was in the hands of the British-Americans (or Anglo-Saxon Protestants), who were not showing any signs of sharing their resources. How could other nationalities realize their distinctives under such unequal conditions? Second, Kallen's view of nationality or ethnicity can very easily be interpreted as racist. That is, after a group accepted the political, economic, and linguistic conventions of the majority, what remained of their ethnicity was its "involuntary" dimensions of a group identity. It appears that Kallen believed that certain features of a nationality were inborn and would continue "even if it loses its memory". And although Kallen did not rank nationalities as superior or inferior, it is implied that the "great tradition" was preferred when it came to politics, economics, and language use. Thus, because Kallen was sufficiently vague about what he meant, his cultural pluralism can be interpreted as another form of assimilation.

The term 'cultural pluralism' would fade from usage after the passage of the 1924 national-origins law. Then, after World War II, Gleason saw the term "designating the actual existence of social diversity and the belief that such diversity was good, provided it was not accompanied by ethnocentrism, prejudice, or discrimination among the diverse groups" (p. 45). Like Kallen's original intent, cultural pluralism represents an alternative to assimilation, but its meaning also continues to be problematic.

As Gleason suggests, one can distinguish these four perspectives on ethnicity and American identity using the national motto, "E Pluribus Unum". The *melting pot* view envisions 'pluribus' assimilating into 'unum'; the unity being a new national culture to which the various ethnic sub-cultures have contributed but eventually disappear themselves. The *cultural pluralism* ideal called for the preservation of 'pluribus' with 'unum' as some transcendent ideology. However, with no explicit strategy for maintaining 'pluribus', or creating equity, and the mysterious nature of the 'unum', this ideal boils down to a liberal form of assimilation. The *Americanization* and *Anglo-Saxonism* perspectives obviously demanded 'unum'; the former creating social institutions to force 'pluribus' into one cultural pattern, and the latter excluding immigrants who did not already fit that pattern.

Ethnicity Recessive and Resurgent (1924-1979)

The salience of ethnicity in American identity reached highs and lows through this half century. The national-origins restriction of 1924 and the crash of 1929 silenced most references to nationality and the issues surrounding it. In the late 1930s, under an atmosphere of New Deal liberalism, several books appeared which described European immigrant histories from a clearly assimilationist perspective: e.g. Marcus Hansen's *The Atlantic Migration* and *The Immigrant in American History,* Oscar Handlin's *Boston Immigrants,* (and three titles which reveal their tone) William Smith's *Americans in the Making: The Natural History of the Assimilation of Immigrants,* Theodore Blegen's *Norwegian Immigration to America: The American Transition,* and Ray Allen Billington's *The Protestant Crusade.* This romanticism of the Americanization of immigrants was reinforced by the entry of the United States into World War II.

Wartime ideology. Gleason points out that "the typical war movie featured an Italian, a Jew, an Irishman, a Pole, and assorted 'old American' types from the Far West, the hills of Tennessee and so on, and this motif was not confined to Hollywood" (p. 47). Much of the wartime propaganda was dedicated to unifying diverse groups in America by focusing on the *Common Ground* (the journal of the Common Council for American Unity, CCAU) to defeat a common enemy. The ideological basis of American identity took center stage during the 1940s. For example, the first purpose of the CCAU was:

> To help create among the American people the unity and mutual understanding resulting from a common citizenship, a common belief in democracy and ideals of liberty, the placing of the common good before the interests

of any group, and the acceptance, in fact as well as in law, of
all citizens, whatever their national or racial origins, as
equal partners, in American society (as quoted in Gleason,
p. 48).

Of course, these kinds of statements were contradicted by the conditions of most ethnic-minorities at that time and especially by the
Japanese-American internment. But, it was clear that an effective way
to mobilize a nation was to instill fear by contrasting the totalitarian
aggressors with the cherished ideals of freedom and democracy.

Social scientists would play a role in the effort lending legitimacy to
the claims of unity. A book initially published as *Our Racial and
National Minorities* in 1937 would change its title to *One America* in
1946. The authors (F.J. Brown and J.S. Roucek) in their prefatory
remarks said "in the crucible of war we are moving toward a cultural
democracy". The imagery of the war turning up the heat on the
melting pot is obvious. The use of the term 'cultural democracy' over
'cultural pluralism' also reveals the appeal for ideological unity and
ethnic tolerance. The Defense Department would also call upon
anthropologists to deal with a variety of intercultural problems such
as minimizing friction between British and American troops and
how to frame the propaganda used to persuade the German and
Japanese people to surrender.

After the war, psychological anthropologists (Margaret Mead is the
best-known example) published a series of 'culture-and-personality'
studies "which combined psychoanalytic assumptions about the
crucial importance of infantile childhood experiences with
ethnographic studies of child rearing and socialization patterns to
identify the 'basic personality structures'" of cultural groups
(Gleason, p. 49). These scientists, like those who supported race theory
before them, were extending a doctrine of cultural superiority under
the guise of scientific objectivity. As an example, the Chinese
personality was described as passive because of their psychological
dependence on orality, presumably brought about by an over-
indulgence of children and little emphasis on toilet training. These
studies also provided, although never explicitly, psycho-cultural
explanations for the results of the war. One typology of child-rearing
practice labelled the preferred style as 'democratic' and troubled
children were the result of a "authoritarian" style (Baumrind, 1967).

In 1956, forty years after introducing the term, Horace Kallen published *Cultural Pluralism and the American Idea*. This time there was no signs of racism within his cultural pluralism. He included all forms of social categorization: "diverse utterances of diversities— regional, local, religious, ethnic, esthetic, industrial, sporting, and political..." (as quoted in Gleason, p.50). Kallen was also more explicit on what held the pluralism together, or what he called the "American Idea":

> Of course, the (American) Idea isn't a 'surrogate' to any religion. Nor is it a substitute for all. It is that apprehension of human nature and human relations, which every sort and condition of Protestant, Catholic, Judaist, Moslem, Buddhist, and every other communion must agree upon, be converted to and convinced of, if they mean to live freely and peacefully together as equals, none penalizing the other for his otherness and all insuring each the equal protection of the law. And this is how the American Idea, is literally religion (as quoted in Gleason, p.50).

This kind of thinking is a good example of what would be called 'civil religion' in the 1960s. To reveal and challenge this trend, Will Herberg wrote *Protestant-Catholic-Jew* (1955). Herberg saw two apparently contradictory trends in American life: a revival of religion and a growth of secularism. To resolve this paradox, Herberg applied what he called "Hansen's Law" that "what the second generation wants to forget, the third generation wants to remember". He argued that the religious dimension of an ethnic heritage was the most likely to be recovered by third and fourth generation Euro-Americans. Since most religious denominations in America had deep roots in Europe *and* had been Americanized to some extent, religion provided an ideal link to the past. Thus Protestantism, Catholicism, and Judaism were considered "the three great faiths of democracy" since they allowed a commitment to the "spiritual values" underlying the American idea. Herberg, like Kallen, embraced the American ideology, but wanted to maintain a separation of the sacred and secular.

The new ethnicity. In 1937, the Carnegie Corporation commissioned an investigation of the situation and prospects of the American Negro. A Swedish sociologist, Gunnar Myrdal directed the project which took seven years to complete. The title of the report, *The American Dilemma* speaks to the contradiction between the treatment of African-Americans and the American ideology. Myrdal pointed to the theoretical demise of race theory and how the war with nazism, which is based on racist assumptions, meant the following:

> Americans had to stand before the whole world in favor of racial tolerance and cooperation and of racial equality... It had to proclaim universal brotherhood and the inalienable human freedoms (as quoted in Gleason, p. 51).

He made predictions that radical change was probable and imminent. Myrdal was half right, new interpretations were made but it took several lives and 21 years to occur. The civil rights act and immigration law of 1965 were long overdue (and they certainly did not signify the end of racism or segregation in America).

One could argue that Stokely Carmichael's slogan "Black Power" in 1966 stands in contrast to the ideals which led to African-American liberation. However, what was emerging was a resurgence of ethnic consciousness and assertive ethnic expression in arenas which had previously been barred—the political, the educational, and the workplace. A parallel phenomena occurred in Canada as the Separtist Party won Quebec, and the election of a French-Canadian Prime Minister challenged the British-Canadian system to re-think its original charter. Red, Yellow, Brown, and White-ethnic power movements developed throughout the United States and the intelligentsia began a formidable attack on assimilation as a historical reality and inevitable immigrant process.

Nathan Glazer and Daniel Moynihan's *Beyond the Melting Pot* argued that "the assimilation power of American society and culture operated on immigrant groups in different ways, to make them... something they had not been, but still something distinct and identifiable" (as quoted in Gleason, p. 53). Ethnicity was now seen as something more durable than it ever had before, and more importantly, it started to be defined dynamically rather than by historical markers, artifacts, food, festivals, and dress. The works of Andrew M. Greeley carried the themes of ethnic persistence and transformation and Michael's Novak's *Rise of the Unmeltable Ethnics* unmasked those who called themselves "100% American" as being just as ethnic as the ethnics! The publication of Thomas Sowell's *Ethnic America* and Anthony Smith's *The Ethnic Revival* both in 1981, perhaps signified the climax of ethnic analyses. In the same year, Stephen Steinberg's *The Ethnic Myth* challenged the ethnic interpretation arguing that it was a ploy by both the rich and poor to advance their economic status.

Gleason attributes the growth of ethnic consciousness to the weakening of the ideological element of American identity. The racial crisis, the Vietnam War, the New Left, radical feminism, and the Watergate scandal all contributed to a "view that America was systematically oppressive and immoral". The founding ideals were nothing but a sham, a smokescreen, or an ideology in the materialist sense of the word. Gleason also argues that the spokespersons for the new ethnicity contributed, unintentionally, to the collapsing statue of liberty. These 'ethnocrats' depended on the ideals of freedom and equality for their liberation, but in their rhetoric often implied that America never had values and ideals that different immigrant groups agreed upon, accepted, and identified with to the extent of defending them together. Perhaps this overemphasis on 'pluribus' contributed to the return of hyphenated identifiers such as the recent shift from Black to African-American.

The existentialist and mass-culture critique of American life attributes the ethnic revival to the urban American living space and techno-bureaucratic work (cf. Isajiw, 1978). The critique argues that the impersonal and highly compartmentalized urban living in America contributed to the crisis of meaning and identity. Ethnicity was one of the many options to wrap one's identity flag around. The resurgence of ethnicity can also be accounted for by a materialist ideological critique. The Equal Employment Opportunity Commission's means of assessing the presence of discrimination[7] actually facilitated hiring practices based on group (ethnic, gender, etc.) quotas. The creation of situations where being ethnic was to one's economic advantage most likely also increased ethnic identification. In sum, the rise of ethnicity during the 1960s and 70s was a quest for power, identity, community, and for some, an economic move to get what the state was distributing.

Gleason is careful to point out that the 'ethnicizing' of America does not mean that there is not a distinct sense of peoplehood among all ethnic Americans. Conventional usage implies a difference between American identity and ethnic-identity. But, as Erikson pointed out earlier, the two cannot be separated. Most Americans are not likely to think of themselves as being ethnic, and ethnic-Americans can easily forget the second half of their hyphenated label. Gleason admits that this "American nationality" is highly abstract and grew out of Protestant British democracy, but he affirms its presence across all ethnic-American groups. He continues:

> To affirm the existence of American nationality does not mean that all Americans are exactly alike or must become uniform in order to be real Americans. It simply means that a genuine national community does exist and that it has its own distinctive principle of unity, its own history, and its own appropriate sense of belongingness by virtue of which individuals identify with the symbols that represent and embody that community's evolving consciousness of itself. American nationality, so under-stood, does not preclude the existence of ethnicity in the subgroup peoplehood-sense, but neither does the existence of the latter preclude the former... (p. 57).

Gleason's argument must be recognized, but it should be emphasized that the "American nationality" is constantly undergoing evaluation and re-interpretation. It is too easy to forget that in 1776 an 'American' did not include women, slaves, and the natives. The meanings of freedom, equality, and justice are not absolute and one might argue that an 'American' is someone trying to discover what these words mean and striving to make these ideals realities.[8]

Summary: American Identity and Ethnicity

Gleason's essay followed the relative salience of the issues represented by the concepts of race, culture, nationality, and ethnicity in American identity. Gleason's history follows the conflicts between British vs. American, Catholic vs. Protestant, South vs. North, Facism vs. Democracy, Black vs. White, and Ethnics vs. Non-Ethnics. Each of these conflicts represent a challenge to some aspect of the founding ideals. Gleason's hermeneutic, or the fundamental assumption he has used to tell his story, is that American history is the history of a vision, a history of a people in search of freedom and equality. This is especially evident in his concluding argument that there is a legitimate "American nationality" which transcends all groups, ethnic, religious, political, class, etc.

It may be that the issue of American identity is only academic. The issue may only be a part of the intelligentsia's role in establishing a nation out of diverse ethnic groups (cf. Smith, 1986). Gleason's story relied heavily on what had been published at different periods in American history. This type of data-base only raises the suspicion that a nation's ideology might be an invention of the intellectuals and power elite. Perhaps the shifting emphasis from America's 'unum' to America's 'pluribus' is only a reflection of how a nation's ideology shifts to meet the needs of its economy and defense.

However, our historical account also supports the argument that ethnicity in American identity is much more than academic ideology. Racism, sexism, ethnocentrism, and discrimination is deeply woven into the narrative of American history. Several examples make this clear. "What does it mean to be an American?" was not even a question for slaves, women, and the American Indians for over a century. Irish Catholics in the early 19th century were encouraged to divorce themselves from their Old World nationality. Immigrants in the late 1800s were forced to speak English and taught to be "100% American" citizens. Immigration of Chinese and other "undesirables" was restricted for over 75 years. Being 'colored' in the South still had legal consequences even after the Civil War. Affirming one's loyalty and being willing to serve in the U.S. armed forces were not enough to stop the internment of Japanese-Americans during World War II. Identifying yourself as either Black or African-American, Chicano or Mexican-American, Indian or Native American, or Amerasian or Asian-American, signifies much more than a concern for brevity. A study of American identity is simultaneously a study of American multi-ethnicity.

Gleason's history supports the claim that American society is ethnically diverse. His history also revealed the racism and ethnocentrism that has been, and continues to be, a part of American life. The same historical argument can be made for Canada's racist and ethnocentric nature. Peter Ward's *White Canada Forever* (1978) does an excellent job of telling the Canadian story without "white-washing" history. Today, it is appalling but not surprising, that it is easy to find incidents of racism on college campuses that are not just "institutional" but explicit and violent.

Part III

Ethnic Identity: Empirical Research

With reference to the *Harvard Encyclopedia's* (1980) definition, is there empirical evidence that ethnic groups exist in North America? Do different language communities exist in North America? Do institutions exist that are specifically designed to serve and maintain an immigrant groups' religion, traditions, values, symbols, literature, folklore, music, food, ties to their 'homeland', and sense of distinctiveness of peoplehood? We present these as rhetorical questions. There are obvious objective signs of ethnic diversity in North America.[9] But, what about the subjective dimension of ethnicity? Does ethnicity exist 'in the minds' of people? and if it does, does it have any significant influence on their behavior? It is these two questions which we turn our attention to now.

Social scientists often hypothesize that unobservable entities or variables exist because of what people say or do. A person's "ethnicity" or his or her sense of peoplehood is an example of one of these unobservables. The most direct method of assessing a person's ethnicity is to simply ask him or her to identify, describe, or define their ethnicity. The first place one can look for this kind of data is the census bureau.

U.S. Census Data

The U.S. Bureau of the Census asks members of the American population to indicate their *"race"*. The categories one has to choose from represent a conglomerate of perspectives. "White" and "Black" reflect race theory, "Asian" and "Pacific Islander" reflect country or place of origin, "Spanish/Hispanic origin" reflects a language categorization, "American Indian, Eskimo, and Aleut" are the closest to ethnic classifiers, and finally, there is the "other" race category. Because of this theoretical inconsistency, there are lobbies to have the question revised or even dropped altogether. The point is that the U.S. Census "race" question tells us very little, if anything, about ethnic identification.

In addition to the race question, the 1980 U.S. Census did inquire into people's ethnic origins by asking the question, *"What is your ancestry?"*. In 1980, English (50 million), German (49 million), Irish (40 million), and "Black" (21 million) topped the ancestry list for the American population. Hyphenated responses, like Mexican-American, Italian-American, etc. were rejected by the census in their coding procedures. That is, a Mexican-American response was coded as Mexican, Italian-American as Italian, and so forth. The instructions discouraged the response "American" by specifying that

> Ancestry (or origin or descent) may be viewed as the
> nationality group, the lineage, or the country in which
> the person or the person's parents or ancestors were born
> before their arrival in the United States.

However, despite the logical contradiction involved (i.e. a person cannot immigrate from America to America), "American" was accepted by the Census as an ethnic ancestry response. Out of the total U.S. population of 226.5 million in 1980, there were close to 13.3 million (6%) people who gave "American" or "United States" as their ancestry. One could speculate that respondents are indicating their loyalty to America, or they simply do not know where their ancestors came from.[10]

It was possible to list more than one country in response to the ancestry question. For example, nearly 75% of the 40 million persons recorded as having Irish ancestry included at least one other ethnic group (Lieberson, 1985). Such multiple entries can be interpreted to reflect the consequence of ethnic intermarriage. The National Opinion Research Center (NORC) has been asking an ethnic origins question since 1972. Multiple ancestry listings have risen steadily since WWII, particularly for Euro-Americans. Combinations of countries from northern and western Europe have accounted for over half of the multiple responses. The NORC asks, "From what countries or part of the world did your ancestors come?", and if the answer is more than one, the follow-up question is "Which one of these countries do you feel closest to?" Alba & Chamlin (1983) review the results of the NORC data from 1977, 1978, and 1980 for native-born respondents who trace their ancestry to European countries. Almost half of the sample reply with a single country, 42% name two countries, and 10% could not give an answer. Of the 42% reporting mixed ancestry, more than two-thirds said that they felt closer to one country over the other. Alba & Chamlin suggest that this result may reflect the ethnic revival among "whites" during the 1970s. That is, the "melting" of Europeans may be occurring but the hybrids are not necessarily thinking of themselves as such (cf. Greeley, 1971).

Canadian Census Data

The Canadian Census for its first 70 years used race theory to categorize the population. The question used was *"What is your racial origin?"*, and if the person did not know they were given various race categories to choose from (e.g. Caucasian). Then in 1951, under pressure from the social scientists, the question was changed to *"To what ethnic or cultural group did you or your ancestors (on the male side) belong on coming to this continent?"* And if the person could not answer they were offered ethnic categories to choose from (e.g. Scottish). When presented with categories, a respondent might feel obliged to pick one even if none of them really fit or had any meaning in their lives. That is, the so called ethnic or cultural "mosaic" which Canada claimed might have been an artifact of the census question.

Prime Minister John Diefenbaker in 1961 tried to have the question deleted from the census arguing that it worked against his nationalistic efforts to affirm a unique "Canadian" identity and culture not tied to any particular ethnic group. But he lost out to the French-Canadians who wanted an indication of their representation. Then in 1977, Statistics Canada announced that the question would be dropped arguing that "ethnic origin and its predecessor racial origin, appear to be among the most ambiguous and ill-defined of any census concept" (Kralt, 1977; p. 3). The academic community disagreed and managed to keep the question in the 1981 census, but they also altered it to allow a person to specify more than one ethnic origin (deleting the sexism and taking into account ethnic intermarriage). Unfortunately, ethnic categories were still provided and the possibility of the "mosaic" being artificial still exists.

In summary, the census data indicates that most North Americans can identify their ethnic ancestry. However, because of the way the question is asked and the response categories given, this probably should not be interpreted as ethnic identification. That is, the censuses' ancestry questions do not really tell us if people currently think of themselves as members of an ethnic group. And, even if they did have an ethnic sense of peoplehood, we cannot tell whether their ethnicity is important in how they conduct their lives.

Social Science Data

Partly in response to the ambiguity of the census question, several Canadian social scientists have conducted research on ethnic identification. Table 1 summarizes the results of eight studies on ethnic identification with adults.

Table 1

Ethnic Identification of Canadian Adults

Researcher(s)	Boyd et al.	Berry et al.	Richmond	Driedeger et al.		Mackie	O'Bryan et at.
Sample	National N=44,000	National N=1,849	Toronto N=3,218	Winnepeg N=332	Edmonton N=398	Calgary N=885	5 Cities N=2433
CATEGORIES							
Ethnic	14%	22.7%	54%	50%	37%	31.7%	17.8
Hyphenated	-	18.2%	8%	10%	8%	.2%	45.8
Canadian	86%	59%	26%	30%	49%	.8%	36.2
Other	-	-	4% Jewish	10%	7%	-	-
No Response	-	-	8%	-	-	67.2%	-

Researcher(s)	Weinfeld						Goldstein & Segal
	Slavs		Jews		Italians		
Sample	Foreign N=296	Canadian N=44	Foreign N=84	Canadian N=83	Foreign N=540	Canadian N=14	Winnepeg N=524
CATEGORIES							
Ethnic	73.8%	40.4%	91.4%	71.7%	81%	65.3%	47.7%
Hyphenated	5.8%	4%	0	9.1%	5.8	14.5%	12.9%
Canadian	20.4%	55.6%	8.6%	19.3%	13.2	20.2%	35.8%
Other	-	-	-	-	-	-	3.7%
No Response	-	-	-	-	-	-	-

Boyd et al. (1981) asked a national sample, *"To which ethnic cultural group do you feel you now belong?"* and included "Canadian" in their list of possible responses. The majority selected "Canadian" suggesting that national identity outweighed or had replaced ethnic identity. But, a hyphenated option, such as French-Canadian was not included in their response list. Berry et al. (1977) did offer hyphenated options and found that they were selected by almost a fifth of their sample.

Richmond (1974) interviewed a stratified sample of households in metropolitan Toronto and asked them the following question:

> *I would like to ask you some questions about the ethnic group you belong to. By ethnic group, I mean race, language, nationality, or cultural background. When you think of ethnic group in this way, what is the ethnic group you feel you belong to?*

This question deliberately forced the respondent to choose between the various ways of categorizing human diversity and did not provide possible answers. That is, the person had to make their own interpretation to respond. Richmond's results show that approximately half his sample used an ethnic term (30% British and 24% other ethnic) and another quarter used "Canadian". Less than 10% selected a hyphenated category which included ethnic and linguistic labels: e.g. Polish-Canadian and French-Canadian. Driedeger et al. (1982) asked two sample of adults, one from Winnepeg and one from Edmonton, the question, *"How would you define your ethnicity?"* with no response categories offered. The greater multi-ethnicity of Winnepeg was confirmed with half the sample using an ethnic or hyphenated term. In contrast, half of the Edmonton residents define their ethnicity as "Canadian". Meanwhile, Mackie (1978) asked a sample of adults in Calgary the question:

> *Canada is made up of many people who have come from all parts of the world—like the Irish, Norwegian, Chinese, etc. Do you identify with any of these people? If so, which one?*

Because the way this question is phrased, the possibility of a national identification is almost nullified: i.e. it is nonsense to immigrate to Canada from Canada. Thus, the two-thirds of her sample who did not identify with an immigrant group might have identified themselves as "Canadian" if the question had been phrased not to preclude that response. If this guess is right, then the two cities in Alberta are more homogenous than Winnipeg and Toronto. The census ancestry data on these cities lends some validity to this pattern of ethnic identification.

O'Bryan et al. (1976) sampled people from non-official language groups (i.e. not English or French) in five Canadian cities. Since the sampling was differentiated on the basis of language, it is not surprising that 46% of their sample used a hyphenated term (e.g. Ukrainian-Canadian). It is interesting that some people (12.5%) switch the terms to form a "Canadian-ethnic" term; for example, Canadian-Chinese. This reversal perhaps signifies a desire to emphasize citizenship, birthplace, language use, and/or national loyalty. Reviewing the same data collected by O'Bryan and his associates, Reitz (1980) observed that ethnic identification varies between ethnic groups. That is, ethnic groups which have experienced racism and/or discrimination in Canada are more likely to use ethnic identifiers than those who have not. For example, 82% of the Chinese in the sample referred to themselves in ethnic or hyphenated terms while only 30% of northern European groups (e.g. Dutch-Canadians) identified with their ethnicity.

Various demographic correlates have been collected at the same time these ethnic identification questions have been asked. This enables some correlations to be calculated and some hypotheses formed about what influences a person's ethnic identification. Richmond (1974) concluded that a person who is third generation (one or both parents born in Canada), was born after WWII, and claims English as the mother tongue is the most likely person to identify his or her ethnic group as "Canadian". Conversely, recent immigrants whose mother tongue is not English are the most likely candidates to identify themselves ethnically. These are, of course, predictions based on correlations; the data does not warrant any inference of causal relationships.

Affective ethnicity. Using the same question as Richmond, Wienfeld (1981) surveyed a sample of Slavs (most of whom were Poles and Ukrainians), Jews, and Italians living in Toronto. He assumed that for these groups, the labels "Canadian", "British", or "English" meant that the respondent considered him or herself to be part of the Canadian mainstream. In reporting the results, Weinfeld divided the groups into those who had been born abroad and those born in Canada (2nd and 3rd generations). As seen in Table 1, there is a definite shift from ethnic (and ethnic-religious in the case of Jews) to hyphenated or national identification from the foreign-born to the Canadian-born.

At first glance this pattern of results supports Gordon's (1964) notion of "identificational assimilation"; i.e. the loss of a distinctive group identity. Nevertheless, the majority of the Canadian-born still felt that they belonged to an ethnic group. This result surprised Wienfeld because it was not consistent with five measures he had taken to assess the behavioral or objective ethnicity of his sample. That is, in comparison to the first generation, the Canadian-born sample were living in less ethnically segregated neighborhoods, rarely (and for some, never) used their ethnic language, were not heavily involved in ethnic organizations, had a more ethnically diverse network of friends, and were definitely more in favor of ethnic intermarriage. The 2nd and 3rd generations had adopted the host culture, or to use Gordon's (1964) term, "acculuturated", but many of them still identified themselves ethnically. Subjective ethnicity was present, but objective ethnicity was absent. Wienfeld likens this apparent paradox to what Herberg (1955) saw between growing secularism *and* church attendance after WWII. Part of being an American was attending a church, but there was no need for personal piety or church participation. Weinfeld continues:

> ... ethnic identification has even less emphasis on active membership and intensive participation. There is little expectation or possibility that an individual move beyond the superficial dimensions of 'affective ethnicity' and embrace fully traditional cultures and lifestyles associated with the ethnic group. It is a value for which lip-service may suffice... Perhaps a strong attachment to an ethnic label, and a strong commitment to the idea of value of ethnic heritage, are privately significant even when not accompanied by discernible, corresponding behavior. (p. 79)

Goldstein and Segall (1985) have explored the relationship between ethnic intermarriage and ethnic identification. To measure the subjective or internal component of ethnicity they asked a sample of Winnepeg adults, the following open-ended question: *"How would you describe your ethnic identity?"*. The responses were coded into four categories and the results are presented in Table 1. This pattern of ethnic identification is very similar to Driedeger et al.'s (1982) sample of Winnepeg adults taken earlier. Goldstein and Segall also asked their subjects to identify the ethnicity of their parents. Forty-one percent of the sample were from ethnic intermarriages, the other 59% were from non-mixed marriages. The relationship between parentage (ethnically mixed or not) and ethnic identification supported Steinberg's (1981) contention that intermarriage is one sign of the disintegration of an ethnic group. That is, children of ethnic intermarriages are less likely to identify themselves with an ethnic label than children of non-mixed parentage. To assess the objective or external component of ethnicity, Golstein and Segall asked only those subjects who used an ethnic or hyphenated label the question, *"Do you belong to any clubs, groups, or organized activities of your ethnic group?"*. Only 18% of this sub-sample said they belonged to one or more ethnic organizations. This suggests once again that Canadian adults who identify themselves ethnically do not necessary display ethnic priorities or behaviors.

To summarize the research listed in Table 1, the number of Canadians who identify their ethnicity as "Canadian" is about the same as those who use an ethnic or hyphenated term. Birthplace, ethnic ancestry, length of residence, region or city, mother tongue, and ethnic group are all able to predict a person's response to some extent. Those people who identify their ethnicity as "Canadian" are usually third generation and from northern European ethnic groups. First and second generation immigrants from southeast European and non-European groups are more likely to identify themselves with an ethnic or hyphenated label. However, this identification for some might be symbolic where it has little influence on the person's behavior and commitments. Gans (1979), speaking of ethnic groups in America, talks about a "new kind of ethnic involvement... which emphasizes concern with identity" and expresses itself through symbols such as ceremonial holidays, food, furniture, etc. that are not potentially stigmatizing like original group language. This idea of "symbolic ethnicity" appears to be applicable to Canadians. Smolicz (1979) has criticized this affective or symbolic ethnicity as being "ethnic residue... (where) ethnic culture gets steadily shallower". Meanwhile, Roberts and Clifton (1982) note that because symbolic ethnicity does not influence values or behavior in any significant fashion, it could "persist for generations".

All the research studies listed in Table 1 were with adult samples during the 1970s. We turn now to research done with university students, most of whom would be adults today.

University student data. Table 2 presents the results of five studies which asked students some form of an ethnic identification question.

Table 2   **Ethnic Identification of University Students**

Researcher(s)	Edwards & Doucette	Bociurkiw	Frideres & Goldenberg	Mackie & Brinkerhoff		
Sample	Xavier University	Univ of Alberta Ukra.-Canadian	Univ of Calgary	University of Calgary		Univ of Nebraska Open
				Closed	Open	
CATEGORIES	N=185	N=734	N=213	N=208	N=147	N=267
Ethnic	31.8%	4%	10.7%	19.2%	7.5%	7.9%
Hyphenated	-	42.8%	11.7%	13.4%	.7%	1.1%
Canadian	-	52.8%	66.6%	54.8%	40.8%	24.7%(Amer)
Other	-	.4%	-	12.0%	14.3%	14.2%
No Response	68.2%	-	11.2%	.5%	36.7%	52.1%

Edwards and Doucette (1987) asked their introductory sociology students at Xavier University if they considered themselves to be members of an ethnic group. One-third said "Yes" and two-thirds said "No". It is likely that the students are interpreting "ethnic" in this question to mean "minority"; particularly those minorities who are "visible" or have some physical marker which sets them apart from the majority. Since most the students were from Scottish and English ancestry, they probably do not think of themselves as members of an "ethnic" group. Edwards and Doucette also asked their students if they thought it was "possible for ethnic identity to remain even if 'visible' markers like language have disappeared?". Over 70% agreed with this statement, which provides support for the notion of "affective" or "symbolic" ethnicity.

In 1968 at the University of Alberta, 734 Ukrainian-Canadian students filled out a 21-page questionnaire exploring their ethnic identification and attitudes (Bociurkiw, 1972). Most of the sample had been born and raised in small rural Ukrainian-Canadian communities and spoke Ukrainian as children. However, only 10% of the sample still spoke Ukrainian at home and less than 20% were involved in any Ukrainian organizations. When asked how they perceived their ethnicity, over half said Canadian and 42.8% used the hyphenated term, "Canadian of Ukrainian descent". Most of those who identified themselves as Canadian were 2nd and 3rd generation males whose mother tongue was English and no longer belonged to Ukrainian churches. There was a correlation between organized religious involvement and perceiving oneself as ethnic, but the relationship is not perfect. That is, some students who identified themselves as "Ukrainian" also indicated that they had abandoned their religion. Interestingly, the hyphenated and ethnic identifiers were children of both farmers *and* professionals. This challenges the argument that ethnic identification decreases as people move up the socio-economic ladder. In addition, Richmond's (1974) sample of Toronto Jews were quite wealthy and strongly identified with their ethnic-religiosity.

When asked to respond to the question, *"Who am I?"*, two-thirds of a University of Calgary sample of students included "Canadian" in their answer (Frideres & Goldenberg, 1977). Twenty percent used an ethnic or hyphenated term and the remainder did not include any national or ethnic descriptors. This pattern of results supports our earlier interpretation of Mackie's (1978) data based on an adult sample from Calgary. It would appear that the majority of the residents in Calgary, when asked to identify themselves, think of their citizenship but not of their ethnicity. The following question was also asked of the student sample:

> *Does the fact that you are a member of an ethnic group play an important part in your life?*

Approximately one-third of the students did not respond to this question, probably because they did not perceive themselves as belonging to an ethnic group. Another third said that their ethnicity is of no or little importance to them. The remainder (27%) indicated that their ethnicity was either important or very important to them. It comes as no surprise that people who do not identify themselves ethnically do not perceive ethnicity has having much importance in their lives.

In 1983, Mackie and Brinkerhoff (1984; 1988) collected some data which enabled them to look at ethnic identification on both sides of the border. The Canadian sample was taken at the University of Calgary and the University of Nebraska was the site for the United State group. The comparison proved interesting since the results supported Reitz's (1980) suspicion:

> The conventional wisdom is that the American 'melting pot' favors rapid immigrant assimilation and the elimination of ethnic differences, whereas the Canadian 'ethnic mosaic' allows for the survival of ethnic cultures while each group is integrated but not assimilated into the larger society. This alleged difference might be just rhetoric. (p. x) [11]

In Calgary, Mackie and Brinkerhoff used two different ways to solicit ethnic identification to see if different questions would significantly influence responses of subjects who were very similar to one another. One type was in a "closed reply" format (after Berry et al., 1977) where students had to select one of six categories in response to the question, *"How do you usually think of your own ethnicity?"*. Almost 20% use an ethnic label, 13% hyphenated, and over half simply select "Canadian" as their answer. The second question used to assess ethnic identification was Driedeger et al.'s (1982) "open" question, *"How would you define your ethnicity?"*. Comparing the two types of questions, ethnic and hyphenated responses drop significantly with the open question and the number of people giving no response jumps from almost none to 37%. This shift most likely represents the students' ignorance of what "ethnicity" is, as well as their interpretation that "ethnic" means "visible minority". The researchers interpret this result as an indication that the ethnic awareness of Calgary students is very low.

Members of the United States sample were only given the "open" form of the ethnic identification question. The number of students using an ethnic or hyphenated term is almost equal for Canadians and Americans. Half of the Nebraska students and one-third of the Canadian sample do not even respond to the question. Forty percent of the Calgary students define their ethnicity as "Canadian" and almost one quarter of the Nebraska sample say their ethnicity is "American".

In essence, the patterns of ethnic identification among university students at Calgary and Nebraska are very similar. Despite the fact that previous research has suggested that Calgary is a very homogenous city, if the "ethnic mosaic" and "melting pot" stereotypes were true, we would have expected a different pattern of ethnic identification.

Ethnic salience. Mackie and Brinkerhoff (1984; 1988) have developed two ways to assess "the importance an individual attaches to being ethnic", or what they have appropriately called "ethnic salience". The first measure requires students to choose the "most important aspect" of themselves from five "social identities": as a male or female, as an ethnic person, as a religious person, as a citizen of this country, and as a resident of their province. The majority of their Calgary sample (62.3%) selected gender as the most important social identity. Only 4.4% selected ethnicity, most of whom were non-Europeans born outside of North America. In the case of the Nebraska students, 42.9% selected gender, 3.8% ethnicity, and 32.1% said that their religious identity was the most important to them. (The salience of religion for a third of the American sample is probably a reflection of Nebraska being part of America's "Bible Belt"). The authors' point out the very low ethnic salience and non-significant difference between the two groups, again challenges the Canadian boast of ethnic plurality.

The second measure of ethnic salience was an adaptation of Roof and Perkins (1975) religious salience scale. The ethnic salience scale is comprised of three questions which are reproduced in Table 3.

Each question is scored so that the minimum is 3 (low ethnic salience) and the maximum is 11 (high ethnic salience). The Canadian sample mean was 5.04 (s.d.= 1.69) and the American, 5.36 (s.d.= 1.69); a very small numerical difference but one that proved to be statistically reliable. This result is in complete contradiction to the "conventional wisdom" Reitz spoke of in the quotation above. Mackie and Brinkerhoff interpret this finding as another piece of empirical evidence for the view that Canada's "ethnic mosaic" is more rhetoric than reality. They admit that the results might be different if samples were taken from different regions of the two nations (e.g. Montreal and Los Angeles), but their findings certainly encourage "further comparative analysis of ethnicity in Canada and the United States" (p. 110).

TABLE 3
Ethnic Salience Scale
(Mackie & Brinkerhoff, 1984; 1988)

1. My ethnicity is: (CHECK ONE)

☐ Only of minor importance for my life, compared to certain other aspects of my life.
☐ Important for my life, but no more important than certain other aspects of my life.
☐ Of central importance for my life, and would, if necessary, come before other aspects of my life.

2. Everyone must make many important decisions during his/her life such as whom to marry and what to teach one's children. When you have made, or do make decisions such as these, to what extent do you make the decisions on the basis of your ethnic background?

☐ I seldom if ever base such decisions on my ethnicity
☐ I sometimes base such decisions on my ethnicity but definitely not most of the time.
☐ I feel that most of my important decisions are based on my ethnicity, but usually in a general, unconscious way.
☐ I feel that most of my important decisions are based on my ethnicity, and I usually consciously attempt to make them so.

3. Without my ethnic background, the rest of my life would not have much meaning to it.

☐ Strongly disagree
☐ Disagree
☐ Agree
☐ Strongly agree

It is interesting to note that for the Calgary sample, females scored significantly higher than males on the ethnic salience scale (5.18 vs. 4.76). Greater ethnic awareness and salience among females was also found in Bociurkiw's (1972) sample of Ukrainian-Canadian students. Contrary to Bociurkiw however, Mackie and Brinkerhoff found that students from working class backgrounds scored higher on the ethnic salience scale than those from middle-class professional families. As one might expect, foreign students scored higher than the Canadian-born. These results most likely reflect the situational nature of ethnic salience. That is, the importance an individual attaches to being ethnic is probably influenced by the situation the person is in (Yancey et al., 1976). For example, if the ethnic salience scale was given to a group of Canadian-born students studying in China, it is likely that their scores would be much higher than the Calgary sample.

TABLE 4
Ethnic Salience by Ancestry
(Mackie & Brinkerhoff, 1984)

SAMPLE CATEGORY	N	Mean	S.D.	Significance Test (t-tests)
TOTAL SAMPLE	355	5.04	1.69	
ANCESTRY				
a. British	116	4.64	1.33	a=b
b. West European	87	4.70	1.46	b=c
c. East European	35	5.14	1.87	c>a; c=d
d. South European	15	5.73	1.75	d>b
e. Non-white	36	6.50	2.05	e>d

Table 4 presents a breakdown of the ethnic salience measure by ancestry. This data is further evidence that an "ethnic hierarchy" exists in Canada which corresponds to the ethnic groups' experience of racism, past and present (cf. Reitz, 1980).[12] That is, there might be a positive relationship between how much racism, ethnocentrism, or discrimination a group has experienced and its ethnic salience score. Being made to feel inferior and/or being denied privileges because of one's ethnicity would make one more ethnically aware and sensitive to how it influences one's life. The ethnic group which holds most of the power (i.e. British) scores low on the ethnic salience measure since its characteristics are taken for granted. A person who is a part of the majority would have a difficult time being aware of his or her's ethnic characteristics because they are the standards or norms. This line of thinking is supported by the situation where students do not realize how ethnic they are until they have experienced a situation where the norms of behavior are no longer their own (e.g. an international travel experience).

Summary. In comparison with adult samples, there is a greater percentage of university students who identify their ethnicity as "Canadian" or "American". This is not surprising given the regional location of the universities. Three of the five studies were done in Alberta, a province which the adult research suggested was very "Canadian". The one study done in the United States was certainly not at a university known for its ethnic diversity. The notions of affective or symbolic ethnicity found some support among the student samples. Very few of Ukrainian-Canadian students displayed what would be considered objective features of ethnic group membership. Mackie and Brinkerhoff's research suggested that ethnic salience was low in both Canada and the U.S.: i.e. students do not attach much importance to their ethnicity. The situational nature of ethnic salience can account for some of this result, but there were still examples of students who identified themselves with an ethnic or hyphenated label whose ethnicity does not appear to influence their lives in any observable fashion. It may be the case that the objective evidence of North American society being multi-ethnic simply reflects the presence of new immigrants. That is, it is the newcomers who live in ethnic neighborhoods and participate in ethnic organizations, not the later generations. This suggestion, however, does not fit with the composition of North American Indian and African-American and African-Canadian communities. It may be that symbolic ethnicity is more characteristic of certain ethnic groups and not others. Perhaps it is predominately within the European or "white" ethnic groups that the later generations acculturate and adopt an affective posture towards their ethnicity. Research with non-European ethnic groups would have to be done to test out this hypothesis.[13]

Summary: Ethnic Identity

Up to this point we have evaluated the usefulness of ethnicity as a construct to describe human diversity in North American culture. Gleason (1980) argued that Americans' sense of identity at any time during the country's history has always been in relation to or in reaction against ethnicity. That is, ethnicity is a useful construct to understand American history. Even the historical materialists, who emphasize economic conditions in the course of history, cannot deny the correlation between ethnic and economic stratification that exists in North American society. It comes as no surprise that Gleason's history also supported the contention that ethnicity can be used as part of an ideology to maintain *or* challenge the economic status quo.

Since objective evidence for ethnic diversity was considered obvious, the subjective evidence of whether or not North Americans think of themselves as members of ethnic groups became the focus of our empirical review. The national censuses told us very little and the social science research on ethnic identification data gave some support that ethnic group membership is still a part of some people's self-perceptions. It is important to note, however, that many of those people who identify themselves with an ethnic or hyphenated term do not display the usual objective features of ethnic group membership. This phenomena was referred to as affective or symbolic ethnicity and appears to exist most frequently among European or "white" ethnic groups.

Canada's Multiculturalism Policy and Ethnic Identity

The official policy of multiculturalism is one reason why most of the ethnic identification and ethnic salience research has been done in Canada. When the policy was adopted by the federal government in 1971, one of its basic assumptions was that if people are to be open to ethnic diversity, they must have confidence in their own ethnicity. The premise was labelled the "multicultural assumption" and was described by Prime Minister Trudeau in the following statement:

> ...national unity, if it is to mean anything in the deep personal sense, must be founded on confidence in one's own individual identity; out of this can grow respect for that of others and willingness to share ideas, attitudes, and assumptions. (Multiculturalism and the Government of Canada, 1971).

The multiculturalism assumption implies at least three prerequisites for constructive inter-ethnic relationships: (1) people perceive themselves as members of an ethnic group *as well as* Canadians, (2) people's ethnic identity is secure enough not to be threatened by each other's ethnicity, and (3) people are willing to enter into dialogues about their differences and similarities. Those people who do not think of themselves as ethnic, but as "Canadians" might think of the multiculturalism policy as being for "ethnic-Canadians" and having very few implications for themselves.

Berry et al.'s (1977) national survey was an attempt to empirically evaluate the multiculturalism assumption. While 40% of their sample usually think of themselves in ethnic terms, it was not clear whether ethnicity was salient in their lives. It is also unclear how the 60% who identified themselves as "Canadian" thought of the multiculturalism policy. Indeed only 20% of the entire sample were even aware of the policy.[14] Despite this ignorance, most people said that they were in favor of maintaining and encouraging ethnic diversity in Canada. Being in favor of the policy, however, did not mean that people were willing to pay additional taxes to support multicultural programs or support curriculum changes in the public schools. As Berry et al. (1977) concluded, it would appear that there is intellectual support for multiculturalism in Canada, but "while the support for the ideal seems high, it seems that many individuals 'do not want to get involved'" (p. 241).

Ten years later, Edwards and Doucette (1987) asked their introductory sociology students if they had any knowledge of Canada's multicultural policy and 86% said that they did not. However, 84% said that they supported ethnic groups' attempts to retain aspects of their identity (including language, religion, etc.). When provided with options about what they thought the government's role should be with regards to ethnic diversity, 47% said "tolerance", 43% said "active promotion" and 10% said "oppose or restrain ethnic diversity". As expected, those students who considered themselves members of an ethnic group (31.8%) all agreed that the government should be actively promoting ethnic diversity. Edwards also administered his questionnaire to a sample of Xavier students, faculty, and local townspeople (Edwards and Chilsolm, 1987). In this sample (N=401), he found that almost two-thirds of the subjects knew of the multiculturalism policy. However, many of the respondents interpreted the policy as government support for bilingualism. With this interpretation, only a slight majority (between 56-60%) reported that they supported the policy. It would appear that there is limited awareness and understanding of Canada's multiculturalism policy among its citizens.

In light of the data just reviewed, one could argue that the "multicultural assumption" may not be warranted. The multiculturalism policy in Canada might be based on mistaken assumptions.

Early in the 1980s, Manoly Lupul (1982a; 1982b; 1983) made this exact argument. Lupul's analysis begins by dividing the Canadian population into four types of "ethnics". These types or groups of people are defined by how they view their ethnicity and the *conscious* salience it has in their lives. The posture that each group takes towards the multiculturalism policy is a reflection of their ethnic identity, or lack of it. Table 5 summarizes Lupul's typology.

TABLE 5
Canadian Ethnic Group Typology
(Lupul, 1982a; 1982b; 1983)

Ethnic Groups	View of Multiculturalism Policy
1.Non-ethnics • British • French	• helped solve the French-Canadian situation • provides ethnic groups the opportunity to display their folklore
2.Disappearing White Ethnics • northern and western Europeans	• symbolic ethnic diversity is fine • real ethnics threaten Canadian unity
3.Real White Ethnics • eastern and southern Europeans	• a false hope • a political device to maintain the bi-ethnic and bilingual status quo
4.Visible Ethnic-Minorities • Asian, African, etc.	• helps confront ethnocentrism, racism, and discrimination

Non-ethnics. People from the British Isles, the English, Irish, Scottish, and Welsh do not identify themselves as ethnics. Over the course of Canada's history their ethnic cultures have been transformed into the Canadian mainstream culture, or the "dominant group" (cf. Millett, 1981). Lupul believes that these "Anglo-Celts" (his term) refer to themselves as "Canadian" and many resent being called "ethnic". Despite their distinctive language, Lupul argues that French-Canadians or Quebecois are also non-ethnics. Since they succeeded in having the British recognize their language officially in 1969, the Quebecois have seen themselves as part of the founding peoples. As stated in Part I and with some empirical support, most of the British and French do not see themselves as ethnics.

Lupul's label might be misleading. He is not saying that the British and French-Canadians are not ethnic, these groups simply do not think of themselves as being ethnic. Since they are the charter groups and since they make up the numerical and political majority, their (ethnic) characteristics are assumed to be the norm or "normal". Those people who are different from them in appearance or behavior are the "ethnics".

Although they introduced and passed the policy, the non-ethnics do not identify with multiculturalism. "They throw no multicultural festivals," Lupul (1983) says, "and when they participate it is as folk troupes doing habitant dances, Highland flings, Scottish pipers, and Welsh choral numbers, very rarely in Gaelic" (p. 101). To the non-ethnics, the policy serves as an ideology. As reviewed in Part I, Lupul views multiculturalism as a political ideology designed to protect the interests of the non-ethnics by making it difficult to challenge the status quo.

Disappearing white ethnics. The peoples from northern and western Europe (e.g. German, Belgians, Swedish, Danes, Dutch, etc.) make up a group that Lupul argues have assimilated into the British-Canadian mainstream. Lupul likes to refer to this group as the "Nordics". Their appearance, religion, education, government, etc. made the blending easy and was even encouraged by most groups. Ethnic awareness and salience for these groups fades with each native-born generation and any residue that remains is "highly romanticized and heavily stylized"; i.e. affective or symbolic ethnicity. That is, disappearing white ethnics in time become non-ethnics.

This group's posture towards multiculturalism is described best by Lupul (1983):

> Not surprisingly, the attitude of the Nordics toward multiculturalism, today's term for cultural diversity, is as tepid as that of the Anglo-Celts. On multicultural councils, they frequently wonder out loud why they or anyone else is there, and they are as quick to remind all present that we are Canadians first, as if announcing an important discovery. Such reminders are usually followed by equally benign professions of loyalty by the more recent immigrants, especially those from non-preferred countries. To the ethnically conscious Canadians with

great-grandparents buried in Canadian soil, the whole
exercise is not only childish but rather embarrassing,
especially when it is meant to be taken seriously. (p. 103)

Multiculturalism to the disappearing white ethnic is patronized,
occasionally used, but mostly criticized by being a threat to national
unity.

In some cases, sub-groups within these disappearing ethnics keep a
measure of distance from the British-Canadian mainstream. This
distinctive is usually in the form of religious beliefs and practices. The
Dutch-Calvinists with their own system of Christian schools and the
German-Mennonites with their ethnic-religious "sales" would be two
examples of sub-groups who have not been completely co-opted by the
British.

Real white ethnics. Lupul refers to the eastern and southern
European ethnic groups in Canada as real white ethnics. Ukrainians,
Balts, Greeks, Italians, etc. have been less eager to assimilate due to a
variety of factors: religion, language, political situation in homeland,
etc. "The main concern, undistinguished in external appearance and
therefore socially invisible," Lupul says, "is language and cultural
retention and development". However, studies by Bociurkiw (1972)
and Wienfeld (1981) suggested that the majority of Slavic and
Mediterranean Canadians had not retained or developed their
ethnicity. Lupul's counter is that these white ethnic groups are the
most heterogeneous. Within these groups there will be entirely
assimilated urban professionals as well as 1st generation immigrants
who cannot and have no desire to learn to speak English. As an
example, in the fall of 1964 the Ukrainians were represented by five
different groups at the Federal Commission on Bilingualism and
Biculturalism. For those white ethnic groups who do wish to
perpetuate their language and culture, multiculturalism is a false
hope. As already outlined in Part I, the policy has no support politically
or financially but serves the charter groups as a rhetorical device to
ward off charges of ethnocentrism and discrimination. To real white
ethnics, multiculturalism is a disappointment, a missed opportunity
to have political support for maintaining and developing their
culture.

Visible ethnic-minorities. People whose roots lie in Asia, Africa,
Central and South American, the Caribbean, East India, Pakistan, and
Canadian Indians cannot help but be ethnic in Canada. The physical

features of these people make them visibly different from the British and French and, therefore, they are perceived as "foreign". For example, a Canadian television news magazine did a story on the number of foreign students in Canadian universities and suggested that an invasion was occurring. Many of the visual images presented were of Canadian-born Chinese-Canadians implying that they were foreign students, part of a new "Yellow Peril" threatening the education, jobs, and neighborhoods of Canadians everywhere. Even if a visible ethnic-minority is Canadian-born and holds a prestigious political or community position, he or she will still experience ethnic slurs and attacks. His or her ethnicity might be only skin-deep and symbolic, but some degree of ethnic awareness and salience is necessary to function in an ethnocentric and racist culture. Visible ethnic-minorities cannot disappear or become invisible; "they wear their ethnicity literally on their sleeves, as did the Jews and others during the war in Nazi Germany" (Lupul, 1982b; p. 5).

Canada's multiculturalism policy to the visible ethnic-minorities is a political lever to combat racism and discrimination. Unfortunately, as we saw in Part I, the policy was not designed to adequately deal with the inequity and injustice which exists in Canadian society.

Lupuls' analysis of how ethnic awareness and salience differs among Canada's ethnic groups is supported by the empirical research we have reviewed. What this implies is that the three prerequisites contained in the "multicultural assumption" are probably not a reality in Canadian society. Most Canadians do not perceive themselves as members of an ethnic group. And, although most Canadians support the idea of ethnic diversity, they are not willing to act any differently. The British and French-Canadians assume that their ethnic characteristics are the norm in their respective regions. They are willing to be entertained by ethnic folklore but do not wish to enter serious dialogues about the values and beliefs which produce the folklore, let alone make any serious compromises which would move the bi-ethnic situation towards ethnic plurality. Lupul's conclusion, once again, is that Canada's multiculturalism policy is a lame duck.[15] The policy was created to solve one ethnic-linguistic issue but did not provide any footholds or resources for other groups except for displaying "ethnic exotica" (cf. Peter, 1981). Canada's multiculturalism, as it is defined now, supports an ethnicity which is symbolic, voluntary, and private. It does not facilitate the "sharing of power and opportunity" as Lupul assumes the intent of multiculturalism policies should be.

Canada's Multiculturalism Policy Revisited

It is obvious at this point how important a definition of multiculturalism is when presented as policy. The same struggle that Horace Kallen had in defining "cultural pluralism" in the first half of this century is repeating itself now with multiculturalism. Rather than build up abstractions in search for a definition of pluralism (e.g. Novak, 1980), it is best to ask what consequences a multiculturalism policy has on a nation or institution. In Canada's case, the multiculturalism policy is serving two purposes. First, for those groups and individuals for whom their ethnicity is salient (i.e. new immigrants, real white ethnics, and visible ethnics), the policy helps them maintain those aspects of their culture which do not threaten the political and economic system. For example, new immigrants can get assistance in offering courses in schools which teach their own language (but the "official" languages are still English and French). Also, they can write grants which help sustain their ethnic folklore. However, new immigrants cannot expect the multiculturalism policy to serve as a foothold to change Canada's system of government or require a re-distribution of wealth and resources. The policy does not provide for any possibility of alternative political, social, educational, or economic structures being established in Canada. At the risk of sounding repetitive, the policy presents a vision of ethnic plurality which is voluntary and symbolic. It does not present a vision of inter-ethnic dialogue and cooperation. Such plurality is too threatening to those ethnic groups who currently hold the balance of power.

Second, Canada's multiculturalism policy provides a formal avenue to confront racism, ethnocentrism, and discrimination. Equity and justice in the areas of education and human resources (i.e. hiring, promotions, etc.) has clearly been an agenda of the policy. However, as Lupul as already pointed out, the Multiculturalism Directorate lacks the political clout to effectively confront discrimination. Furthermore, the Directorate's posture has been reactive in nature. It has not struggled to define discrimination and establish policies to correct past incidences, confront present practices, and offer preventive measures.

The ideological interpretation of Canada's multiculturalism policy appears to have the most support. It is probably best seen as a piece of rhetoric designed to maintain the status quo while giving the appearance that change is possible.

Multiculturalism in Higher Education: Lessons from Canada?

In the fall of 1989, close to 300 people gathered in Oakland (CA) to discuss what the conference organizers called "From the Eurocentric University to the Multicultural University: The Faculty's Challenge for the 21st Century". With 18 panel discussions, 5 keynote lectures, and 4 workshops, a wide range of topics were addressed such as demographics, curriculum reform, teaching and learning, language, access, racism, and equity. While we fully support these initiatives, it is important to recognize that these concerns are not new to American higher education. Offices and departments that were started during the 1960s to address these issues had the terms "minority" and "ethnic" in their titles. Now, the word "multicultural" is appearing in our vernacular. As stated earlier, American colleges and universities have borrowed a term from their northern neighbor to describe *and* provide a vision for their curricular and institutional reforms. Just as Canada's multiculturalism is both a descriptor and policy, the "multicultural university" is an ethnically and culturally diverse academic community helping society move towards a vision of peaceful and just plurality of all the world's peoples.

Although there are probably more differences than similarities, it might be instructive to draw parallels between Canada's multiculturalism and the multiculturalism that is appearing on college and university campuses. Both nation and academy would agree that North America is ethnically diverse, and that the globe is shrinking on all fronts from the marketplace to ecological interdependency. Also, the primary goal of multiculturalism, (despite its ambiguity)—ethnic and cultural plurality—is the same for both nation and academy. Both must confront similar issues: e.g. sharing of power, language diversity, racism, sexism, ethnocentrism, discrimination, assimilation, symbolic ethnicity, etc. The methods or strategies vary in size, but the process is essentially the same: i.e. separate offices or departments within the governance structure are given the mandate to "multiculturalize". From our perspective, it seems essential that colleges and universities moving towards the vision of ethnic and cultural diversity look closely at Canada's efforts of multiculturalism to avoid making faulty assumptions and impotent programs or policy.

Part IV

A Case Study of Ethnic Identity and Multiculturalism at a Christian College

Calvin College is a liberal arts colleges owned and operated by the Christian Reformed Church (CRC) of North America. In the 1987-88 academic year, 4,359 students were enrolled at Calvin. On a forced-choiced question, 89% of the students identified themselves as "U.S. citizen, White". Seven percent selected "Canadian", another 2% said they were foreign students or U.S. Aliens, and the remaining 2% choose one of four "U.S. citizen, ethnic-minority group" response options (38 Black, 33 Oriental, 12 Hispanic, and 4 Indian).[16] Calvin is located in Grand Rapids, the second largest city in the state of Michigan with a metropolitan population of approximately 600,000. In the 1980 census, 93% of Grand Rapids identified their race as White, 3% selected Black, 2% Spanish-origin, .5% Asian/Pacific Islander, .5% American Indian, Eskimo, or Aleut, and 1% chose the Other category. From these statistics, one could conclude that Calvin College is a predominately "white" college in a predominately "white" city.

A closer look at Calvin and Grand Rapids reveals an ethnic-religious presence. There are 166 Christian Reformed churches in the metropolitan area, which represents 28% of the total number. The next largest denomination in the city is the Reformed Church of America (58 churches) whose college and seminary are located a few miles away in Holland, Michigan. In a Grand Rapids Chamber of Commerce publication introducing newcomers to the city, nine ethnic groups (including Jewish) are briefly described. Here are the two paragraphs written for the "Dutch":

> The largest ethnic grouping in the area, the Dutch came to West Michigan where Dr. Albertus Van Raalte established a colony at what is now Holland on Lake Michigan's shore.

The greater Grand Rapids area houses the largest enclave of Dutch in North America, and they are to be found in all sectors of the city. Known for their strict Calvinistic religion, hard work, and extreme thriftiness, the Dutch had great influence on GR. The headquarters for the mainly-Dutch Christian Reformed Church in North America is in Grand Rapids, as is the college supported by the denomination, Calvin College. Here, too, is the world's largest religious publishing house, associated with the Dutch name of Zondervan.

It is obvious from several phrases that a non-Dutch Christian Reformed person wrote these paragraphs. Not many CRC people would refer to their church as "mainly-Dutch", although it is an accurate description. Also, the CRC *owns* Calvin College and the Seminary. The college and seminary share a Board of Trustees which is comprised of 52 representatives from the CRC, and thus the relationship between church and college is much more than just "support".

The label that outsiders place on a group of people is called an *exonym*. From the above quotation and our personal experience, it is probably safe to conclude that to many people on the outside, Calvin College is a Dutch or Dutch-American community. The label that insiders place on themselves is called an *autonym*. When asked to define their ethnicity, do Calvin College students use the same label as the outsiders? If Lupul's analysis is applicable to America, the majority of Calvin's students who are Dutch-Americans are "disappearing white ethnics". That is, they have assimilated into the British-American mainstream and probably do not see themselves as being ethnic. We addressed these question and predictions empirically.

Subjects and Questionnaire

A two-page questionnaire was administered to 547 students enrolled in a January interim course in 1988. Since the course offers core curriculum credit, several different types of majors take the course. The first page of our questionnaire included demographic questions. Fifty-eight percent of the sample were women and 42% were men. The majority had been raised in middle-class urban homes in Michigan. Sixty-five percent indicated that they were members of the Christian Reformed Church. These demographics are almost identical to those compiled by college's Registrar for all students. The majority of the sample (94%) were either freshmen or sophomores but over half the student body are in their first two years. Thus, it is probably safe to consider our sample to be representative of the entire student body.

It is well known in survey research that respondents' answers can largely depend on how the questions are phrased. Thus, we used three different types of questions to evaluate ethnic identification. Table 6 presents the three versions.The first two versions were taken from Mackie and Brinkerhoff (1984) and the third was constructed to further evaluate how students would interpret their ethnicity.

Mackie & Brinkerhoff's (1984; 1988) ethnic salience scale (see Table 3) followed the ethnic identification question to replicate their question order. Students were instructed to read and answer the questions in order. They were also told not to look at the second page until after they had completed the first page of demographic information.

Results

Ethnic Identification. Table 7 presents the results of the three ethnic-identification questions. When presented with options, about half the sample make use of an ethnic or hyphenated label (i.e. Dutch or Dutch-American) and the other half simply equate their ethnicity with their citizenship (American or Canadian). The coding of the responses given for the Open and Two-Part Versions were done by two different people who agreed on over 90% of the response classifications. For the open-ended question (where no suggestions are given about what "ethnicity" is), 38% used an ethnic or hyphenated label, 25% used an ethnic-religious label (i.e. Dutch-CRC), and 24% chose not to respond (probably because they did not understand the question). Eight percent of this sub-sample define their ethnicity as "white", perhaps implying that they interpret ethnicity as "race" or skin-color.

Sixty-two percent of those students who received the Two-Part Version said that they rarely or never see themselves as being a member of an ethnic group. This percentage is almost identical to what Edwards and Doucette (1987) found with Scottish- and English-Canadian students in the Maritimes. That is, when left undefined, ethnicity is probably interpreted to mean "minority" by those people who make up the majority; i.e. the majority do not see themselves as being ethnic.

TABLE 6
Ethnic Identification Questions

I. **Closed Version** (after Mackie & Brinkerhoff, 1984):

How do you usually think of your own ethnicity? (*Check only one.*)

☐   In terms of my ancestral country of origin on my father's side
☐   In terms of my ancestral country of origin on my mother's side
☐   As a hyphenated American or Canadian (e.g. Italian-American) (your father's ethnic origin—American or Canadian)
☐   As a hyphenated American or Canadian (your mother's ethnic origin—American or Canadian)
☐   As an American or Canadian

II. Open Version (after Mackie & Brinkerhoff, 1984):

How do you define your ethnicity?

III. **Two-Part Version:**

1. Do you ever think of yourself as a member of an ethnic group?

☐   Yes
☐   Sometimes
☐   Rarely or never

If you responded "Yes" or "Sometimes," please answer the next question.

2. How would you describe your ethnicity?

Table 7

Ethnic Identification of Calvin College Students

Sample	Closed Version N=186	Open Version N=171	2-Part Version N=190
Ethnic	38	19	14
Hyphenated	12	19	5
American or Canadian	49	5	0
White	-	8	7
Ethnic-Religious	-	25	12
No Response	1	24	62

Those subjects who do think of themselves as a member of an ethnic group define their ethnicity with an ethnic or hyphenated label (19%), an ethnic-religious term (12%), or use the racial term, "white" (7%).

It is clear that how our subjects identified their ethnicity depended on what question they were asked. Ethnicity is an ambiguous to most people, especially to those who do not think of themselves as being ethnic. It is also clear that the majority of Calvin's students do not see themselves as they are perceived by outsiders. Their autonym does not match their exonym. Most perceive themselves as non-ethnic Americans, but the Grand Rapids Chamber of Commerce continues to refer to them as "mainly-Dutch". Lupul's description of the Dutch-Canadians appears to apply to the Dutch-Americans. Most of our sample, many of whom are from a Dutch ancestry, are disappearing ethnics. Most do not think of themselves as being ethnic. Those who maintain an ethnic consciousness probably do so because of the religious dimension of their ethnicity. Given this pattern of ethnic identification, one would not expect high ethnic salience scores, except perhaps for those who do *not* make a clear separation between their ethnicity and religion.

Ethnic Salience. Table 8 lists the ethnic salience scale means for various classifications of the subjects. The overall mean of 5.51 is not statistically different than the University of Nebraska sample (mean = 5.36) collected by Mackie & Brinkerhoff (1988), but it is reliably greater than the University of Calgary sample mean (5.04). Again, the conventional opinion that Canadians are more ethnically conscious is contradicted. The "Region" reflects where the subjects have lived the majority of their lives, and again we see no difference between Canadians and Americans. The students who had lived most of their lives outside North America had higher scores but not reliably so.

The "Community of Origin" refers to the type of environment in which the subject grew up. Using an analysis of variance, there was no reliable relationship of this variable with ethnic salience. "Family Income" and "Church Membership" could not predict ethnic salience either. A multiple regression analysis was also conducted using gender, region, community of origin, family income, and church membership as predictors and ethnic salience as the criterion. A stepwise procedure allowed only two predictors to be entered into the equation: church membership and family income (in that order). The multiple R statistic was .13 which accounts for only 1.7% of the criterion variance. With such a small amount of variance being accounted for it would be a mistake to infer that any of the demographic categories could reliably predict ethnic salience.

Ethnic identification and ethnic salience. Interestingly, the type of ethnic identification question that a subject received influenced their ethnic salience score. If a person had to define "ethnicity" for themselves (i.e. the Open Version) then their ethnic salience score would in general be higher than if they had received one of the two other types of questions. This relationship is understandable given the order of the questions. First, the subject is asked to identify their ethnicity in response to one of three questions. Then, all subjects are given the questions which make up the ethnic salience scale. A respondent's interpretation of the ethnic salience questions was probably influenced by how they had just defined their ethnicity.

For example, it is the Open Version of the ethnic identification question that yielded the highest percentage of "ethnic-religious" responses. It is possible that the high ethnic salience score reflects the respondents religious salience as well.

TABLE 8
Ethnic Salience Scale Means

SAMPLE CATEGORY	N	Mean	S.D.	Significance Test
TOTAL SAMPLE	540	5.51	1.64	
GENDER				
Female	314	5.60	1.64	
Male	226	5.38	1.64	t-test n.s.
REGION				
United States	490	5.50	1.66	
Canada	33	5.58	1.37	
Outside N.A.	17	5.82	1.59	
				F test n.s.
COMMUNITY OF ORIGIN				
Rural	59	5.85	1.73	
Small town	107	5.40	1.56	
Small city	152	5.39	1.74	
Medium city	151	5.62	1.56	
Large city	70	5.44	1.63	F test n.s.
FAMILY INCOME				
<$30,000	117	5.33	1.58	
$30-$50,000	193	5.59	1.63	
$50-$75,000	132	5.42	1.59	
>$75,000	86	5.79	1.74	F test n.s.
CHURCH MEMBERSHIP				
Christian Reformed	355	5.59	1.51	
Reformed Church	29	5.97	1.78	
Presbyterian (all)	24	5.46	1.96	
Baptist (all)	30	4.90	1.65	
Other Protestant	58	5.24	1.85	
				F test n.s.
ETHNIC IDENTIFICATION QUESTION				
Open Version	169	5.86	1.72	
Closed Version	183	5.43	1.57	
Two-Part Version	188	5.27	1.58	F test sig.

$F_{(2,537)} = 6.30$, MSe = 2.64; p = .002   5.86 > 5.43 = 5.27 (N.K.)

For example, if persons defined their ethnicity as "Dutch-CRC", and then were asked a series of questions concerning the importance their "ethnicity" had in their lives, they most likely answered those questions using the definition they had just generated. This interpretation is confirmed by looking at the ethnic salience scores of those people who received the Open Version question and defined their ethnicity as "Dutch-CRC". Their mean ethnic salience score is 6.71 (s.d. = 1.69 and n = 42), the highest of all sub-groups. Meanwhile, the Two-Part Version had 62% of its repondents indicating that they never think of themselves as ethnic group members. These people probably carried their definition of ethnicity (i.e. "ethnic-minority") over to the ethnic salience questions yielding the smallest mean. Logically, if you don't perceive yourself as a member of an ethnic group, then you would not perceive your ethnicity has having much, if any, importance in your life.

If the type of ethnic identification question a subject received influenced his or her ethnic salience score, it follows that how a person identified their ethnicity would predict ethnic salience. Table 9 presents the mean ethnic salience scores for ethnic identification categories.

Table 9
Mean Ethnic Salience Score by Ethnic Identification

ETHNIC IDENTIFICATION	N	Mean	S.D.	Significance Test
1. Ethnic	128	5.59	1.57	
2. Hyphenated	64	5.36	1.59	
3. American or Canadian	101	5.26	1.50	
4. White	26	5.73	1.43	
5. Ethnic-Religious	63	6.40	1.81	
6. No Response	158	5.28	1.65	F test sig.

$$F_{(5,534)}=5.20, MSe=2.59; p=.0001$$
$$5 > 4 = 1 = 2 = 6 = 3 \ (N.K.)$$

An analysis of variance revealed that only the ethnic-religious identification could be distinguished from the other five categories. That is, those students who defined their ethnicity as "Dutch-CRC" judge their ethnicity to be of more importance in their lives than do the others. As with other ethnic-religious groups (e.g. Jews), it is very difficult for some "Dutch-CRCers" to separate their religious beliefs and practices from the other criteria used to distinguish the group. No reliable differences occurred between the other groups, but they are ordered as we might expect them to be; e.g. ethnic identifiers score higher than those who do not respond.

In sum, very few students in our sample consider their ethnicity to be of much importance in their lives. Those students who do score high on the ethnic salience score interpret their ethnicity to be a combination of their ancestral origin (Dutch) and religious beliefs or church membership (CRC). This pattern of ethnic salience is what we expected given the ethnic identification data we collected. Ethnic awareness and salience is very low among students at Calvin, with the exception of a small number who identify themselves in ethnic-religious terms.[17]

Calvin's Multiculturalism Policy: The Comprehensive Plan

In 1986, Calvin's faculty and board accepted "in concept" a set of recommendations which was contained in "The Comprehensive Plan" (1985). Its complete title reveals its vision: "Comprehensive plan for integrating North American ethnic minority persons and their interests into every facet of Calvin's institutional life". This vision is rooted in the colleges' conviction that a truly Christian community is culturally and ethnically diverse. The demographic and economic realities of a "global village" is also recognized and that an education relevant to today world's is necessarily multicultural in nature.

In essence, the Plan is an affirmative action policy and curriculum reform document. All levels of the institution—students, staff, faculty, administration, and the board—were targeted for increased ethnic-minority representation. Also, steps towards multiculturalizing the curriculum were taken as changes in the core requirements were proposed. Two additional administrative positions and a standing committee were created to implement the Plan. These positions and committee are only a few administrative steps away from the college president and board, but they do not enjoy budgets necessary for their task. And, as with most policies, the faculty and student support ranges from fervent conviction to apathy or ignorance.

Calvin's Comprehensive Plan and Ethnic Identity

If the ethnic identification and salience of our sample of Calvin students and faculty has any degree of validity, then Calvin could greatly benefit by considering Lupul's analysis of the Canadian situation (see Table 5). Like Canada, the majority of Calvin's population do not perceive themselves as being members of an ethnic group. And, although they have expressed support for the vision behind the Comprehensive Plan, they might not be prepared or willing to act any differently. That is, since their ethnic-religious characteristics are the norm in the college *and* they are not aware of their own ethnicity, any substantive changes are going to perceived as a threat. As Lupul argued, "disappearing white ethnics" will only support symbolic ethnic and cultural diversity. Ethnic folklore, multicultural lecturers, and even increased representation is acceptable. But, the dialogues and compromises necessary to bring about real plurality are viewed as a challenge, a threat to the college's identity and unity.

Similar to Canada's non-ethnics and those who are disappearing, it is our impression that most people at Calvin perceive the Comprehensive Plan as having very little to do with them. To many, the Plan is simply for increasing the numbers of ethnic-minorities on campus. Thus, we have heard the criticism that the Plan has made some students victims of "reverse discrimination"; i.e. they have been denied financial aid that has been directed to less qualified ethnic minorities.[18] Also, since there are very few ethnic-minorities within the CRC, some people are concerned that increasing the number of "other-than-CRC" faculty members will dilute the "Reformed" character of the college.

In two college publications, the first author (Lee, 1988; Lee, 1989), has tried to encourage the Dutch-Americans at Calvin to take a closer look at their own ethnicity. One of his central arguments is that it is possible to be ethnic without being ethnocentric. Inviting people to dialogue over their ethnic-religiosity and exploring ways in which ethnic and cultural differences can co-exist and inform one other have been the goals of his essays.

Using Lupul's typology once again, one of Calvin's "real white ethnics" has recognized that the Comprehensive Plan is crippled until the rest of her clan confront their own ethnicity. Mary Vander Goot, a Dutch-American CRC professor, in her attempt to incorporate cross-cultural and ethnic-minority examples in the teaching of introductory psychology made the following evaluation:

> It is my impression that introductory level students lack experience with other cultures and groups, and that lacking experience they also do not have constructs into which they can assimilate material concerning persons unfamiliar to them. In the process of learning they tend to use the constructs they already have in place, and these are constructs which deal with their own experience and life-setting. In other words, they go back to what is personal and familiar to them. (1987, p. 33)

In order to remedy this situation, Vander Goot suggests that students be immersed in another culture to facilitate their awareness and motivate them to take differences seriously. She also suggests that other members of her ethnic group begin taking their own ethnicity more seriously. Since both of us (the authors) are "outsiders", it is appropriate that we quote an "insider" at length on this issue.

> Understanding ethnicity and cultural diversity is a two-sided process. It seems that the more we understand and take ownership of our own ethnicity (for better or worse) the more open we can be to the ways in which others are like us and different from us. At the same time it is also the case that the more exposure we have to people who are not like us, the more conscious we can become of our own ethnicity.
>
> The two-sided character of ethnic, minority, and cross-cultural awareness has some especially important implications for Calvin College because it is, at least by tradition, an ethnic school. If ethnically Dutch persons are to become polycultural in their awareness, they need to come to terms with their own ethnic experiences. Many of the ethnic Dutch belong to an invisible minority in a majority culture into which they assimilate but never

quite feel as fully in place as they believe Anglo-Americans are. Ethnic awareness involves noticing and understanding habits which shore up ethnicity. Ethnic awareness involves overcoming ethnic shame and denial. Ethnic awareness includes expressing ethnic pride in fair and appropriate ways.

Because Calvin College is an institution with a strong ethnic base, the position of Anglo-Americans in this community is a particularly complicated one. Anglo-Americans have more difficulty than almost any other ethnic group in forming a sense of their own ethnicity because it is the majority. It is very easy to construe Anglo ethnicity as the standard against which every other ethnicity is measured.

It must be confusing for Anglo-American members of the Calvin student body and faculty when they encounter ethnic Dutch persons who do not behave as the general cultural majority, but who nonetheless behave as a majority in the Calvin College setting. This is a peculiar role reversal that can take place in ethnic enclaves.

Allow me to elaborate the previous point with an example. Majorities are usually allowed to make references without explanation to common events in their group experience. Minorities are expected to introduce and explain the meaning of their ethnic experiences or habits if reference is made to them in the present of majority members. In short, minorities are expected to know majority ways: majorities are not expected to know minority ways. Given these characteristics of majority and minority behavior, who are the majority and minority members of the Calvin College faculty and student body? In an enclave of ethnic Dutch where Anglo-Americans are a minority, the majority is actually more familiar with minority ways than the minority is with majority ways. This is a truly unusual pattern.

Consider a further example. Majorities and minorities use different patterns of rhetoric. The notion of 'tolerance' belongs to majorities; majorities can afford to be tolerant. It is ironic when a minority member professes tolerance of the majority; minorities have less choice regarding tolerance. Minorities are inclined to pursue plurality and they are often critical of the powerful majority. Once again it is interesting to consider who the majority and minority are at Calvin. In some sense everyone is a minority here, and that makes this situation peculiar.

If students and faculty could begin to understand the dynamics of diversity and plurality on this campus, this campus could become a model environment for learning about diversity around the globe. If we could get to the point amongst ourselves where we could express ethnic and cultural differences rather than defend them, and if we could build the courage to deal with ethnic and cultural misunderstandings rather than deny them, ours might indeed become an extraordinarily progressive community.

Wouldn't it be interesting, for example, if the Dutch-ethnic majority of the Calvin college faculty were so confident of its ethnicity that it dared to offer an "Introduction to Dutch Ethnic Ways" as part of its orientation process. If the majority is not confident enough of its own ethnicity to do that, because it is ashamed or fears criticism, can it really be tolerant of any one else's ethnicity and cultural identity? Can an ethnic minority group which downplays its own ethnicity engage in genuine affirmative action with respect to other ethnic and racial groups? (pp. 36-39)

When a group of people are not aware of, or deny the presence of their ethnicity, they behave as if their way of life is normative. Members of the majority have a difficult time becoming aware of their ethnicity since it is the norm. Santayana captured this principle nicely when he said, "We don't know who discovered water, but we know it was not the fish". Becoming aware of one's own ethnicity is often painful and confusing. However, when a group of people become aware of how their ethnicity impacts their life, they are better prepared to respect, interact with, and learn from people who are different than themselves.

Calvin's Comprehensive Plan as Ideology
Another "insider" Calvin faculty member, Roland Hoksbergen (1987), has criticized the college for not willing to adjust two of its tenure requirements which acts as a barrier to attracting ethnic-minority faculty to Calvin. The two requirements are (1) that faculty children attend Christian schools and (2) that, for tenure, faculty must be members of the Christian Reformed Church. Again, a quotation is appropriate:

> The basic problem here is that most ethnic-minority evangelicals, while perhaps devout Christians, do not share the same loyalty to Christian Reformed institutions as do traditional Christian Reformed members. In fact, many view such requirements not only as pretentious, but also as indictments of their own Christian traditions and practices. Ethnic-minority professors tend to be both jealous of their own Christian traditions and suspicious of other Christian communities' call to conform. When ethnic-minority prospects see before them these two requirements, more then anything they see an institution not really committed to change, and not really willing to accept people from other Christian cultures. Instead, they recognize the institution as wanting the exact same kind of people it has always had (except with different skin color). (p. 28)

With regards to the church membership requirement, the policy allows for exceptions. Thus, Hoksbergen's recommendation is simple: use the exception and establish a quota of the number of tenured faculty who are not CRC members. He is careful to point out that the quota should not be a quota of ethnic-minority faculty, but a quota of tenured faculty who are members of some other church than the CRC.
Although the Christian school policy does not state it, is has become expected that faculty children attend a certain type of "Christian" school, one that is a member of Christian Schools International (CSI). Not surprisingly, the CSI schools, although institutionally separate, are largely administered, staffed, and attended by CRC members. Hoksbergen calls for a serious review of this policy and its practice

which he views as a blatant contradiction to the vision of the Comprehensive Plan.

Since these two policies are still intact at Calvin, one could easily argue that the Comprehensive Plan may be able to increase ethnic-minority representation, but it cannot bring about *real* ethnic and cultural plurality until some policy alterations are made. If these policies are not changed, then Calvin's attempts at multiculturalism could be interpreted as a part of an ideology which maintains and protects the status quo. That is, perhaps the Plan is simply a marketing tool in addressing the increasing numbers of ethnic-minorities in North America and the decreasing number of Dutch-American CRC high school students. Also, perhaps the Plan is simply a way to ward off charges of ethnocentrism and to create administrative structures which are mandated to deal with racism and discrimination, but are ill-equipped to bring about any significant changes. It is our belief that Calvin's attempts at multiculturalism are sincere and have a good chance of success. The basis of our optimism is the level of administrative support that the Comprehensive Plan has received. Unlike, Canada's situation where the Prime Minister ignored the multiculturalism policy after having passed it, Calvin's administrators have owned the Plan. Whether or not it remains their priority and will translate itself into adjustments to policy and budget has yet to be determined.

Summary and Recommendations

This chapter has tried to review the concepts, history, research, and policies which have addressed ethnicity in North America. As evangelical Christian colleges move towards some form of multiculturalism we suggest five things:

(1) As we enter discussions concerning human diversity we should pay special attention to the words and concepts we employ. The meaning and social consequences of words are constantly changing. Thus, it is imperative that policy-makers select their words carefully, treating them as powerful tools. Words are like finely calibrated instruments, in need of constant evaluation to see if they are still doing what they were intended to do.

(2)   The dictum that "the roots of the present are deep in the past" should be respected. Historians do much more than describe events and dates. A history tells a narrative. It is a story with primary and secondary characters. It also has a plot that involves conflict, a climax, and an ending: all of which reflect the storyteller's beliefs and values. Historians are able to change the social consequences of our words because they re-write the narratives from which the meaning of words are derived.

(3)   Keeping in mind their assumptions and limitations, empirical studies can often assist in describing some phenomenon. When it is possible and feasible, accurate assessment should always precede policy proposals.

(4)   The majority ethnic groups or those in power should become aware of and evaluate their own ethnicity and ethnic-religiosity. Ethnic awareness is a prerequisite for constructive multicultural dialogue and interaction. In most cases reconciliation between ethnic groups will be necessary as well. Injustices in the past have consequences in the present. That is, reconciliation should be seen as an ongoing process that spans generations, just as the effects of injustice spans generations.

(5)   Multiculturalism policies can describe and present ideals, but without political clout and the support from those people in the top positions of power, these policies are expressions of ideological rhetoric. The sharing of power has never been easy for those who have it. However, most evangelical Christians have a belief system which can enable harmonious plurality. Matching our actions with our beliefs continues to be our challenge of the modern age.

References

Alba, R.D. & Chamlin, M.B. (1983). A preliminary examination of ethnic identification among whites. *American Sociological Review, 48,* 240-247.

Anderson, A.B. & Frideres, J.S. (1981). *Ethnicity in Canada: Theoretical Perspectives.* Toronto: Butterworths.

Baumrind, D. (1967). Current patterns of parental authority. *Developmental Psychology Monograph,* Part 2, 1-103.

Berger, K.S. (1983). *The developing person through the life span.* New York: Worth Publishers.

Berry, J.W., Kalin, R., & Taylor, D.M. (1977). *Multiculturalism and ethnic attitudes in Canada.* Ottawa: Minister of Supply and Services.

Bociurkiw, B.R. (1972). Ethnic identification and attitudes of university students of Ukrainian descent. In C.J. Jaenen (Ed.), *Slavs in Canada,* Vol. 3. Toronto: Ukrainian Echo.

Boyd, M., Goyder, J., Jones, F.E., McRoberts, H.A., Pineo, P., & Porter, J. (1981). Status attainment in Canada: Findings of the Canadian Mobility Study. *Canadian Review of Sociology and Anthropology, 18,* 657-673.

Bratt, J. (1984). *Dutch Calvinism in modern America: A history of a conservative subculture.* Grand Rapids, MI: W.B. Eerdmans.

Burnet, J. (1978). The policy of multiculturalism within a bilingual framework: A stock taking. *Canadian Ethnic Studies, 10,* 107-113.

Calvin College's Comprehensive Plan (1985), Minority Concerns Task Force.

Cronbach, L. (1977). *Educational Psychology.* New York: Harcourt, Brace, Jovanovich.

Driedger, L., Thacker, C., & Currie, R. (1982). Ethnic identification: Variations in regional and national preferences. *Canadian Ethnic Studies, 14*, 57-68.

Edwards, J. & Doucette, L. (1987). Ethnic salience, identity, and symbolic ethnicity. *Canadian Ethnic Studies, 19*, 52-62.

Edwards, J. & Chisholm, J. (1987). Language, multiculturalism, and identity: A Canadian study. *Journal of Multilingual and Multicultural Development, 8*, 391-408.

Erikson, E. (1950). *Childhood and society.* New York: W.W. Norton.

Erikson, E. (1975). *Life history and the historical moment.* New York: W.W. Norton.

Frideres, J.S. & Goldenberg, S. (1977). Hyphenated Canadians: Comparative analysis of ethnic, regional, and national identification of Western Canadian university students. *Journal of Ethnic Studies, 5*, 91-100.

Gans, H. (1979). Symbolic ethnicity: The future of ethnic groups and cultures in America. *Ethnic and Racial Studies, 2*, 1-20.

Garrett Park Press, (1987). *Minority organizations: A national directory.* Garrett Park, MD: Garrett Park Press.

Glazer, N., & Moynihan, D.P. (1975). *Ethnicity: Theory and experience.* Cambridge: Harvard University Press.

Gleason, P. (1983). Identifying identity: A semantic history. *Journal of American History, 69*, 910-931.

Gleason, P. (1980). American identity and Americanization. In S. Thernstrom (Ed.), *Harvard Encyclopedia of American Ethnic Groups.* Cambridge: Harvard University Press.

Goldstein, J. & Segall, A. (1985). Ethnic intermarriage and ethnic identity. *Canadian Ethnic Studies, 17*, 60-71.

Gordon, M. (1964). *Assimilation in American life.* New York: Oxford University Press.

Greeley, A.M. (1971). *Why can't they be like us?* New York: Dutton.

Herberg, W. (1955). *Protestant-Catholic-Jew.* New York: Doubleday.

Higham, J. (1955). *Strangers in the land.* New Brunswick, NJ: Rutgers University Press.

Hoksbergen, R. (1987). The recruitment of ethnic minority faculty at Calvin: Are we doing all we should? *Dialogue, 19,* 28-31.

Isajiw, W.W. (1985). Definitions of ethnicity. In R.M. Bienvenue & J.E. Goldstein (Eds.), *Ethnicity and ethnic relations in Canada,* 2nd Edition. Toronto: Butterworths.

Isajiw, W.W. (1983). Multiculturalism and the integration of the Canadian community. *Canadian Ethnic Studies, 15,* 107-117.

Isajiw, W.W. (1978). Olga in Wonderland: Ethnicity in a technological society. In L. Driedger (Ed.), *The Canadian ethnic mosaic: A quest for identity.* Toronto: McClelland & Stewart.

Isajiw, W.W. (Ed.) (1977). *Identities: The impact of ethnicity on Canadian society.* Toronto: Peter Martin Associates.

Ishwaran, K. (1983). Religious socialization and ethnic identity among the Dutch-Canadians. In K. Ishwaran (Ed), *The Canadian family.* Toronto: Gage.

Kallen, E. (1982). Multiculturalism: Ideology, policy, and reality. *Journal of Canadian Studies, 17,* 51-63.

Kralt, J. (1977). *Profile studies: Ethnic origins of Canadians.* Ottawa: Statistics Canada.

Lee, D.J. (1989). Calvin's multicultural Christian academic community. In *Christian Perspectives on Learning: Readings,* 8th Edition, Grand Rapids: Calvin College.

Lee, D.J. (1988). I'm not Dutch, can we still have lunch? *Chimes,* May 6.

Li, P.S. & Bolaria, B.S. (1983). *Racial minorities in multicultural Canada.* Toronto: Garamond.

Lieberson, S. (1985). Unhyphenated whites in the United States. In R.D. Alba (Ed.), *Ethnicity and race in the U.S.A: Toward the 21st century.* Boston: Routledge & Kegan Paul.

Lipset, S.M. (1986). Historical traditions and national characteristics: A comparative analysis of Canada and the United States. *Canadian Journal of Sociology, 11,* 113-155.

Lupul, M.R. (1982a). The political implementation of multiculturalism. *Journal of Canadian Studies, 17,* 93-102.

Lupul, M.R. (1982b) The tragedy of Canada's white ethnics: A constitutional post-mortem. *Journal of Ukrainian Studies, 7,* 3-15.

Lupul, M.R. (1983). Multiculturalism and Canada's white ethnics. *Canadian Ethnic Studies, 15,* 99-107.

Mackie, M. (1978). Ethnicity and nationality: How much do they matter to Western Canadians. *Canadian Ethnic Studies, 10,* 118-129.

Mackie, M. & Brinkerhoff, M.B. (1988). Ethnic identification: Both sides of the border. *Canadian Ethnic Studies, 20,* 101-113.

Mackie, M. & Brinkerhoff, M.B. (1984). Measuring ethnic salience. *Canadian Ethnic Studies, 16,* 114-131.

Millett, D. (1981). Defining the "dominant group". *Canadian Ethnic Studies, 13,* 64-79.

Montagu, A. (1964). *Man's most dangerous myth: The fallacy of race.* New York: Columbia University Press.

Muchinsky, P.M. (1987). *Psychology applied to work*, 2nd Edition. Chicago: The Dorsey Press.

Myers, D.G. (1987). *Social psychology.* New York: McGraw-Hill.

Novak, M. (1980). Pluralism: A Humanistic Perspective. In S. Thernstrom (Ed.), *Harvard Encyclopedia of American Ethnic Groups.* Cambridge: Harvard University Press.

O'Bryan, K.G., Reitz, J.G., & Kuplowska, O.M. (1976). *Non-Official languages: A study in Canadian multiculturalism.* Ottawa: Minister of Supply and Services.

Peter, K. (1981). The myth of multiculturalism and other political fables. In J. Dahlie & T. Fernando (Eds.), *Ethnicity, power, and politics in Canada.* Toronto: Methuen.

Petersen, W. (1980). Concepts of ethnicity. In S. Thernstrom (Ed.), *Harvard Encyclopedia of American Ethnic Groups.* Cambridge: Harvard University Press.

Reitz, J.G. (1980). *The survival of ethnic groups.* Toronto: McGraw-Hill.

Richmond, A.H. (1974). Language, ethnicity, and the problem of identity in a Canadian metropolis. *Ethnicity, 1,* 175-206.

Roberts, L. & Clifton, R. (1982). Exploring the ideology of Canadian multiculturalism. *Canadian Public Policy, 8,* 88-94.

Roof, W.C. & Perkins, R.B. (1975). On conceptualizing salience in religious commitment. *Journal for the Scientific Study of Religion, 14,* 111-128.

Smith, A.D. (1986). *The ethnic origin of nations.* New York: Basil Blackwell.

Smolicz, J. (1979). *Culture and education in a plural society.* Canberra: Curriculum Development Center.

Steinberg, S. (1981). *The ethnic myth: Race, ethnicity and class in America.* New York: Atheneum.

Stocking, G.W. (1968). *Race, culture, and evolution.* New York: Free Press.

Sumner, W.G. (1906). *Folkways.* New York: Ginn & Company.

Thernstrom, S. (Ed.), (1980), *Harvard Encyclopedia of American Ethnic Groups.* Cambridge: Harvard University Press.

Vander Goot, M. (1987). Cross-cultural and minority concerns: A program for introductory psychology. Unpublished manuscript.

Van Ginkel, A.M. (1982). Ethnicity in the Reformed tradition: Dutch Calvinist immigrants in Canada, 1946-1960. M.A. Thesis, University of Toronto.

Ward, W.P. (1978) *White Canada forever.* Montreal: McGill-Queen's University Press.

Weinfeld, M. (1981). Myth and reality in the Canadian mosaic: "Affective ethnicity". *Canadian Ethnic Studies, 13*(3), 80-100.

Yancey, W.L., Ericksen, E.P, & Juliani, R.N. (1976). Emergent ethnicity: A review and reformulation. *American Sociological Review, 41,* 850-867.

Yinger, J.M. (1985). Ethnicity. *Annual Review of Sociology, 11,* 151-180.

Zangwill, I. (1917). *The Melting-Pot: Drama in four acts* New York, The Macmillan Company.

Footnotes

1. The details of this interaction are not known for any attribute, including intelligence, and are unknowable if ethical standards remain in genetic research with human beings.

2. Since we are writing for educators, it is appropriate to say more about educational power. In the earlier 1970s, a study group was commissioned by the U.S. government to review policies and practices affecting exceptional children. The group challenged the viewpoint that defined exceptional or deviant children by comparing them against racist and ethnocentric standards. We quote Nicholas Hobbs, the spokesman for the group:

> What can be said then about what it means to be 'normal' or 'acceptable' in our culture? First it seems to mean that one is prepared to participate, in an independent fashion, in one specific cultural milieu, what has been referred to as the 'Anglo-American mainstream'... The norm is essentially a monocultural one. The 'rules whose infractions constitute deviance' have been made largely by a single group, the custodians of the Protestant, Anglo-Saxon culture. Within the framework of the monocultural rules, the following characteristics can be identified as normal, good, and acceptable:
>
> 1. to be rational
> 2. to be efficient in the use of one's time and energy
> 3. to control distracting impulses and to delay gratification in the service of productivity
> 4. to value work over play
> 5. to be thrifty
> 6. to be economically and socially successful and ambitious
> 7. to be independent and self-reliant
> 8. to be physically whole, healthy, and attractive
> 9. to be white
> 10. to be native-born
> 11. to be Protestant
> 12. to be intellectually superior
> 13. to inhibit aggressive and sexual behaviors except in specially defined situations

14. to be fluent in American English
(as quoted in Cronbach, 1977; p. 50)

In secularized North America, the power to define what is normal, good, and acceptable is largely in the hands of the intelligentsia. Social scientists and their practitioners (psychologists, social workers, etc.) are specifically involved in setting the parameters of normality and maturity. Unfortunately, these people have not always been sensitive to their ethnic and cultural biases with regards to what constitutes a healthy and mature person.

3.   It is significant that Laurier analogy uses a Gothic building in England. He did nothing to reverse the continuing genocide of Native Canadian Indians. He did nothing to reverse the anti-Asian legislation and sentiment during his tenure. That is, Laurier's plurality was European in nature.

4.   The extent of ethnic diversity in Canada varies from region to region. Much like the U.S., the greatest diversity is found in the large cities. Anderson and Frideres (1981) agree with us that "multi-ethnic" is a more representative term than "multicultural" to describe Canadian society.

5.   We have limited our historical review to America for two reasons. First, there are only a few Christian colleges in Canada who will be interested in this chapter. Second, our ethnic identification data was collected at Calvin College, where the majority of the students are U.S. citizens. Although there are important differences between the U.S. and Canada (cf. Lipset, 1986), some Canadians might find Gleason's analysis useful. We also recommend *Identities: The impact of ethnicity on Canadian society* (Isajiw, 1977) for a look at the question of Canadian identity.

6.   It is interesting to note that some Catholics protested the reading of the King James version of the Bible in the common schools. This also contributed to the Protestant outrage, but also reveals the Protestant nature of the so-called 'public' schools.

7.   In 1964, as part of the Civil Rights Act, the Equal Employment Opportunity Commission (EEOC) was created to reduce employment discrimination by ensuring compliance with the law. The equal

employment opportunity (EEO) law focuses on employer's selection or hiring practices. If a company's selection procedures result in "adverse impact" to a group of people, then it has broken the EEO law and various reprimands can be applied. Determining whether adverse impact has occurred is essentially a numbers game. The EEOC has used what is called the "4/5 rule", which states that adverse impact occurs if the selection ratio for any subgroup of people is less than 4/5 of the selection ratio of the largest subgroup. For example, if 100 men apply for a job and 20 are selected, the selection ratio is 20/100 or .20. If we multiply .20 by 4/5, we get .16. This means that if fewer than 16 percent of any subgroup applying for the positions are hired, the selection procedures have adverse impact. Thus, if 50 women applied for a job, at least 8 (50 x .16) would have to be hired.

Unfortunately, some companies simply started using quotas to avoid being charged with discriminatory hiring. This practice was judged to be illegal in 1978 when a white male (Allan Bakke) was denied entry into the University of California, Davis, medical school because of the university's quota system. In other cases, however, "race" has been allowed as one of the criterion used for college admissions. More recently, the Supreme Court decided that a city's (Richmond, VA) policy of setting aside 30% of the city's construction dollars for minority contractors was unjust. The debate over what is and what is not discrimination will likely continue well into the 21st century.

A critical distinction should be made between the EEOC and its 4/5ths rule and affirmative action. Affirmative action is *not* part of the EEO law. Affirmative action is a voluntary agreement between employers and the government. Muchinsky (1987) explains:

> ...(affirmative action) is basically a social policy directed at the personnel function of recruitment and aimed at righting previous wrongs in the work force. Employers are expected to recruit minority group members as vigorously as they do others. Recruiters may (1) visit colleges with mainly black or female students or (2) advertise job openings in magazine or newspapers read by minority groups or on radio or TV programs favored by minorities. Affirmative action programs require employers to recruit minority applicants who might not otherwise seek employment with the company. Also,

companies must prepare affirmative action goals and timetables (not quotas—*ours*) for employing a certain percentage of minority employees. This is required because many employers have a disporportionate small percentage of minorities in their work force compared to the population at large. Since affirmative action is not law, a company cannot be sued for not having an affirmative action program. But economic pressures can be brought to bear against the company for lack of participation. (p. 234)

8. It is interesting to extrapolate how Gleason might review the 1980s. From our vantage point, the last decade has seen a steady increase in American patriotism. The Iranian revolution and American hostage situation turned up the flame of nationalism and kept the Statue of Liberty's torch burning as she received her face lift. Reagan's invasion of Grenada sent a message to the world, especially those Central American nations aligning with the Soviet Union. Dichotomizing the world into the "good guys" and the "bad guys" fueled the American perception that the United States is the global protector of life, liberty, and the pursuit of happiness.

However, there is another side to this rising tide of American nationalism. The recent flag burning controversy nicely symbolizes this situation. On one hand, more Americans are realizing that we are partly responsible for the hunger and poverty throughout most of the Two-Thirds world. The revolutions in the Philippines, Iran, Nicaragua, El Salvador, Panama, etc. were not simply reactions to corrupt governments. The media kept the Euro-American involvement hidden and put all the blame on individuals. What were reasons to criticize and evaluate American policy were twisted into opportunities to raise the flag of freedom. A nice example of this deception was the Iran-Contra affair where the media coverage made a hero of a man who mocked the authority of congress and the democratic process.

American ethnic diversity in the 1980s was not salient and popular culture painted a picture that ethnic-minorities had climbed up the socio-economic ladder. Television's "Cosby Show" depicts an African-American family which has almost completely assimilated except for an occasional symbolic expression of their ethnic identity. Again, behind these media images poverty statistics continued to increase and racism came out of hiding everywhere, even on the nation's most progressive college and university campuses. It is a nation with ideals of freedom, equality, and justice, but continues to live with, and in some cases contributes to, slavery, inequity, and injustice.

9.   The objective evidence supporting ethnic plurality in North America is obvious to us. However, we realize that some of our readers have never visited (or left their own) a clearly delineated ethnic community in Canada or the United States. Some people who have lived their entire lives in Vancouver have never visited the city's Chinatown. Similarly, some residents of Chicago have never been to the south side except for driving through on the interstate. Many people who have been raised in the rural midwest have never left their ethnic-religious communities. It is possible to live in an ethnically diverse society but never take seriously the presence of other groups of people. Besides the obvious recommendation of "go see for yourself" we can refer to two sources to support our contention that objective evidence of ethnic plurality exists in America: (1) the *Harvard Encyclopedia of American Ethnic Groups* (1980) reviews over 100 groups, and (2) the 3rd Edition of Garrett Press' *Minority Organizations: A National Directory* (1987) lists 7,700 organizations, some of which serve more than one minority group.

10.   Another possibility is that a new ethnic group has been formed in America made up of "unhyphenated whites". Lieberson (1985) has made this argument using the census and ethnic identification data. Most certainly, visible ethnics may also be using the term "American" to describe their ancestry. Our historian, Gleason might interpret this finding as support for his contention that a unique "American nationality" exists independent of ancestry or immigration history.

11.   Isajiw (1985) suggests that the basic difference between ethnicity in Canada and in the United States is not the speed or presence of assimilation, but how ethnic groups are perceived by the "powerholding, policy-making, and influence-exerting bodies of the two societies" (p. 16). Canada appears more willing to recognize ethnic diversity, but less willing to take legislative measures to facilitate equity and minimize discrimination. The United States is very slow to admit its ethnic diversity, but have passed legislation directly aimed at discrimination and correcting inequities.

12. An ethnic hierarchy or "pecking order" is further evidenced by considering the distribution of Canadian immigration posts: United States—13, northern and western Europe—18, eastern Europe—4, Mediterranean and Middle East—11, Asia—6, South and Central America—3, Caribbean—3, and Africa—1.

13. O'Bryan et al. (1976) did look at the ethnic identification of ten non-official language groups in five Canadian cities, but no measures of ethnic salience were reported.

14. In 1973, O-Bryan et al. (1976) also found that only 22% of their sample were aware of Canada' multiculturalism policy, but the majority (70%) said they were in favor of maintaining ethnic diversity.

15. Isajiw (1983) responded to Lupul's analysis by arguing that ethnicity can persist over generations and exists even if it is not perceived (i.e. is involuntary). Isajiw also looks more favourably on what multiculturalism policy has done for Canada, but he agrees with Lupul's criticism that the Multiculturalism Directorate needs more support and political clout to implement its ideals.

16. This distribution by "race" has not changed much over the last decade at Calvin. The ethnic-minority representation (Indian, Black, Oriental, and Hispanic) in the fall of 1989 was 2.35% and this represents a change of 1% from 1979-80.

17. Ishwaran (1983), using ethnographic methods, found similar results among Dutch-Canadians living in Ontario. The "ethnic-religious" nature of Dutch immigrants in North America is a central hermeneutic for historians. For example, Van Ginkel (1982) argues that the assimilation patterns of Dutch-Calvinists in Canada are best explained by the different theological postures found within the churches. Bratt (1984) has written the most recent history of Dutch-Calvinism in America. He freely uses ethnicity to interpret and predict the course of his "conservative subculture".

18. New need-based and merit scholarships for ethnic-minority students were created in response to the Plan. But, the Plan was also explicit that admission standards would not be lowered.

Racial-Minorities and Evangelical Colleges: Thoughts and Reflections of a Minority Social Scientist

Henry L. Allen

Although detrimental to the impact of the corporate mission of the evangelical church throughout the nation, and especially in the urban United States, structural or constituent relationships between evangelical colleges and minority communities are typically ineffectual or virtually nonexistent. With the exception of a very few prominent evangelical minority individuals, who are usually employed in Christian service professions, the majority of evangelical colleges have no minority persons on their boards of trustees, few minority students, and few, if any, minority representatives on the faculty. Many of these institutions generally ignore local minority leaders or clients. Furthermore, minority students and alumni who have graduated from evangelical colleges and universities may be placed along an attitudinal spectrum from disenchantment to racial schizophrenia, based on their undergraduate experiences. Indeed, if a casual observer were to visit a representative college, he or she would have to search intently throughout the campus in order to identify the few minority faces speckled in a predominantly white populace.

*Reprinted with permission from *Faculty Dialogue,* 1985, 4, 65-78.

The regrettable depiction given above is easily discernable to those who are perceptive and have been intimately acquainted with evangelical colleges and universities, particularly in the last two decades. Obviously, these institutions as well as the minority communities are not visualizing the potential importance of a constructive structural or constituent relationship between them. Despite infrequent articles that describe the present dilemma (e.g. Nicklaus, 1981), progress in alleviating the situation is painstakingly slow. Why is this the case? Based on my personal experiences as a minority student and an instructor at two different evangelical colleges and on my intensive intellectual curiosity about these particular institutions, the following impressions, reflections, and observations are offered in a brief attempt to conceptualize the structural dimensions of the problem and propose a partial solution.

Social scientists who seriously examine the nature and function of an evangelical college or university must analyze its social structure (cf. McGee, 1971). Basically, the concept social structure refers to a set or composite of human relationships which are systematic, recurrent, and predictable (Dobriner, 1969). In a collegiate setting, this set of relations has *formal* and *informal* dimensions. The formal dimension manifests itself in the traditional expectations and behavior of alumni, students, faculty, administrators, and trustees. For example, alumni, who are usually presumed to be satisfied customers, function to support the college inspirationally and financially. As consumers, students exist as the immediate constituency of the faculty who serve as their teachers and personal mentors. Administrators manage the needs, activities, or conflicts among these groups, as well as, the institution's resources and obligations. Finally, trustees have legal jurisdiction over policy matters at the college. Within the formal dimension of the social structure, relationships between these groups define and propagate the explicit educational agenda of the collegiate community.

Yet the most critical structural dimension probably exists informally in the *voluntary* social interactions among the college's constituencies. These interactions include social and cultural activities such as dating, concerts, worship, and recreation: activities where personal values and tastes acquired through prior socialization influence the nature and degree of participation. From such voluntary interactions the rudiments of social networks emerge and the social ethos of the college is determined. These relations are also indicative of whether cultural homogeneity or diversity prevail. Ultimately, it is the informal dimension of an institution's social structure which discourages minority participation and encourages attrition.

When the social structure of a typical evangelical college is scrutinized, its religious subcultural heritage becomes evident. As a theological and social movement that has evolved from the Fundamentalist-Modernist controversy in American Protestantism at the turn of the century (cf. Marsden, 1980), evangelicalism shapes the basic cultural milieu of the evangelical college. Within this context, however, the current interests, perceptions, and social interactions among alumni, students, faculty, administrators, and trustees also determine the nature and scope of the institution's social structure.

Resembling other predominantly white institutions of higher education in this society, the evangelical college has minimized or ignored minority participation in establishing or reforming its social structure in the direction of racial and cultural pluralism. For the most part, despite theological similarity or conformity among majority white and racial minority students, cultural and social dissimilarities prevail and are most problematic to the social structure of the institution. Perhaps this is because, essentially, evangelical colleges were founded by white persons (who despite their religious sincerity were products of the dominant white culture in America) and have been historically supported by white constituents for the purpose of educating and socializing white students. Furthermore, these institutions have been staffed and administered by white administrators and faculty who have neither had personal social experiences with a representative number of minority persons nor have they been formally or informally educated about the social dynamics of minority relations. As a result of all these proclivities, evangelical colleges are ignorantly insensitive to the contributions and needs of minorities. In short, the social structure of these institutions is inherently ethnocentric. Ethnocentrism may be defined as attitudes and behavior, informal and formal, which implicitly or explicity affirm the contributions and heritage of one's own racial and cultural group to the detriment or minimization of other groups (Vander Zanden, 1983). Minority communities are especially adept at recognizing this racial and cultural ethnocentrism, based primarily on their extensive historical experiences with the same basic phenomenon in the dominant white society in the United States. Consequently, the existence of this ethnocentrism discourages and prevents minority participation in the constituency of the evangelical college.

The manifestation of racial and cultural ethnocentrism occurs throughout the social structure of the evangelical college. Internally, the relative absence of minorities in the student body, as well as on the staff, administration, and faculty, is considered visible evidence. Since minorities constitute nearly twenty percent of this nation's population and many of their communities have Christian churches reasonably compatible with evangelical doctrines, how can this absence be legitimated? This absence of minorities is probably responsible for many of the difficulties experienced by minority youth, especially in the extracurriculum of the college (e.g., social activities, church involvement, and dating). Since peer group relationships have an important role in the maintenance of the institution's social structure and in the cognitive and affective socialization of undergraduates, a devastating social deficiency characterizes the collegiate experiences of minorities at evangelical colleges. How can the sensitive evangelical collegiate community continue to condone this situation? Obviously, elements of ignorance, inexperience, and conformity to the norms of the dominant white culture are crucial variables in answering this question. It is tragic that white evangelicals are no more capable of successful social interaction with minorities than their unregenerate white counterparts, especially given the supernatural love that should be indicative of Christ's true followers.

In order to avoid various external social problems, many evangelical colleges and universities have also isolated themselves from or have minimized their participation in minority communities. The latter generalization is especially pertinent to those colleges located in geographical proximity to large minority communities, which are characteristically in urban settings. These schools have not endeavored to seek, create, and cultivate the same type of associations with minority communities as they have successfully accomplished with their majority white constituencies. Few institutions have established formal and informal relations with minority pastors and churches, minority business person, educators, and other civic or community representatives. Minority persons from local communities have generally not been welcomed or encouraged to participate, where appropriate, in campus activities; they have also not been asked to assist in altering the social structure of the college by accepting trustee, faculty, administrative, or staff appointments. Assuming that minority persons with compatible theological or religious qualifications are either available or can be developed from minority alumni, it seems that the most fundamental impediment to effective interaction between minority communities and evangelical colleges is the absence of or failure to develop a structural or constituent relationship.

Given the structural composition of the evangelical college described previously, what should or can be done to modify the institution's cultural and racial ethos from an ethnocentric one to a more pluralistic one? Why is a modification in the social structure desirable or necessary? What are the obstacles that must be confronted before such a modification can be accomplished? The answers to these questions are not simple but a few reasonable suggestions can be inferred. First of all, the evangelical college must devote itself to establishing a constituent relationship with minority communities as a crucial priority. Therefore, college officals must seek and develop a functional and reciprocal relationship with compatible minority churches and leaders in all appropriate dimensions of the campus. In order to achieve this, minority persons should definitely be recruited to serve as faculty, administrators, and trustees of the institution. This recruitment of minority persons will not be easy in the short term both because of the social and economic barriers minorities confront in securing advanced degrees, as well as the current paucity of minority evangelicals in the existing pool of graduate students. However, assuming a sincere desire to recruit minorities, faculty and administrators could encourage present minority students or minority alumni to seek advanced degrees in order to qualify for faculty positions at evangelical colleges. Minority faculty members who are Christians but are employed in other academic or professional settings, might also be targeted for recruitment. Since many of these persons are not privy to evangelical social and professional networks, a substantial effort may be required to identify them. Minority professional organizations and churches would be logical places to begin in this endeavor.

Once substantive progress in recruiting minority faculty, administrators, and trustees has been made, a major impediment to minority student recruitment and retention will have been curtailed or perhaps, even eliminated altogether. In essence, evangelical college leaders would have to challenge and overcome the ethnocentric social norms of the dominant white society in order to promote constructive social and professional interaction with minority communities. Since most of them live, worship, and socialize in ethnocentric social settings, a tangible and visible commitment to implementing racial and cultural diversity in the college would demonstrate authentic Christian faith.

The rationale for altering the white ethnocentric subculture endemic to the evangelical college has spiritual, cultural, and practical aspects. As educational institutions nurtured by Christians mandated to disciple all peoples or nations, these colleges can not obediently avoid the educational and leadership needs of minority communities. Minority communities across the nation and particularly those located in relatively impoverished urban settings need Christian leaders who are committed to evangelical doctrines as much or more so than majority white communities. At the present time, where can this type of educated leadership be produced, except in an evangelical college? Ultimately, the college needs to do for minority youth and communities what it has rather successfully done for majority white young people. To the extent that it fails to do so, the evangelical church will continue to be regarded with suspicion, irrelevance, or overt hostility by minority communities. Minorities are well-acquainted with the hypocrisy of evangelicals who profess to really love them while they exhibit the same oppressive and insensitive attitudes and actions of the dominant white society.

Young white evangelicals need also to benefit from cultural interaction with minority communities in order to function and minister effectively in this increasingly multiracial and multiethnic society. White students who have not been formally and informally educated about racial minorities are probably doomed to repeating the same ethnocentrism of their progenitors. Thus, the historical American pattern of racial segregation among those professing exclusive allegiance to Jesus Christ would continue to inhibit the impact and integrity of the Christian message in society. Currently, most white students, faculty, administrators, staff, and trustees at evangelical colleges tend to display an excessive naivete about racial minorities. One might grievously speculate about the devastating consequences of a pivotal social confrontation between naive whites and offended minorities, even if both, were compatible in their evangelical beliefs. Hence the need for all participants at evangelical institutions to understand and experience the adjustments and contributions of a racially and culturally pluralistic collegiate social structure.

Several obstacles threaten to impede or minimize progress in modifying the social structure of the evangelical college from its current white ethnocentric subculture to a more pluralistic social environment. None of these may be more decisive than the financial limitations experienced by these institutions of higher education in the present period. Establishing structural relations and recruiting minority faculty, staff, administrators, and students may require financial resources, especially until minority communities are incorporated into the informal and formal channels of the social, professional, and financial networks which characterize white constituent relationships. Funds could be solicited both from sensitive, committed minority and majority persons or organizations. Creative techniques to circumvent financial limitations can be researched by competent faculty and administrators at the college, as well as by minority leaders.

The management of the inevitable social or interpersonal conflicts which arise between majority white and minority persons is another crucial obstacle to altering the social structure. Since ignorance of and inexperience with the dynamics of a racially and culturally pluralistic social environment is normal for citizens of this society, the creation and legitimation of representative advisory or policy committees, which could be composed of an equal number of whites and minorities on and off the campus, might be attempted to curtail and manage these conflicts. If these committees are genuinely based upon and constructed with patience, prayer, acumen, competence, and cooperation, they might prove effective, no matter where they are placed within the governance or administrative structure of the institution. Since the feasibility of this specific suggestion for conflict management may be debatable, the expertise of other colleagues might be sought to generate more practicable and effectual alternatives.

Perhaps the most pertinent obstacle to achieving reform in the social structure of the evangelical college is insufficient motivation among prevailing constituents. Ethnocentrism is indeed capable of blinding college officals and constituents for viewing the educational needs and contributions of minority communities. As a result, these officials have little impetus or incentive to risk alienation from a white constituency in order to accomodate minority concerns. Undoubtedly, this is a crucial dilemma devoid of simplistic solutions.

It may be that the evangelical community has matured enough to recognize the need for appreciating the racial and cultural diversity of all people who are committed to Jesus Christ. One can only hope that this generalization would prove true. Nevertheless, more than hope is required to remove the vestiges of a white ethnocentric subculture from the social structures of evangelical colleges and universities and from the evangelical community at large. Only God's supernatural power and guidance can supersede or eliminate evangelical conformity to the social norms of the dominant society in the United States. For the sake of majority white and minority communities, even now let this be so! Unless evangelical colleges and universities genuinely transform their ethnocentric social structures, however, the reality of substantive minority participation in them will remain an elusive and impossible dream.

> *Editors' Note: Professor Allen's article appeared in two parts. To maintain the integrity of his thoughts, we have not altered the text by adding any transitional comments.*

In response to my previous essay about the relationship between evangelical colleges and racial minorities, three essential questions which require answers have been posed by concerned colleagues: (1) Why should evangelical colleges be responsible for taking the initiative in establishing a structural relationship with minority communities? (2) What are the anticipated outcomes of constructing such a relationship? and (3) What responsibilities should minority communities have in becoming a constituency of a college? These questions are very complex and indicative of the larger issue concerning what evangelical colleges would look like if they actually had a structural relationship with minority communities. Admittedly, the brief explanations which follow are partially speculative and visionary, given that few tangible examples of racially and culturally pluralistic institutions exist within the evangelical collegiate community.

The motivation for evangelical colleges to initiate constituent relationships with minority communities is implicit in the Christian world view and mandate. Since evangelicals recognize the supernatural authority of the Bible, the need for a personal experience of salvation in Christ Jesus, and the necessity of evangelizing the nations and peoples of the world, they are consequently mandated to disciple and serve the needs of all people, including racial minorities. In fact, the witness of Christ's kingdom on earth demands incorporating minority believers so that their communities can also be confronted with the reality of Christ's reign. Furthermore, evangelicals and their colleges, because of their expertise and resources, have been blessed to serve as leaders in the Christian world. Obviously, this leadership carries the responsibility to meet the needs of racial minorities where possible. There is little doubt that evangelical colleges can assist in enhancing Christ's kingdom in minority communities if they would only incorporate these groups into their social structures and educational agendas. Thus, evangelical colleges should initiate structural relations with minorities as an extension of their ongoing mission to educate believers and to serve Christ's kingdom.

Assuming the recognition of this basic Christian mandate, the more problematic issue is the anticipated outcomes of establishing a structural relationship between minority communities and evangelical colleges. Because these colleges have experienced a cultural lag in minority relations, they have most often reacted to the reverberations of social unrest between the dominant white society and minorities. Consequently, they have provided little moral, spiritual, or practical leadership in resolving areas of tension between these social groups. To redress this situation, evangelical collegiate leaders must be careful to avoid popular misconceptions about the needs and desires of minority communities.

One immediate misconception about a structural relationship between minority communities and evangelical colleges is the notion that this relationship *has* to be based upon numerical or statistical parity. Persons who adhere to this misconception seem to believe that statistical parity is a guarantee of minority influence in collegiate affairs. However, it should be apparent that the nature and quality of minority participation is probably more salient than mere statistical presence. For example, a few minority individuals who genuinely participate in the social structure of an evangelical college may conceivably have more influence and be able to accomplish more than a large number of minority persons with token or symbolic representation. Minority participation should therefore be based on substantive participation in the social structure, rather than exclusively on numerical quotas. The key to pluralism is found not in statistical gimmicks but rather in tangible and real cooperation. In reality, the only guarantee of actual minority participation in campus affairs is the integrity and authenticity demonstrated in the commitments of evangelical collegiate leaders and their constituencies.

A second misconception which should be avoided by college leaders is that achieving a pluralistic social structure can be done easily. To alter a pattern of social relations which has characterized an institution for decades is a task not achieved overnight. A carefully developed and implemented strategy for reform takes time to develop, but it will yield more lasting results than hastily conceived efforts undertaken because of social pressure or guilt. The unsuccessful experiences of many evangelical institutions in trying to recruit minority students during the late 1960s should indicate the wisdom of this statement. Instead of devising plans to reform their social structures, college officials recklessly recruited minority students who could or would not cope in the ethnocentric social environment typical of many campuses. Consequently, neither minority communities nor evangelical colleges benefited from this episodic fiasco.

To avoid repeating past mistakes, plans for achieving pluralism in the evangelical college should be constructed carefully with professionalism and minority cooperation. An institution's mission, social structure, and heritage must be critically evaluated along with its capacity to identify and meet the educational needs of minority communities. Social and professional contacts should be made with potential minority participants and consultants, especially those readily available in minority communities in the immediate locale of the college. Communities and advisory boards might also be established to formulate a feasible strategy for promoting cultural pluralism in the evangelical college. Throughout the planning process, those involved should view as their ultimate task the incorporation of minority constituencies into the social fabric of the institution, without compromising the mission, purpose, or objectives of the college or purposefully alienating historic constituencies. Since this objective cannot be achieved without the highest standards of integrity, sincerity, humility, and Christian love, only the most devout and creative persons from both majority white and minority groups should participate in planning the strategy.

The last misconception which needs addressing is that changing the social structure of an evangelical college will inevitably lead to a fundamental and intimate modification in social relations between white evangelicals and minorities, especially with respect to interracial dating or marriage. There is, indeed, a risk that these intimate social relationships would become more prevalent but this is not automatically assured. Nevertheless, even in a pluralistic social structure, intermarriage between different racial, ethnic, or cultural groups would still be infrequent, due primarily to the deeply entrenched sociological norms and sanctions in the dominant society. In other words, the ethnocentric social pressures in this society will continue to insure that intermarriage remains a deviant and precarious venture. As white evangelicals and minorities interact within a pluralistic social structure, each occurance of interracial dating must therefore be evaluated on its own merits. Since the Bible neither condones nor condemns interracial dating or marriage among Christians, the possibility that a pluralistic social structure might encourage these relationships is not a sufficient and credible excuse for maintaining white ethnocentrism at evangelical colleges, to the chagrin of white parents who use these institutions as safe racial havens for their sons and daughters. The existence of a racially and culturally pluralistic social structure at an evangelical college does not in itself either encourage or discourage interracial dating or marital relationships; but rather, it simply provides a milieu in which majority and minority persons can be educated about themselves, their religious and cultural heritages, and about the world around them. In short, altering the social structure of the college is not a panacea for all problems in racial and ethnic relations.

What then are the expected outcomes of a structural relationship between evangelical colleges and minority communities? Precisely, the same as those anticipated from relations with the college of other white constituencies. The colleges generally seek a constituency that is loyal, supportive (inspirationally and financially), and interested in its affairs. Minority communities typically request involvement, participation, or incorporation into the social structure and affairs of the college so that their youth can be educated socially, spiritually, and intellectually. Given the possibility of a mutually beneficial relationship, it seems that historic deficiencies in race relations among white evangelicals and racial minorites are the prime impediment to promoting the awareness, reciprocity, and compromise needed to begin building a constituent relationship. Consequently, the specific outcomes of such a relationship actually depend on the timing, type, quality, and maturity of existing and future relations between particular colleges and the minority communities they might serve.

Having explained the role evangelical colleges should assume in promoting a structural relationship with minorities, the responsibilities of minority communities toward the colleges must now be succinctly identified. As implied in the preceding paragraph, minority communities must be expected to appropriate the same essential duties as other constituencies of the college. Hence, they must cooperate with and support the college by investing their youth and financial resources. Minority communities should not unrealistically expect evangelical colleges to absorb exclusively all the practical costs and responsibilities of providing and financing the education of minority youth. Neither should minorities expect to receive unjustified preferential treatment over other white constituencies in regular collegiate affairs. However, minority communities can reasonably anticipate that their substantive participation in the social structure of the college requires a corresponding participation in responsibilities that all constituencies of the institution have. In other words, as minorities are incorporated into the social structure of an evangelical college, they must also assume those responsibilities endemic to other constituencies of the college. Majority white evangelicals and minorities, as Christians under the lordship of Christ Jesus, actively and submissively must cooperate in order to insure the survival and growth of evangelical colleges. Unless this cooperation is secured, alienation and conflict will continue to characterize race relations among sincere Christians within these institutions. Undoubtedly, only persons and forces opposed to the advance of Christian truth and discipleship could relish such a development.

The ideas presented in this and my previous essay are neither revolutionary nor complex. Hence, they should be easily comprehended by those who have been sincerely concerned about the relationship between evangelical colleges and racial minorities. Hopefully, these ideas have clarified the perennial, yet necessary, estrangement that exists between Christians in minority communities and evangelical colleges, primarily because of historic patterns of racial and social relations. Although this estrangement may be repulsive to most, if not all, of us in the evangelical collegiate community, it will nevertheless remain characteristic of Christian higher education unless the status quo is drastically and decisively changed on most campuses. A resolute commitment to progressive and tangible action is needed by the entire evangelical collegiate community if genuine and substantial progress in incorporating minority evangelicals into the social structures of our colleges will be achieved. To the extent that this commitment to action is ephemeral or nonexistent, an effective and continual evangelical witness among racial minorities in this nation will be disregarded. Surely the Lord Jesus Christ cannot be pleased with those who intentionally or apathetically sanction this inexusable neglect.

References

Dobriner, W.M. (1969). *Social Structures and Systems*. Pacific Palisades, CA: Goodyear Publishing.

Marsden, G.M. (1980). *Fundamentalism and American Culture*. New York: Oxford University Press.

McGee, R. (1971). *Academic Janus*. San Francisco: Jossey Bass.

Nicklaus, R.L. (1981). Can Christian colleges mix with minorities? *Christianity Today, 25* (Nov. 6), 44-48.

Vander Zanden, J.W. (1983). *American Minority Relations, 4th Edition*. New York: Alfred A. Knopf.

Evangelical Tribalism at Christian Colleges

Donald N. Larson

One morning many years ago in Wheaton, Illinois, at the corner of Main and Front, the crossing signals began to announce the arrival of the "roarin' Elgin" with its load of Chicago-bound commuters. The gates came down as the 7:50 rolled into the station. Making a mad dash across Front Street was a commuter, briefcase in hand, trying desperately to make the train. Right there in the middle of the street he was collared by a young man matching him stride for stride trying to shove a religious tract into his hand and engage him in a conversation. Wearing a pained expression on his face and struggling to break the young man's grip, the commuter, tract in hand, finally broke loose, darted under the gate across the track in front of the train and, presumably, jumped on board.

I stood on the corner and watched the whole thing in open-mouthed amazement. What else could I do? From start to finish the event took less than a minute, but it has etched its way into my permanent memory. As a matter of fact, it has become one of those life-shaping experiences that occurred during my college years, like finding my wife-to-be, laying the foundation for a career and making some lifelong friends. But why? Why has the "Wheaton Tract Passer" had such impact? Another story will help to answer this question.

The story is told of Charley who thought he was dead. It is one thing to keep a thought like this to yourself and quite another to make it public. Well, in Charley's case, he blabbed it all over the neighborhood, and this came to be an embarrassment to his family. So they brought Charley to one counselor after another, but he got no help. As a last resort, one day they brought Charley to a world-famous psychiatrist. The psychiatrist invited Charley to sit down across the desk, and they began to get acquainted. Not many minutes had passed when Charley announced, "I'm dead, you know." Urging him to continue, the psychiatrist reached into his desk drawer, drew out a pin and asked, "Charley, dead men don't bleed, do they?" Charley laughed out loud. "Of course, not. Of course dead men don't bleed!" At that moment, the doctor grabbed Charley's index finger, pricked it and squeezed out a drop of blood. "Well, Charley, what do you have to say now?" "Well,"Charley replied, "what do you know. Dead men *do* bleed!"

It's a silly story, but it makes a point that helps us to understand ourselves. Like Charley, we process our experience by means of our *folk theories*. At the core of these theories are certain *presuppositions* that are sometimes hard to recognize or even identify, yet they are so powerful that we rarely, if ever, successfully challenge them. Some specialists refer to them as *incorrigible*. Most everyday events just fall into place, like telling people what you believe about yourself. Our folk theories are merely reinforced by such events. Every once in a while, however, things happen that challenge them, like the Wheaton Tract Passer or like Charley's unexpected drop of blood. They shake us at our roots and cause us to reconfigure our explanations of why things happen as they do, often without being conscious that we are doing so. [1]

That morning in Wheaton, Illinois, I saw what I now call a *Standard Evangelical Christian in America (SECA)* relating to a person whom he presumed to be something other than a SECA himself, a *non-SECA*. I saw myself in the commuter and also in the Wheaton Tract Passer, and I didn't like what I saw. I think that is why the incident has become so important to me. I wanted to identify and understand my own presuppositions and explain how and why SECAs do what they do.

Although it is hard to do so, this chapter attempts to get in touch with some of those incorrigible presuppositions that shape our lives and account for the state of affairs that has been described in earlier chapters of this book. It seeks to answer a couple of questions. Why do Christian colleges hold ethnic-minorities at arm's length? What can be done about it?

This chapter presents an idea. If it is a sound idea, it carries with it an answer to these questions. The idea is simple to state. Standard Evangelical Christendom in America, the great sugar daddy of so-called Christian colleges, is an *emerging ethnicity* characterized by a ubiquitous tribalism that keeps members of one ethnic group from accepting members of another. The idea is not simple to elucidate or defend.[2]

Analytical Framework

"There are two kinds of people in this world," Robert Benchley used to say, "those who divide the world into two parts and those who do not." Like people of old who divided our species into Jews and Gentiles or Greeks and Barbarians, Standard Evangelical Christians of America (SECAs), like most readers of this book, are in good company when they commonly divide the world into two parts, like "Christians" and "non-Christians," or "believers" and "unbelievers," or "saved" and "lost." Thinking of ourselves as something quite special, we Christians, at least some of us, tend to separate ourselves from the rest. However, this leads to some strange interpretations of history, like "I was a Lutheran and became a Christian two years ago," and to some awkward relationships with non-SECAs, like trying to get along with Roman Catholics or Mormons or Ethiopians.

This example, along with the Wheaton Tract Passer and Charley, makes it clear that we all have *perspectives* from which we view the world, *theories* by which we organize what we see and *conceptual tools* that we use to examine it as we go about our daily business. The following section provides an analytical framework for examining these perspectives, theories and tools, especially those with special importance in answering our questions about Christian colleges and ethnic-minorities.

In this chapter, I turn the searchlight of anthropological investigation, not on tribal peoples where we traditionally direct it, but on Standard Evangelical Christendom in America and on its colleges where such statements as those above are common. I explicate and support the notion that Standard Evangelical Christendom in

America is a case of *ethnogenesis* and show its significance for understanding the relationships of ethnic-minorities and Christian colleges.

My major premises are three. *First*, of all the congregations and organizations of Christians in America, there is a subset which can be identified as Standard Evangelical Christians in America. *Second*, ethnic groups, like individuals, go through life cycles, and there is evidence to support the notion that Standard Evangelical Christendom in America is an emerging ethnicity, an instance of ethnogenesis. *Third*, understanding Standard Evangelical Christendom in America as an emerging ethnicity helps to explain why so-called Christian colleges affiliated with Standard Evangelical Christendom in America relate to ethnic-minorities as they do.

In this chapter I will try to defend two hypotheses. *First*, when Christians develop an ethnicity of their own, they lose not only the divine birthright that they believe is theirs but their assumed power. *Second*, when they create institutions of higher learning, it is primarily for ethnic reasons, not to pursue transcendent goals as Christians are challenged to do.

Perspective

We all have "stand points" from which we view the world, as well as the limitations that they entail. For example, in a two-dimensional world, no citizen sees all sides of a square. In fact, cubes look square. About the best one can hope to do is to see two sides. So Fred sees sides A and C, Frieda sees sides C and B, Ford sees sides B and D and Ferne sees sides D and A. Each has a perspective which in one sense is overlapping and in another *unique*.

Yet in spite of the fact that neither Fred nor Ford sees what the other sees, as they talk to one another, each comes to develop at least a version of what the other knows. By the judicious use of their *communication faculties*, they overcome the handicap of *mutually exclusive* perspectives. They transcend their limitations and utilize the perspectives of each to enhance their understanding. Each slowly but surely comes to some awareness of what is obvious to every other. Understanding and accounting for another's perspective is crucial in a *fair fight*. For example, it is unfair of Fred to accuse Ford of blindness when he does not share his perspective, but it is *not unfair* of Frieda to disagree with

Fred on the nature of side C and to argue about it. Quite obviously, the more we know of one another's perspectives, the more likely we are to *fight fair*, and even to agree. In answering the questions that we have posed, then, we need to *fight fair*—to see things from one anothers' perspectives while maintaining our own uniqueness.

Figure 1

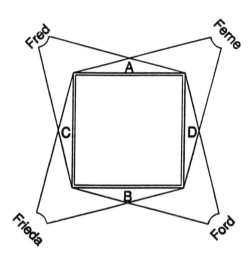

In principle, it is important for members of Christian colleges and members of ethnic-minorities to see things from one anothers' points of view. The perspective of each one is *part* of the whole story, *not* the whole story. Thus Christian colleges and ethnic-minorities do not see their relationship in the same way because their "stand points" differ. Yet as each examines things from the other's perspective, they may be able to draw closer together.

Theory

From our perspectives, we look at the "stuff" out there, like the Wheaton Tract Passer's goals and objectives, or a drop of Charley's blood, or the relationship between Christian colleges and ethnic-minorities, or whatever the contents of the box in Figure 1 may be, in terms of *theories* by which we organize what we see. We all work with theories. So statements made in a book like this rest on the theories of their authors and are interpreted by the theories of the readers.

When leaders of Christian colleges confront representatives of ethnic-minorities, therefore, it is not in a *theoretical vacuum* but in terms of the theories of each. In a fair fight it is good to know "where we are coming from" and to do this, we need to make our theories as explicit as possible.

In examining our theories, we discover that some rest on presuppositions, others on evidence and still others on proof. Our primary concern is to identify the *incorrigible presuppositions* that support the *folk theories* of SECAs that account for its relationships with ethnic-minorities. Although what I have to say in this chapter rests on my own folk theory, I try to go beyond my own naked presuppositions and present *evidence* that *explains* some things; namely, why ethnic-minorities and Christian colleges relate to one another as they appear to do.

The constitution of such evidence varies. What may be evidence to one person may be nonsense to another. In any case, evidence in support of such *explanatory theory* is collected by various methods. That which is gathered here comes primarily by way of *ethnography*—a way of processing and presenting data on ethnic groups.

By way of definition, ethnography is the art and science of describing a group in terms of its culture (Fetterman, 1989). The ethnographer aims through observation and interview to collect data from one member after another and to make sense of this data from the external perspective of social science. Ethnographers approach their task from a variety of explanatory theories, and in most of them what people say about themselves and others plays a significant role. This chapter is written in the spirit of such ethnography.

Conceptual Tools

From the *perspectives* by which we view the world , we organize what we see in terms of *theories* and use certain *conceptual tools* to examine our experience. Five of these concepts are of special importance in answering our questions about the relationships of Christian colleges and ethnic-minorities: *class, group, culture, religion, and life cycle.*

Class and group. The principal audience of this book name certain institutions as *Christian colleges* and certain populations as *ethnic-minorities*. If we are to engage in a fair fight and improve relationships between Christian colleges and ethnic-minorities, we need to understand precisely what is meant by these terms.

It should be noted in the first place that *Christian college* refers to a *group*, whereas *ethnic-minority*, like Asian-American, refers to a *class*. The terms *group* and *class* are of primary importance in this chapter. A *group* is a population whose members are *organized* in terms of culture. It is an organism with a life of its own, like *Overeaters Anonymous*. A *class*, on the other hand, is merely a collection of individuals with one or more common *attributes* or *characteristics*, like people who overeat. The Minnesota Orchestra is a *group*. Musicians belong to a professional *class*.

It should also be noted that perspectives on *group membership* vary. Members may differ among themselves concerning the matter of *inclusion* or *exclusion*. Non-members may view such inclusion or exclusion differently from members. For example, even though as a Swedish-American I prefer to be *included not excluded* from the category of ethnic-minority, many people would not think of me in this way. They would exclude me. Furthermore, some of my friends, associates and acquaintances who call themselves and their institutions Christians would be *excluded not included* from the SECA groups described in this chapter.

To improve their relationships, it is important for Christian colleges and ethnic-minorities to clarify who is and is not to be *included* or *excluded* in these categories.

Finally, it should be noted that some groups create their own names for themselves (autonyms) and others borrow the names that others use to describe them (exonyms). For example, members of groups who practice the rite of baptism may call themselves *baptists* today. In all probability what is today for them an autonym began as an exonym that non-Baptists applied to them. While people have a right to call themselves and others what they wish, in a book of this kind, the fundamental terms *ethnic-minority* and *Christian college* need to be clear and precise in their meanings.

In addition to seeing the *ethnic-minority* as a *class*, we also need a clear understanding of what we mean by *minority, majority, ethnic-*

majority and ethnic-minority. When we describe a population as a *minority*, we imply the presence of a *majority*. Although the constituents of Christian colleges belong to a *majority* of some kind, often they are not identified precisely.

Culture. The term *ethnic*, as employed by ancient Greeks, was used to designate a population with certain racial, social, cultural and linguistic characteristics. Thus an ethnic group had a certain *culture*, often defined today as "the acquired knowledge that people use to interpret experience and generate social behavior,"[3] and an *ethos* or "dominant emotional tone"[4] of its own.

Therefore, in describing a given population as an *ethnic-minority*, we imply not only certain characteristics but also the presence of other kinds of minorities, such as factory workers, lawyers and residents of certain neighborhoods.

Although the characteristics of *ethnic-minorities* are rarely described in detail, we are even less precise concerning the cultural features of a dominant *ethnic-majority* that shares an ecological niche with ethnic-minorities. Often such dominant ethnic groups do not recognize their own *ethnicity* as such but are quick to recognize it in others. In fact, the title of this chapter suggests that there is a certain population evangelical that can be characterized in terms of *tribalism*. Few members of this population would normally recognize themselves as *ethnics or recognize their own tribalism.*

Ethnicization is a process that touches all of us. We all undergo the process. None of us escape it. We are all ethnic. The majority population's tacit assumption that it is non-ethnic, and this *ethnic blind spot*, will be challenged later in this chapter. One result of ethnicization is a set of incorrigible presuppositions shared by all members.

As we shall explain below, there is a population that can be identified as Standard Evangelical Christians of America (SECA). This population, as we shall show, is an *emerging ethnic group* which when in full bloom will have lost its original reason for existence. We shall show that it is in its emerging ethnicity that SECA finds reasons for keeping ethnic-minorities at arm's length. We shall also show that the presence of so-called ethnic-minorities in so-called Christian colleges have a vital role in retarding SECA's tribalism and revitalizing evangelical Christendom in this country.

Religion. This book is also about *Christian colleges,* and clarifying this term rests on a clear understanding of what we mean by *college, Christian, and Christian college.* First of all, when we describe an institution of higher learning as a *college,* we usually imply a focus on the liberal arts, although it is evident that many so-called Christian colleges are liberal in letter but not in spirit. Second, in describing a college as *Christian,* we not only imply a certain *religious* orientation but the presence of colleges associated with other religious traditions, such as Jewish, Muslim, Hindu, Buddhist. For our purposes, *religion* is "the cultural knowledge of the supernatural that people use to cope with the ultimate problems of human existence."[5]

For most people, a *Christian college* is one that is founded by, operated by and populated with Christians. However, the term *Christian* has many definitions. Some people who call themselves Christians use it in an *exclusive* sense while others use it more *inclusively* to include anyone who calls himself or herself a Christian. The term *Christian college* as used in this chapter refers exclusively to those which are private, not public, religious, not secular, oriented to the Christian tradition, not some other religious tradition, and *evangelical, not mainline protestant or catholic,* and more specifically to institutions with certain characteristics associated with Standard Evangelical Christendom in America.

For example, when leaders of such organizations as the Christian College Consortium or the Christian College Coalition named themselves as they did, it was *to include* Christian colleges that used the term as a synonym for *evangelical* and *exclude* those that used it with reference to Christian colleges of mainline American Christendom. By choice, they rendered judgment on colleges that did not meet their criteria for *Christian* and *excluded* many that stand in the Christian tradition. To be honest, they should have referred to themselves as Evangelical (Christian) College Consortium or Evangelical (Christian) College Coalition. Quite clearly, where *Christian college* is defined more inclusively, many more representatives of ethnic-minorities are eligible for enrollment.

From what we have said thus far, a few things should be crystal clear. First, in this country, it is sometimes convenient, or pleasurable, to deny our ethnicity. However, to recognize it and to understand wherein we are all ethnics is to get along better with those whom we dub as ethnic-minorities. Second, while we are all *ethnic*, none of us *chooses* our parents or our birthplace or our ethnicity. It is thrust upon us, and we are thrust into it. If we happen to belong to an ethnic-majority, we can take some comfort in it. However, along with the pleasure, there is also the pain of recognizing how we may have treated ethnic-minorities in our own ecological niche.

Life Cycles. Imagine yourself in a situation where two ethnic communities, Squaresville and Roundsville, are found in the same ecological niche. Every normal individual is born into one group or the other. It is typically the source of certain biological characteristics, one's identity, communication system, primary relationships, name, history, tradition, heritage, home territory, marriage partners, shared visions, rituals, group self-consciousness and boundaries between members and non-members. Imagine that you are a Square, one of two fundamentally different ways to live. Squaresville is where your essential humanness is fashioned, where you shape your perspectives on reality, your theories and the conceptual tools used that you use to process your experience. In one sense, the formation of your Squareness begins at birth and continues through the first critical years of life. In another, the formation of such ethnicity is a lifelong process.

In certain respects Squares and Rounds are very similar. In certain others they are very different. These similarities are valuable because they provide similar readings on the environment, thereby enhancing survival and well-being in their common eco-niche. But sometimes these similarities are disturbing because they tend to attenuate the boundaries which separate the two groups. Thus differences are valuable because they provide the basis for sharp separations between groups.

But Squares and Rounds sometimes find a way to value their differences. As members of Squaresville or Roundsville with their sharp boundaries, Squares and Rounds sometimes form sets around new centers. Old boundaries weaken in favor of new centers. But boundaries are latent functions in all groups, so before long, this new set begins to establish new boundaries of its own.[6]

Ethnic groups, like individuals, go through life cycles. In the course of time, as members of the two ethnic groups contact one another, the groups spread and change. Each group splits in various ways, and new mergers occur. They are born in historical circumstances, two sometimes merging into one or one splitting into two. They spring to life and mature. So long as internal and external change is managed well, life goes on. It seems that no other groups outlive ethnic groups. After generations, and in spite of many different kinds of change, their incorrigible presuppositions prove durable. But eventually they probably die, although cases like the Egyptians seem to challenge such an assumption.

However, as groups go through these cycles, they tend to develop different *postures* toward other groups in their eco-niche:

Figure 2

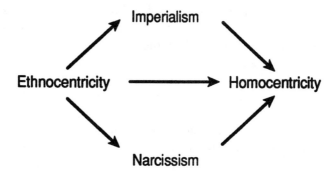

Starting from a basic "default" position, Squaresville assumes an *ethnocentric posture* toward Roundsville. In some cases, this ethno-centrism turns into a *narcissistic posture* in which Squares see Rounds as deviants or distortions from Square norms; in others an *imperialistic posture*, seeing Rounds as new fields to conquer; in still others a *homocentric posture,* seeing the possibilities of new levels of understanding and cooperation with Rounds as they cross boundaries and identify similar centers.[7]

Tribalism, as we shall use the term in this chapter, is the product of ethnocentrism, narcissism and imperialism. It stands in contrast to a transcendence of ethnicity in which homocentric Squares and Rounds learn to survive in one anothers' shoes, a quality known as *ultrastability*.[8] In one assessment of the Biblical evidence, tribalism is an inherent flaw in every ethnic group. Insofar as this is assessment has merit, SECA as an emerging ethnicity will become more and more tribal and less and less true to its Biblical mandates.

The Squaresville scenario illuminates what has happened in the history of Standard Evangelical Christendom in America and lays the groundwork for understanding why their relationship with ethnic-minorities exists as it does.

Sizing Up the Situation: What's Happening?

According to the dominant tone of this book, the visibility and impact of ethnic-minorities in Christian colleges is more limited than it should be. We will examine this position in three stages? what's happening, what's wrong, what's the cause.

According to the collaborators of this book, representatives of ethnic-minorities are at a disadvantage as they struggle to increase their visibility, to close the gap and to gain access to Christian colleges. Christian colleges separate themselves from ethnic-minorities, and contributors to this volume find this separation unacceptable because it denies Christian members of ethnic-minorities access to such institutions. In this chapter my purpose is to show that ethnic-minorities struggle not simply with Christian colleges but with the forces of Standard Evangelical Christendom in America. *While members of such ethnic-minorities may themselves be evangelicals, they are not standard.* Therein lies their disadvantage. This first section has three parts. The first is a description of the roots of Standard Evangelical Christendom in America and its emergence as a *class* of Christians with certain characteristics. In the second part, my purpose is to show that SECA is a *group* with certain organizational attributes. In the third part, my purpose is to show that SECA is an *emerging ethnicity* and in so doing to account for the present relationship between Christian colleges and ethnic-minorities.

SECA Roots

The history of Standard Evangelical Christians in America (SECAs) begins in Palestine two thousand years ago, continues in

Europe, works its way across the Atlantic and grows up as a new and distinct American expression of Christian faith.

Early Christians. The Christian movement got underway in Palestine among ethnic Jews in their *territory*. They were *insiders*. In its original form, the Christian community consisted almost exclusively of Jews who had become Christians. These Christian Jews expressed the core of their Jewish ethnicity in Christian ways. They were *Christian Jews*. By definition, the Christian Jew is a *Christian ethnic*, an ethnic who expresses his or her ethnicity in Christian ways.

As a result of the *diaspora*, Jews found themselves in the traditional territories of other ethnic groups where they were *outsiders* among *insiders*, as in the Greek communities of Ephesus, Galatia, Corinth and Colosse. As a result of their contact with Jews and Christian Jews, Greeks underwent a similar split when some Greeks became Christians and, like the Christian Jews before them, expressed the core of their Greek ethnicity in Christian ways. They became *Christian Greeks*, another breed of Christian ethnics.

At this point, *Christian Jews did not stop being Jews and Christian Greeks did not stop being Greeks.* However, they did struggle with some new alternatives. One was to accept Greeks into congregations on Jewish terms, to *homogenize* the differences in such a way that Jews would not be offended. Another was to develop a *heterogeneity* in which both Jews and Greeks *transcended* the limitations that traditional views imposed on their relationships.

A remarkable thing occurred. Christian Jews and Christian Greeks chose the second of these alternatives and formed ethnically *heterogeneous congregations* in which each processed their new found experience in terms of their own ethnicity, modifying them as necessary in similar ways. Each helped the other to process their new found faith in terms of their own ethnicity. Indeed, such congregations provide a striking historical example of different ethnic groups learning to value one another at points of difference, not merely at points of similarity. In spite of radically different world views, theologies and religious traditions, they found in Jesus Christ a common Lord.

However, as time passed and as the Christian community spread from one place to another, at least some of these ethnically heterogeneous congregations *began to develop a homogeneous ethnicity of their own—a Christian ethnicity.* Unlike what happened in the first century, *Christian ethnics became ethnic Christians.* Whereas *Christian ethnics,* finding their Christian faith to be of primary importance, *used their ethnicity to express it, ethnic Christians,* finding their ethnicity most important, *used their Christian faith to express it.*

In certain respects, this was an understandable development. From the very first, Christians struggled with Jewish ethnocentrism, as exemplified in Peter's struggle to relate to Cornelius. The early Christian community demonstrated a certain narcissism in its preoccupation with reflection and self-examination, exemplified in the problems that Paul addressed in his letters to the Thessalonians. Early Christians demonstrated imperialistic tendencies and sought to expand the range of their own authority and power, as exemplified in the position of the Judaizers addressed in Paul's letter to the Galatians. At the same time, the Christian community made a noble effort to come to grips with its ethnicity and sought to influence others in the direction of recognizing what all persons have in common, including the separation from its Creator (as exemplified in the Garden of Eden) and from one another (as exemplified in the account of the Tower of Babel) and the possibility of new unity in Christ leading to re-establishment of relations with its Creator (as in the Garden of Gethsemane when Jesus prays that the will of his Father be done) and with one another (as on the Day of Pentecost when the same message is delivered in familiar languages by people who are apparently unfamiliar with them).

In focusing on the Garden of Eden and the cross, SECAs emphasize re-establishment of relations with the Creator, losing sight of the importance of the Tower of Babel and the Day of Pentecost in re-establishing relationships with one another, something that occurs only when we get the message of the Garden of Gethsemane back into perspective.

At this stage in Christendom's history then, we can distinguish three types of congregations. *First,* there were ethnically homogeneous congregations of Jews and perhaps Greeks. *Second,* there were ethnically heterogeneous congregations consisting of mixtures of Jews, Greeks, Romans, and others. *Third,* there were new congregations emerging with a Christian ethnicity of their own, with diminishing traces of Jewish, Greek or Roman past. Unlike the earlier *ethnically heterogeneous congregation* in which members of two or more ethnic groups express their ethnicity in Christian ways, but like the first type, this congregation was ethnically *homogeneous* members whose Christian ancestors came from different cultural backgrounds develop a *Christian ethnicity* of their own. Some see this new wrinkle of *homogenization* as a step forward. Others see it as a step backward, for when Christians develop an ethnicity of their own, tribalism will soon reappear.

Thus it was in this crucible of *inter-ethnic interaction* that the early church developed. Not only were Greeks as insiders and Jews as outsiders faced with the challenge of getting along with one another in their congregations, but Christian Jews and Greeks also faced the further challenge of identifying their common centers and learning to survive in one anothers' shoes, a quality referred to earlier as *ultrastability.*

In these early stages then, no Greeks became Christians without contact with Christian Jews. This placed the burden on Christian Jews to pass into the worlds of Greeks and allow Greeks access to their own worlds. In addition to such "bi-passing," Christian Jews faced the additional burden of becoming acceptable to Greeks. Even more, they faced the challenge of communicating *effectively* with those whom they ostracized as gentiles, the very people whom as Jews they had traditionally avoided.

No doubt many Jews and Greeks were put off by Christian Jews and Christian Greeks having *fellowship* with one another. What clearly happened, however, was that congregations emerged in which Jews and Greeks *incarnated themselves* among one another, *reconciled* their differences, *discipled* themselves to one another and *confessed* their sins to one another. In fact, where there are Christians, there should always be *incarnation, reconciliation, discipleship and confession*, one group learning to live among another, both learning to reconcile differences, members of one group discipling themselves to members of another and members of one group confessing their sins to members of another.

To recapitulate, a cycle has been in operation for nearly two millenia. The cycle starts when an ethnic group begins to express its ethnic core in Christian ways. A split occurs as Christian ethnics emerge. Christians of this ethnic group then begin to contact members of another ethnic group. As Christians of the first ethnic group contact members of the second, a new variety of Christians emerges. Christians of the two groups merge and continue to express their ethnic cores in Christian ways. Ultimately, these Christians homogenize their ethnic differences and become *ethnic Christians*, a new formation.[9]

The issues which this book confronts then are in most ways no different from what repeatedly happens when people of one background confront those of another. The confrontation of members of ethnic-minorities and leaders of Christian colleges is nothing more or less than a new wrinkle on an age old confrontation of *ethnic Christians* and *Christian ethnics*.

European Christians. After countless cycles, the Christian movement gradually reached Europe, and patterns of congregational growth and spread established in the earliest generations of Christians continued without interruption. In some cases, ethnic Christians assumed a *tribalistic posture* and came as powerful invaders, imposing their will on helpless insiders. In others, ethnic Christians recognized their limitations, assumed a *homocentric posture* toward other groups and once again formed new ethnically heterogeneous congregations.

By way of example, during the ninth century, ethnic Christians from the mainland of Europe came to Sweden, the homeland of my ancestors who were pagan Vikings. Many of these were slowly absorbed into the homogeneous congregations of ethnic Christians of Europe and the British Isles. The *state church* of Sweden, became the stage in which ethnic Christians expressed their own blend of Christian faith and Swedish citizenship.

Long after the Roman Catholic church began to *reform* itself in the 15th century, the impact of this *reformation* ultimately reached into Scandinavia, and in time, Martin Luther's version of the Christian experience was reinterpreted and applied in Sweden's *state church*. So scratch a Swede and you'll find a Lutheran. Scratch deeper and you'll find a Catholic. Scratch even deeper and you'll uncover a pagan Viking.

As time passed, among these Swedish Lutherans were those who began to separate Viking seeds and Swedish seeds and Lutheran seeds and seeds that they read about in the Bible. In fact, they were widely known as the *"readers,"* and later as the *Free Church*, thus distinguishing themselves from, I guess, the *bound church*. My own ethnic roots reach back into congregations of the so-called Free Church.

All my great grandparents were born and raised in Sweden. Some were brought up as Lutherans and others were part of the Free Church movement. Most of them immigrated to America. Three of my grandparents were born and raised in Sweden and one in America. All were members of the Evangelical Free Church, and it was among people like my grandparents that the Evangelical Free Church of America was formed.

If asked to choose, my parents would have referred to themselves as Swedish-Americans in ancestry or ethnicity, as Americans in nationality and as Free Church in religious tradition. Like their parents, they were members of the Evangelical Free Church of America, the descendant of the Swedish Free Church of America and before that the Evangelical Free Church of Sweden.

Depending upon the occasion and circumstances, I call myself by different names. In nationality, I am an American. In ethnicity, I am a Swedish-American. In religious affiliation, I am a Christian. In terms of group memberships, I am a member of the Evangelical Free Church of America. This group is a principal shaper of my cultural experience.

American Christians. Contrary to what many Americans seem to believe today, American history did not begin when the Pilgrims arrived at Plymouth Rock. During the first period of American history, this continent was occupied solely by ethnic groups now designated as *Native Americans.* These people were *animists.* There were no Christians among them. But after many more cycles, *ethnic Christians* landed in the "new world." For many of these rebel Episcopalians, Congregationalists, Baptists, Lutherans, Methodists, and Presbyterians, this new land meant freedom from state religion to follow Christ in new ways, like converting the nearby Pequot Indians.

Many of these early arrivals began to undergo *Americanization*, a new kind of *nationalization*. Thus ethnic Christians from Europe and the British Isles learned to express their old Christian ethnicity in new American ways. But others resisted the pressures of *Americanization* in favor of retaining their English or European ways in America. Gradually their earlier characteristics were reshaped and replaced with new ones. As generations passed, a new breed of ethnic Christians began to develop—*American Christians.*

SECA

In this new mainstream of American Christendom, where a new brand of ethnic Christian was forming, lone congregations or loose federations of like-minded congregations sought to break out of this new formation—American Christendom and its new ethnocentrism. Some of these "evangelical" branches had their roots in Europe, like the Evangelical Free Church of America (Sweden and Norway), the Baptist General Conference (Sweden), North American Baptist Convention (Germany) and Evangelical Covenant Church (Sweden). Others were "made in the USA," including Nazarenes, Assemblies of God, the Christian and Missionary Alliance, Pentecostals, Mormons, Seventh Day Adventists, Jehovah's Witnesses and Christian Science, none of which had roots in Europe.

As time passed, some of deviant mainstream branches began to recognize one another, to identify their common core and their shared differences from the mainstream. Some consolidated, and as they grew more and more autonomous, they separated further and further from the mainstream of which they had been a part, either in colonial America or in Europe. Others did not, and new evangelical coalitions began to form, like the American Sunday School Union in the 1800s, and in more recent times, the National Association of Evangelicals, the World Evangelical Fellowship, the Evangelical Foreign Mission Association, and the International Foreign Mission Association, have all facilitated alliances among evangelicals.[10] Meanwhile, "free lance" individuals and congregations with evan-gelical fervor continued to cultivate relationships within the mainstream itself.[11]

After World War II, the evangelical star began to rise higher and faster. Billy Graham gave it a great boost in the 1950s. In the 1960s, the media blitz began. In the 1970s, its visibility increased in the wake of post-Vietnam backlashes, the conversion of Charles Colson and the election of Jimmy Carter. In the 1980s and the reign of Ronald Reagan, it reached what may have been its apex.[12]

Today as evangelicals cut their teeth (or sharpen their swords) on such life and death issues as rights of women, abortion, military readiness, prayer in the schools, AIDS, gun control and evolution, they are working out guidelines for the formation of a cultural core, carving out a new view of the world and finding new identity.[13] To be an evangelical today is to respect certain *standards*. I refer to those who are undergoing this standardization today as Standard Evangelical Christians in America (SECA). SECAs are drawing new boundaries today to separate themselves from non-SECAs. Included among non-SECAs, then, are many who designate themselves as Christians, including Roman and Eastern Catholic, most mainline groups and various other evangelical groups like charismatics.

SECAs tend to be insensitive to their own ethnicity partly because of a lack of interest in their own pasts. In developing their standards, it is not surprising to find SECAs rewriting church history. Thus one frequently hears young evangelicals saying things like "I was a Lutheran and became a Christian" on the grounds that Lutherans do not meet their standards. Insensitive or not, this covert ethnicity grows and deepens, and as it does, SECA's lack of *ethnic consciousness* blinds them to the fact that they are really tightly controlled by their ethnicity.

In the United States today, most self-designated Christians are *ethnic Christians, not Christian ethnics.* They tend to sort themselves out in terms of a wide variety of groups and classes. Included among them is a class known as *evangelical. American evangelicals* are like all other Christians, like some other Christians, and like no other Christians. With all they have certain holidays in common, with some they have a common citizenship. With some they share hymns and scriptures. Yet they have a unique set of characteristics that sets them off from all other Christians. Only an evangelical says things like "I was a Lutheran and became a Christian two years ago."

This class of American evangelicals is important for a number of reasons, one of which is their emphasis on taking their version of the Christian gospel to the ends of the earth. Why then, and here is part of the puzzle which this book is trying to solve, do the colleges of American evangelicals often hold members of ethnic-minorities seeking a closer affiliation at arm's length?

SECA as a Group. People are typically classified by social scientists as *social aggregates* and *social groups.* Social aggregates are classes of people with common lifestyles, status, strata, rank, etc. *Social groups* are collectivities organized in such a way that members interact with one another. Their essential feature is *internal organization*. Social groups are further differentiated as *primary* or *secondary* on the basis of such factors as size, identity, unity, scope of activity, face-to-face relations, and intimacy. Primary groups tend to be smaller than secondary, with a greater sense of identity and unity, a broader scope of activity, and more intimate face-to-face relationships. The process of being a member is more important than anything that is produced.

The class of American Christians identified as Standard Evangelical Christians in America is more than a *class*. Numerous signs indicate that this *class* is at least a *secondary group* for many evangelical Christians in America. Standard party lines on many issues are developing and boundaries between American Christians who follow these standards and those who don't are rapidly becoming evident.

SECA as Emerging Ethnicity. By way of review, one type of primary social group is referred to by specialists as an *ethnic group*. Every normal individual is born into an ethnic group. The ethnic group experience is fundamental. It is where essential humanness is fashioned, particularly through the influence of the kinship group. The formation of ethnicity is a process that begins at birth and continues through the first critical years of life. It is a lifelong process, and ethnic groups, like individuals, are born in mergers, spring to life, mature, grow old and eventually die. No other groups or aggregates outlive ethnic groups.

Standard Evangelical Christians in America are not just a *class of people*. To view it as such is to overlook or minimize its complex and powerful internal organization. Nor is it just a *secondary social group*. To view it as such is to overlook or minimize the importance of many characteristics that it shares with primary groups.[14] The similarity of SECA to *ethnic groups* is seen in a number of features. *First*, there is a growing sense of "we-ness" that demolishes earlier distinctions in theology, polity and ecclesiology. SECA's solidarity is unmistakable. Boundaries between members and nonmembers are based on such things as race, culture, behavior and lifestyle, and are well-marked and carefully maintained. *Second*, there is a strong tendency for the young to marry other SECAs, a pattern known as group endogamy. *Third*, membership is ascribed not achieved and exclusive not inclusive. If "they say" you are a SECA, you are. *Fourth,* SECA's emphasis on "family of God" (as the Gaithers sing, "We're so glad we're a part of the family of God") is more than a cliche. It is a living and powerful metaphor resting on such Biblical concepts as "fictive kinship" (Hello, Brother Jim!) or "new birth" and adoption" as modes of reproduction and internal growth. *Fifth,* its internal relationships are to a great extent face-to-face, as exemplified in fellowships of many kinds. *Sixth,* its language variety is unique. For example, the words 'blessing' and 'joy' are common markers by which Christian radio broadcasts can be identified. New words, like 'to bible-study' (as in "we bible-studied together for a few months last year"), are part of a growing SECA vocabulary. SECAs have their own style of praying. There is a marked contrast between the language used when SECA meets SECA (homogeneous communicative events in which insider meets insider) and when SECA meets non-SECA (heterogeneous communicative events in which insider meets outsider). *Seventh,* process is clearly more important than product. That is to say, it is more important to participate in the "evangelical process" than to produce anything substantial. To summarize, for a SECA, to be a "Christian" means more than participating in the beliefs, practices and rituals of a religious tradition. It is a way of life emerging around a core of premises, values and strategies, an ethos that shapes the SECA's entire cultural experience.

Like any emerging movement, SECA has been developing its ideology[15], and the SECA ideology emerging today is likely to be in full bloom tomorrow, but like a loose wheel, SECA's various attempts to strengthen itself, as well as its growing tribalism, will ultimately weaken its usefulness within world Christendom. SECAs as *ethnic Christians* are increasingly becoming what their progenitors condemned. SECA real estate holdings increase in value. SECA buildings increase in complexity and ornateness. SECA congregations increase in size. SECA sports a professionalized clergy with salaries, fringe benefits and degrees that were unheard of a few years ago. SECA is fast developing internal cohesion. The organization known as the National Association of Evangelicals has played a crucial role in this emerging ethnicity. *Christianity Today,* the periodical, has also had a significant role. Institutions like Wheaton College have played a crucial role. Trinity Evangelical Divinity School may be on the way toward becoming SECA's single most important seminary.

All these developments notwithstanding, the mission of the church is not to turn itself into a homogeneous ethnic group. It is to develop and maintain a heterogeneous community of witnesses from every tribe, tongue and nation with global scope and homocentric concerns.

Thus SECA's tribalism becomes a critical issue. If it doesn't conflict with SECA belief structures, then it isn't a threat, but if it reinforces SECA beliefs, which it does, then tribalism, while actually strengthening SECA as a group, weakens it as an instrument in what we understand to be the building of the kingdom of God.

By way of conclusion, the group of evangelical Christians in America which we have identified as Standard Evangelical Christians in America (SECA) is not just a group. It is a group characterized in terms of its *emerging ethnicity*, and to see this is to understand why ethnic-minorities are held at arm's length in Christian colleges: *SECA tribalism is alive and well.*[16]

SECA and I. SECA has played a significant and uninterrupted role in shaping my own experience, two aspects of which are important in examining the issues in this book. Much of my own *learning experience* after high school and *work experience* after college has occurred in SECA institutions and organizations. For many years, my own SECA tribalism remained intact, out-of-awareness, powerful.

My learning experience in higher education includes a semester at the Free Church Bible Institute and Seminary (now called Trinity College and located in Deerfield, Illinois) in the fall of 1943, a few courses in an undergraduate college of the University of Oklahoma, not at all a SECA institution, a degree from Wheaton College, my first venture as a student in a SECA institution, two degrees from the University of Chicago, hardly a SECA institution and short courses at the Summer Institute of Linguistics, a quasi-SECA institution and a Linguistic Institute at the University of Michigan, not SECA.

My professional career includes twelve years of teaching Greek and Linguistics at Trinity College and twenty years of teaching Linguistics and Anthropology at Bethel College, St. Paul, Minnesota, as well as a few courses at Jaffray School of Missions, Nyack, New York (now known as Alliance Theological Seminary). It also includes a two-year stint in the Philippines to organize and direct the Interchurch

Language School (now known as Christian Language Study Center), a three-year stint as special secretary for translations at the American Bible Society in New York, and a one-year assignment as linguist-in-residence at the Union Language School, Bangkok, Thailand.

Summer activity includes twenty-five years of teaching and twenty years of leadership at the Toronto Institute of Linguistics, ten years of teaching at the Outgoing Missionary Conference, National Council of Churches, eight years of service to two Lutheran bodies during their Summer Schools of Mission as consultant on cross-cultural learning, and several summers at the Tekak witha Conference, an association of Roman Catholics engaged in evangelistic work among Native Americans.

After retiring from Bethel in 1987, I joined the staff of Link Care, Fresno, California, as Senior Consultant for Cross-Cultural Learning. Whereas its programs, services and resources are utilized by many SECAs, Link Care serves a wider Christian public.

I make this report simply to underscore the fact that I am a SECA and have had opportunities to see SECA from within and without and to see it in its relationships with other Christians and people of other traditions in a variety of situations. From this vantage point, it appears to me that SECA controls the doors of Christian colleges and thereby the access of ethnic-minorities to their programs, services and resources. This comes as no surprise since members of other ethnic-minorities, Christian or not, are not SECAs.

As an emerging ethnic group, SECAs attitudes toward other ethnics is predictable. It partakes of all the tribalism that one would expect when one ethnic group confronts another. Like eating grape-fruit, there is more to SECA than what meets the eye. Take skin color, for example. SECA is essentially deaf, dumb and blind when it comes to the presence and participation of Blacks, Asians or Native Americans in their typical congregations. Consider, for example, the flight of SECAs from urban to suburban areas, not to mention the size and shape and cost of the churches that are constructed in these areas. Among SECAs, Christian members of ethnic-minorities are acceptable in token quantities, but it is only the rare SECA congregation that hears a call to stay among them in the urban centers and minister to their needs.

By way of summary, SECA is more than a group. It is moving toward the full status of an ethnic group that shapes and forms its young in ways which are virtually identical to those found in other ethnic groups.

Christian Colleges as Captives of SECA

Having discussed SECA in terms of *ethnogenesis,* it remains in this section to account for the present relationships between Christian colleges and ethnic-minorities. Insofar as Christian colleges are dominated by SECA constituencies, it comes as no surprise to find them taking on the same attitudes, beliefs and values with reference to ethnic-minorities as the constituencies which sponsor them. What else could they do?

It makes sense, I suppose, to call what goes on in a tower, like an ivory tower, *higher* education. And it probably also makes sense to refer to what goes on in an ivory tower occupied by Christians as *Christian higher education.* As noted earlier, in this book institutions of Christian higher education known as *Christian colleges* are typically members of the Christian College Consortium and the Christian College Coalition, and as noted earlier in this chapter, to refer to them as *Christian Colleges* reflects SECA's emerging ethnicity.

In so designating themselves, they (purposely, though sub-consciously perhaps) separate themselves from colleges which are as fully a part of the Christian tradition as any in the Consortium or Coalition. In this *exclusivism,* they reveal their presuppositions about people who call themselves Christians but do not meet SECA standards. *Only an evangelical institution could be so crass as to refer to itself as a Christian college* to the exclusion of colleges which are true to their Christian heritage, like Luther College, Notre Dame, Hamline, etc.

The Christian college as understood in this book is clearly a captive and a tool of SECA. SECA uses the Christian college to indoctrinate, not liberate. Christian colleges are really and rapidly becoming 4-year puberty rites for late adolescents in SECA families. Consider, for example, the hectic and frenetic dash for Fort Lauderdale, and other spring break sunspots. In a kind of annual SECA Woodstock, SECA parents spend millions of dollars to treat their kids to a little *sunshine* as a part of some college's *Operation Sonshine.* To the kids it's partying in the sunshine, and to the paying parents, it's a way for their kids to "*do Christian work.*"

Or consider summer adventures to Japan and more recently to China to "teach English," advertised by one evangelical agency as a way to do missionary work "without crossing the cultural barrier." Or consider the pledges to conform to lifestyles to which wealthy members of constituencies themselves subscribe. Or consider the chapels, some daily and others several times a week, to which students are required in some cases, obliged in others and "strongly encouraged" in others to attend. Or consider the devotionals or prayers before classes which faculty members are required in some cases, obliged in others and "strongly encouraged" in others to conduct. Or consider the passive listening, woolgathering and mind-wandering characteristic of students resembling typical participants in Sunday worship. Or consider that SECA roots were so well-established at Bethel that a professor of chemistry was allowed to teach a course on the Four Spiritual Laws during more than one January interim.

In these instances and others Christian colleges unmistakably reflect the emerging ethnicity of SECA. Interestingly enough, these practices tend to attenuate over time as Christian colleges establish clear boundaries that meet the requirements of SECA constituencies.

SECA Colleges and Ethnic-Minorities. Members of ethnic-minorities are as rare in Christian colleges as they are in SECA congregations. These are not unrelated observations. Clearly if SECA congregations had more representatives of ethnic-minorities in their ranks, so would the Christian colleges that they sponsor.

In respect to the presence of ethnic-minorities, as in other cases, the Christian college tends to assume a reactive posture with reference to SECA. "What SECA wants, SECA gets." One outcome of this is the low visibility of ethnic-minorities in Christian colleges. Consider some examples.

After the war, during 1946-1949, apart from an occasional Black or Asian, members of ethnic-minorities at Wheaton College were scarce. Most of these rarities were international "trophies of grace" imported from mission fields abroad. A few were American citizens. At that time, none were "big men on campus."

During 1949-1961, at Trinity, the situation was much the same, although there were even fewer members of ethnic-minorities. One whom I remember was a Chinese Indonesian caught in the USA during Indonesia's struggle for independence. Another was a young Japanese converted through the ministry of Inter-Varsity who will probably go down in Trinity history for his prayer in chapel one day in which he asked the Lord for forgiveness because "we don't give a damn about your word."

In my brief exposure to Nyack, the picture was somewhat different. I seem to recall a higher percentage of internationals and ethnic-minorities from America, perhaps in keeping with its posture as a "missionary college" of the Christian and Missionary Alliance.

The late 60's and early 70's at Bethel College were days of students running around in "Jesus is Neat" tee-shirts. For many, Bethel was a nine-month summer camp where SECA's learned that *ethnic-minorities* were people who needed the gospel, not an education at Christian colleges. Make no mistake about it, these children never thought of themselves as ethnic, and when their ethnic roots were pointed out and described, few were willing to engage in serious introspection or investigation of its significance. At Bethel, like Wheaton and Trinity, members of ethnic-minorities from America were virtually non-existent, although there was the occasional international who had been "saved by grace."

On one occasion early in my Bethel sojourn, I refereed an imbroglio between a student from Nigeria and a faculty colleague. The Nigerian complained of ethnic and racial harassment. When I confronted the colleague involved with information gleaned from the student, he told me that "since he couldn't get into medical school himself, he was not going to do internationals any favors by helping them."

Only rarely did these international "trophies of grace" speak out objectively about their experiences with and attitudes toward the first Christians whom they had encountered. On one occasion, however, I recall an African student's description of missionaries as "living up on the hill and commuting to the 'billage,'" as she put it. On another occasion she told about her cooking classes in the mission school where missionaries taught them how to cook turkeys in electric ovens but where, as she put it, "we had no electric *obens* and had never seen a *tuhkey.*"

Like other Christian colleges, I suppose, Bethel College recruited a few Blacks, mostly athletes, in the late 60's and early 70's, and this was not without its problems, for the college and also for the students involved.

To sum up, in addition to various problems with student representatives of ethnic-minorities, it seems that virtually every one of the ethnic-minorities recruited for faculty positions ran into trouble, including a black Haitian and a Norwegian Baptist in the language department, a Korean in physics, a Messianic Jewish woman in the Bible department, and a South Indian in the economics department.

To recapitulate, in this section I have tried to establish SECA as an emerging ethnicity and to show the consequences of such emerging ethnicity in the relationship of so-called Christian colleges and ethnic-minorities. This *ethnic dimension* in SECA has remained hidden from view. It is a blind spot not only in SECA but in their so-called Christian colleges. When this ethnic dimension is fully recognized, we will better understand how to improve the working relationships between Christian colleges and ethnic-minorities.

Sizing Up the Situation: What's Wrong?

At the outset of this chapter, we referred to *fair fights* and in the interest of fighting fair, it should be pointed out first of all that it is just as impossible for a *class* to fight a group as it is for a group to be expected to accommodate an entire class of people. In charging one another with wrongs, Christian colleges and ethnic-minorities should *fight fair.* Members of ethnic-minorities as such cannot wage war against Christian colleges, as groups, and expect as a class of people to win, nor can Christian colleges be expected to care for all members of ethnic-minorities. These would not be *fair fights.*

Leaders of Christian colleges know that they cannot be expected to care for all members of ethnic-minorities, and from their perspective, they do no wrong in taking this position. From the perspective of Christian members of ethnic-minorities, however, this position is wrong because it deprives them of what they consider a right: access to Christian higher education. If members of ethnic-minorities don't know it, they should know that Christian colleges cannot be expected to care for all members of a class, like ethnic-minorities.

If leaders of Christian colleges don't know it, they should recognize that they hold ethnic-minorities at arm's length because of their identity with Standard Evangelical Christendom in America. They should recognize their tribalism for what it is and admit that they are unready, unable and unwilling to practice the transcendent ideals to which they give lip-service. To put this somewhat differently, the Christian college, from its unrecognized ethnic perspective, looks at the ethnic-minorities as any other ethnic organization would look on ethnic-minorities in its own context. It excludes them. As humans see themselves as part of a species that includes all humans and excludes all else, so an ethnic postulates a group that includes all members and excludes all else.

The leg on which Christian leaders stand is *right* because ethnic-minorities are not SECAs and Christian colleges are. From the SECA point of view, the *Christian college is of SECAs, by SECAs and for SECAs*. But it is *wrong* because it fails to recognize the *dissonance* between its own ideals of transcendence and the reality of its tribalism.

From the viewpoint of Christian members of ethnic-minorities, as Christians they should have the same access to Christian colleges as other Christians. However, in failing to recognize the ethnicity of SECA and its so-called Christian colleges, many fail to see why Christian colleges treat them as they do. Instead they assume that Christian colleges transcend their own ethnicity. This unwarranted assumption is responsible for their disappointment and the need for this book.

To put this somewhat differently, each party suffers from an *ethnic blind spot*. Neither recognizes the ethnicity of SECA and its Christian colleges for what it really is. *Each assumes that the Christian college operates in a culture-free posture or ethnic vacuum.*

In arrogating the right to classify other self-designated Christians as *non-Christians* and act toward them from a *tribalistic posture*, SECA and its Christian colleges fail to act from the *ideal transcendent posture* that they allege to respect.

Sizing Up the Situation: Causes

Why does a group of Christians like Standard Evangelical Christians in America develop a *tribalistic posture*? Why does it lose or abandon its earlier *homocentric posture*? Why do members not retain a more symbiotic relationship between themselves and members of other groups? The answer to these questions is hinted at throughout this chapter. *First*, there is a failure to cope with natural tendencies toward *tribalism*. *Second*, there is a failure to measure up to standards for *church* set in Scripture and history. *Third*, there is a failure to recognize and correct certain counter-productive presuppositions.

1. Natural Tendencies toward Tribalism

Humans are inclined naturally toward *tribalism*, and the postures of *ethnocentrism, narcissism and imperialism* that one group takes toward another is predictable. From a Christian point of view, tribalism is the fundamental flaw in ethnicity, for it results in all sorts of murder and mayhem between people of different groups. We are disinclined toward holism or the unity of our species.

Not surprisingly, SECA is blind to its own emerging ethnicity. It is gripped by a myth in which ethnic-minorities are its adversaries. This leads them to exclude or at least harshly limit the access of members of ethnic-minorities, even though Christians, to the programs, services and resources of its colleges. SECA is mired down in a set of mistakes that it attributes to non-SECAs. Its narrowness of experience is coupled with an attitude of arrogance. It reduces the dimensions of the non-SECAs' world to terms which are congenial to SECA. It manifests its own special variety of xenophobia toward people of other backgrounds.

As a consequence of its tribalism, the posturing of Christian colleges over *liberal arts* is mostly phony. As an ethnic group cannot *intentionally liberate*, liberal arts has a hollow ring on the lips of SECAs. Trapped in its own tribalism, it cannot foster the affirmative action that it alleges to espouse.

2. Standards of Measurement

SECA fails to measure itself by its own belief that Jesus Christ came to create and lead a kingdom that overcomes tribalism. Christian colleges fail to apply these same standards of measurement to themselves. In Christ, SECA says, there is neither Jew nor Greek, yet it is not policing its own attitudes toward non-SECAs in terms of this Pauline argument. A group can properly claim to have met this standard when it demonstrates that it can cope with its natural tendencies toward tribalism.

But SECAs operate quite unconsciously on the principle of "one down for them is one up for us." If they take their words at face value, in the best of all possible worlds, there are no Mormons or Pakistanis or Buddhists because SECAs have won them all for Christ, one at a time. Measuring their effectiveness by increments in this way but believing intuitively that the way leading to eternal life is "narrow" and only few find it and that the way leading to destruction is "broad" and many choose it, SECAs find themselves moving toward an impossible goal.

3. Counterproductive Presuppositions

Certain SECA presuppositions are really inimical to what it hopes to be. For example:

Salvation/Redemption. SECAs deep ethnocentrism leads them to focus on *salvation, a matter of life and death, not on redemption, a matter of freedom and bondage.* This allows those who have been delivered from poverty, disease and ignorance and no longer carry its burden, to be free to contemplate the past, with all the mysteries of creation and history, and the future, with all the mysteries of the seals, trumpets and vials of John's revelation, without a thought about where their next meal is coming from. And even worse, it allows those who have developed technological means to exploit the resources of their own back yard to buy their way into non-SECA communities around the world and use this technology to consume the resources of the non-SECA back yard to enhance their own way of life. Unfortunately, not understanding history in linear terms as SECAs do (more often thinking of it as a "cycle of life" in many parts of the world), many non-SECAs are not turned on by "Christ the Savior," the messiah of linear history whom God announces and then sends and then takes away and then offers again as Savior and then some day returns. But non-SECAs do understand this world around them and their bondage to the elemental spirits of the universe and to principalities and powers, and perhaps if SECAs understood the world as non-SECAs see it, they would talk to them more about "Jesus the Lord" who brings deliverance, who redeems from bondage. SECAs need to remind themselves that while they consider Christ is Savior, leading the world from death to life, he also spoke of himself as Lord, delivering the world from bondage to freedom. To be free enough to ignore their fellow humans in need is to be in bondage to their own self-interests. In relating to non-SECAs, SECAs may learn to talk about "Christ the Savior" and "salvation" and "life and death" in terms of Western Christian Evangelical Theology that they learn so well, but they may fail to learn how to talk in terms which are meaningful to non-SECAs about "Jesus the Lord" and "redemption" and "freedom and bondage."

Of course, in the Christian college, much of this is beside the point, so to speak, since the Christian members of ethnic-minorities who seek access are "already saved." As long as the main SECA responsibility is seen in terms of "salvation," no charge against the Christian college will really stick. In fact, this may help to explain why Christian colleges seem more open to recruiting internationals than American Christians from ethnic-minorities.

Poor, Lazy, and Dumb. A more pernicious evil, and an expression of deep-seated narcissism, lies in the presupposition that SECAS are rich, industrious and smart because they heeded God's revelation, worked hard and saved their money. SECAs often look at non-SECAs among whom they work as poor, lazy and dumb. The task that SECA carves out for itself is to help non-SECAs to become rich not poor, hardworking not lazy, and smart not dumb. So they reach out to non-SECAs through giving to the poor, preaching to the lazy and teaching the dumb. Unfortunately, this means that they build a wall between themselves and non-SECAs, those whom they seek to reach, and when non-SECAs think of themselves as reasonably well off, industrious and intelligent, and find that SECAs think of them differently, they build a wall of their own to shut SECAs out.

Some of the frustration that leaders of Christian colleges feel as they deal with the issues of this book no doubt are due at least in part to the tensions between intuitions telling them that it is wrong to think of some non-SECAs as poor, lazy and dumb and the actions which they take to reinforce it.

Leaders of Christian colleges find themselves on the horns of a dilemma. They need Christian members of ethnic-minorities on their campuses to properly offset the criticism aimed at them, yet to give them a more visible presence is to invite change that SECA supporters may disapprove of, unless, of course, they can insure supporters that recruits from ethnic-minorities are truly poor, lazy and dumb, thus qualifying them as targets of mission, evangelism and discipleship.

Incrementalism. As stated above, SECAs operate quite unconsciously on the principle of "one down for them is one up for us," a kind of covert imperialism. This *bigger-is-better syndrome,* clearly out-of-synch with Biblical revelation and standing in stark contrast to Jesus' words about "narrow is the way," leads the Christian college to the untenable position that it is better to have more students than less, more faculty than less, more administrative levels than less, more money than less, more equity than less, more endowment than less. Members of ethnic-minorities cost more. They don't bring in as much revenue. Over the long haul, they are not as profitable. So any change in present policies toward the enrollment of ethnic-minorities would not be cost-effective.

Summary

SECA today is hardly to be mistaken for a roving band of hetero-geneous Christian ethnics like their ancestors of the first Christian century. Rather it is a critical mass of increasingly homogeneous ethnic Christians assuming one of two postures in the presence of non-SECAs. Some are perceived as *cooperative*—"one among many." Others are seen as *competitive* ("soul winners") "one versus many."

SECA somewhat schizophrenically thinks of itself in two ways. On the one hand, it is a group of *Christian ethnics* who have emerged from a variety of ethnic origins and are moving toward a goal of world service. On the other, it is a group of *ethnic Christians* caught up in tribalism and moving toward a goal of survival by nourishing itself, controlling predators and reproducing itself. Tribalism and transcendence are engaged in mortal conflict. As *ethnic Christians,* SECA's separate themselves from non-SECAs, whereas *Christian ethnics* at their best are uniting to demonstrate in their own rela-tionships that the homocentric principle provides a better foundation for the Christian way of life. But such homocentricity doesn't come easily. It requires openness to non-SECA's. It means risking contact with them. However, the driving forces of tribalism lead SECAs to seek and maintain privacy and protection.

This goal conflict is not without its negative consequences. First, in becoming an ethnic group, SECA further fragments the human species. Second, if we take the writings of first century Christians at face value, SECA's increasing attention to its own survival is clearly contrary to their aspirations. Third, certain core-presuppositions that nurture its ethnicity are actually counterproductive in cultivating transcendance. Non-SECAs often view SECAs merely as religious colonialists or inveterate navelgazers.[17]

Unless this goal conflict is recognized, this emerging ethnicity will go unchecked. If recognized, SECAs can reconstitute themselves, with God's help, from their emerging status as ethnic Christians to Christian ethnics in the best sense of the Christian tradition of ethnic heterogeneity. SECAs can rise above their ethnocentrism, fight off their narcissistic and imperialistic tendencies and give themselves to the development and nurture of homocentricity, as Christians have done repeatedly throughout the history of Christendom. "Through ethnicity (nomos)," said Paul, "I died to ethnicity to live for God."

It is *not* the *ethnic group* that is *called to* a species-wide mission. It is the *remnants called out from* ethnic groups that are challenged to a world mission, not to form a new ethnic group but among other things to confess and forsake their tribalism. When SECA is fully ethnic, a matter of another generation perhaps, it will have lost its reason for existence.

The solution to the problem of ethnic-minorities on the campuses of Christian colleges is all tied up in their status as a tool of SECA. A truly Christian college, if it were to exist, would draw no ethnic boundaries. Such a Christian college is not yet on the horizon.

SECAs have not dealt with this goal conflict because we have not yet seen what our emerging ethnicity is doing to us. Any attempt to reform SECA's role in the world must begin with a clear perception of this goal conflict.[18] Insofar as this formulation is accurate, it is significant to the concern of this book because it explains why Christian colleges tend to exclude or at least curtail the visibility of Christian ethnics on their campuses.

Sizing Up the Situation: What Can Be Done?

It remains then to offer some guidance for reforming the present situation. Of course, much of this book is devoted to the search for a solution to the problems which ethnic-minorities face in gaining greater access to evangelical Christian colleges, especially in the chapters to follow. I will therefore focus simply on the special problem of evangelical tribalism that I have posed.

To save itself from the inevitability of ethnicity, in which it loses its birthright and mandate, SECA must become aware of itself as an emerging ethnic group and the ethnicization process which it is undergoing and forswear any exclusivism or tribalism that makes it impossible or awkward to carry out its commission. In this, the true evangelical Christian college has a key role. Future SECA leaders to a great extent will move through such institutions of higher learning to positions of influence. There their world views will be modified or reinforced. It is the laboratory in which *transcendence* of ethnicity can be developed. In the evangelical Christian college, Christian ethnics can and should have a key role in heightening awareness of SECA's emerging ethnicity as they serve in the experimental laboratory where they will work with SECA leaders of the future to confront tribalism and to develop a transcendent posture before the world.

Given that the mission of Christian ethnics, as students, faculty, staff and administration, is to join SECAs in a common struggle to transcend tribalism, a working coalition of ethnic-minorities and evangelical Christian colleges is necessary in order to lead thinking SECAs away from ethnic entrapment and toward the transcendence for which the Church is intended.

Implementation

Such an idea is not easy to implement. It demands careful discrimination between a "one among many" posture in which homo-centricity is pursued and a "one versus many" posture that nurtures tribalism. It requires SECAs to eschew all attempts to get non-SECAs to abandon their own ethnicity in favor of a new one, something that is humanly impossible and biblically reprehensible.

But still implementation won't come easy. *First*, if it is true that a properly understood and applied gospel yields heterogeneous

Christian ethnics, educators need to be ethnics who have become Christians, not Christians who have become ethnics. Their posture shapes the approach that they take toward higher education. *Second,* if it is true that a properly understood and applied gospel leads to transcendence, educators need to make sure that they eschew all forms of tribalism. The goals of educators, ideal or actual, likewise shape their approaches to education. *Third,* if educators hope to do justice to an appropriate application of the gospel, they must seek to relate to non-SECAs in a "one among many" posture. By insisting or seeming to insist that non-SECAs give up their ethnicity (which is impossible), educators would appear to arrogate to themselves the right to guard the purity of their good news. That may be God's prerogative.

At its best, the evangelical Christian college is in the vanguard of cultural change. At its worst, it merely indoctrinates, and in so doing, it perpetuates traditional tribalism for another generation. The evangelical Christian college plays a crucial role within the church in *bending the trend* away from tribalism and toward transcendence and ethnic-minorities provide the essential element in the academic environment to bring about the confrontation that is necessary in change.

By way of prescription, there are four medicines to be recommended.

First, we humans are endowed with great potential for creating barriers of various kinds. At the same time, we also have great potential for developing bonds with those insiders on the other side of the barriers that we create. Christian colleges are most effective when their graduates are in an *incarnational posture*—when they are identifying with the insiders and their point of view. The Christian college must specialize in programs, services and resources for *de-alienation*—the process which outsiders undergo in order to become acceptable to their hosts, interweaving insights from psychology, anthropology, linguistics and sociology. We best cut through barriers when we are *incarnationally* oriented.

Second, we humans are also endowed with great potential for living within the walls which we erect. At the same time, we also have great potential for passing in and out of the worlds of those on the other side of the walls that we erect. Christian colleges are most effective when they are in a *reconciling posture*—when they are confronting similarities and differences constructively, cooperatively and creatively. The Christian college should specialize in programs, services and resources for *bi-passing*—the process which outsiders and insiders undergo when they pass in and out of one anothers' worlds. We are at our best when we are demonstrating reconciliation in the way we as outsiders conduct ourselves among insiders.

Third, we Americans have designed and developed an educational system that tends to nurture passive dependent students, yet living among those of other backgrounds in this incarnational and reconciling posture is an ongoing process that demands active and independent learning. The Christian college is at its best it is in a *learning posture.* The Christian college must specialize in programs, services and resources for learning in which one's potential for learning from those of other backgrounds is cultivated by insights into learning from psychology, anthropology, linguistics and sociology. We are at our best when we are first learning from those whom we hope to teach.

Fourth, mistakes are inevitable when people of different backgrounds try to live and work together, yet we are endowed with great potential for recognizing, admitting and correcting them. Christian colleges are at their best when they are in a *confessional posture.* The Christian college must specialize in programs, services and resources for heightening awareness of *alleged mistakes*—mistakes which members of one group attribute to those of another and helping outsiders to deal with them constructively. We are at our best when we are one group of beggars telling another where to find bread.

These four principles provide a framework within which the Christian college conducts its business. It would be difficult for the Christian college to work effectively without such a set of assumptions.

This means that the Christian college must aim to develop students who enter the work force equipped to play four roles.

In the role of *ombudspersons,* the alumni of Christian colleges help people of different backgrounds to resolve conflicting points of view, not to reinforce them. They encourage diversity without alienation and unity without sameness. They find reasons in the principle of incarnation for helping people of different backgrounds to undergo de-alienation and try to discover one anothers' reality.

In the role of *interpreters*, the alumni of Christian colleges help people of different backgrounds to analyze when they cannot see the trees and to synthesize when they cannot see the forest. They encourage individuality and wholeness, not fragmentation. They find reasons in the principle of reconciliation for people of different backgrounds to be more complete persons through *bi-passing*.

Like *patriarchs* and *matriarchs* that provide experience and expertise, the alumni of Christian colleges help people of different backgrounds to find footing when everything is going down hill and to find momentum when everything is grinding to a halt. They help people of different backgrounds to find moorings in midstream instead of swimming for shore. They find reasons in the human's potential for learning to help people of different backgrounds to learn from one another.

Like *prophets* that provide visions of new alternatives, the graduates of the Christian college help people of different backgrounds to strive for new levels of competence and to develop untapped personal resources. They help to maintain order in relationships without letting order become conformity. They encourage the development of creative potential, not the reward of mediocrity. They find reasons in the principle of confession for helping people of different backgrounds to confront their *alleged mistakes* and rectify them.

These four roles provide another part of the framework with in which the Christian college carries out its mission. It would be difficult for the Christian college to work effectively from a contradictory set of assumptions.

Treatment

Prescription is one thing. Taking the treatment is another, and boards of directors of colleges and the leadership of constituencies which support them is where policy must begin to change.

But policy won't change until it is resisted, and this resistance must come in different forms and be brought to bear on boards of directors, often the most tribalistic of all.

There are a number of affirmative actions that can be taken. First, boards of directors can appoint members of ethnic-minorities to their boards. Second, students can be encouraged, not just allowed to critique and even resist policies driven by ethnocentric boards of directors.

Third, leaders can hire members of ethnic-minorities to tenure-track positions.

Finally, it should be noted that *openness toward pluralism* is not enough. Pluralism is not enough. Assuming a "one among many" or "live and let live" posture is to settle for too little. For its SECA constituency, the Christian college must *model transcendence*, thereby assuming a proper prophetic role. Young people growing up ethnic need to be confronted with the *homocentricity alternative* to ethnocentrism and tribalism. For them to do so, they need to confront *inter-ethnic* differences and issues which separate one ethnic group from another. Ethnic-minorities must not just be *"present"* but must be in a position of *power* when this confrontation takes place if it is to take root in the lives of young SECAs.

Conclusion

SECA has alternative futures, one planned and another unplanned. Without planning ways to deal with its own tribalism and emerging ethnicity, SECA will line up alongside everyone from Arabs to Zulus as full-fledged ethnics, equally ethnocentric, equally preoccupied with survival and well-being, equally concerned with itself more than with others. Administrators, often establishment SECAs, and educators will be influenced by SECA's tribalism working its will on whomever it can touch and control.

By planning and developing ways and means of heterogenizing itself and giving itself to the pursuit of transcendence, SECA can offer itself in service to a wider world as one among many. Educators will become catalysts in helping Christians among Arabs and Zulus to create a global Christian mosaic, not a pot which melts out all unacceptable differences. Dealing redemptively with their privacy and insecurity, educators will open themselves to the world and risk fuller and deeper contacts with non-SECAs. As long as they are trapped in their own tribalism, none of this is possible.

Most important, then, is the *de-tribalization* of the leadership of Christian colleges. An old Chinese parable makes the point:

> Once upon a time a monkey and a fish were caught up in
> a great flood. The monkey, agile and experienced, had the
> good fortune to scramble up a tree to safety. As he looked

down into the raging waters, he saw a fish struggling
against the swift current. Filled with humanitarian
desire to help his less fortunate fellow, he reached down
and scooped the fish from the water. To the monkey's
surprise, the fish was not very grateful for his aid.

The leadership of Christian colleges who themselves have not
developed serious relationships with members of ethnic-minorities
high on their own personal agendas need to do so before any
significant changes can take place. Until they develop some genuine
empathy with minorities, they cannot really be trusted with the
delicate process of *education for homocentricity leading to ultrastability.*
In a word, if things are to change, we must certify the credentials of
educators, not just debate principles and guidelines for allowing
ethnic-minorities greater access to Christian colleges.[19]

Various options are open to the Christian college. One is to hold to
its present course: reinforcing evangelical tribalism. Another is to
prepare leaders of the future to bring SECA to a greater awareness of its
emerging ethnicity and its need for a more transcendent posture in
its context. If SECA doesn't take the message of this book and this
chapter seriously, no change in the status of the Christian college and
no change in the role and presence of ethnic-minorities is likely to
occur. But if the Christian College takes this message to heart, change
is inevitable and the present rate of change toward tribalism will
diminish.

References

Adams, D. (1960). "The Monkey and the fish: cultural pitfalls of an educational adviser," *International Development Review, Volume 2* (2), 22-24.

Bateson, G. (1958). *Naven*. Stanford, CA: Stanford University Press.

Brushaber, G.K. (1989). Playing the Oxymoron Game, *Christianity Today*. December 15.

Cadwallader, M.L. (1966). "The Cybernetic Analysis of Change in Complex Social Organizations," in Smith A.G. (1966), *Communication and Culture*. NY: Holt, Rinehart and Winston, Inc.

Fetterman, D.M. (1989). *Ethnography Step by Step* (Applied Social Science Research Methods Series, Volume 17). Newbury Park, CA: Sage Publications.

Flake, C. (1984). *Redemptorama: Culture, Politics and the New Evangelicalism*. Garden City, NY: Anchor Press, Doubleday and Co. Inc.

Foster, G.M. (1962). *Traditional Cultures: And the Impact of Technological Change*. New York: Harper and Row.

Gerlach, L.P. (1969). "Personal Transformations and Revolutionary Change," (Program II) in *Lifeway Leap: The Dynamics of Change in America*. Television series produced in association with KTCA, Minneapolis, MN.

Greeley, A.M. (1974). *Ethnicity in the United States: A Preliminary Reconnaissance*. New York: John Wiley & Sons.

Hiebert, P. (1982). The Flaw of the Excluded Middle, *Missiology* 10:35-47.

Kuhn, T. (1970). *The Structure of Scientific Revolutions*, 2nd ed. Chicago: University of Chicago Press.

Larson, B.E. (1985). The Masters of Sociological Thought: Application to the Lakewood Evangelical Free Church. Unpublished manuscript.

Larson, D.N. (1984). *Guidelines for barefoot language learning.* St. Paul, MN: Communication Management Services.

Mehan, H. and Wood, H. (1975). *The Reality of Ethnomethodology.* New York: John Wiley and Sons.

Spradley, J.P. and McCurdy, D.W. (1980). *Conformity and Conflict: Readings in Cultural Anthropology.* (4th Ed.) Boston: Little and Brown.

Spradley, J.P. and McCurdy, D.W. (1975). *Anthropology: The Cultural Perspective.* NY: John Wiley & Sons, Inc.

Wallace, A.F.C. (1956). Revitalization Movements. *American Anthropologist, 58,* 264-281.

Footnotes

1. Mehan and Wood (1975) develop the notion of incorrigible propositions.

2. In the development of these ideas over the past years, I am in debted to a number of colleagues, for regular feedback, counsel, critique and suggestions. Drs. Thomas C. Correll, Kenneth E. Gowdy, James Hurd, William A. Smalley, Paul D. Wiebe, Kevin Cragg and Paul Spickard, and especially to Henry Allen, who led me back to Greeley's work on ethnogenesis and ethnicization (1974), the "process by which immigrants from one society become ethnic in another."

3. This definition is developed in Spradley and McCurdy (1975). Much to the chagrin of SECAs who are professional anthropologists, Hebrew did not have a close natural equivalent to what we mean by "culture." But perhaps the Greek "kosmos" and perhaps even "nomos" come close. For example, "nomos" in the generic sense, formal or informal, oral or written, is first a "regularity," much like the "law of gravity." Culture, to the cognitively oriented anthropologist, defined as the knowledge, belief, feeling and attitude used by a group to generate behavior and interpret behavior, is the source of "nomos." Thus the translation in which "nomos" is rendered as "culture" or "ethnicity," while cheating a bit, serves to remind the reader of the role that ethnicity places in responding to the gospel.

4. The concept of *ethos* is developed in Bateson (1958).

5. The definition of *religion* is developed in Spradley and McCurdy (1975).

6. Hiebert (1982) develops the concepts of bounded and centered sets.

7. The concept of *homocentricity* is developed in the introduction to Spradley and McCurdy (1980).

8. The concept of *ultrastability* is developed in Cadwallader (1966).

9. Greeley (1974) refers to this process as ethnogenesis.

10. These and others are principal enablers of ethnic SECA. It should also be noted that parachurches were also developing in the mainstream. They are still represented by YMCA and YWCA. Parachurch organizations also began to develop within the branches, like Moody Bible Institute, Pacific Garden Mission, Youth for Christ, Young Life, Inter-Varsity Christian Fellowship, to mention a few. Some of these, like the Salvation Army, the Navigators and Campus Crusade for Christ, almost look like denominations themselves. SECA has also developed educational institutions and umbrella organizations that manage education from the cradle (Awana and Pioneer Girls) to the grave, so to speak. Beginning with Scripture Press and Gospel Light, with Christian High Schools and the Christian College Consortium and Christian College Coalition, it carries through in such programs as that of the Institute for Advanced Christian Education, the American Scientific Affiliation and the Creation Research Society. Organizations like the Billy Graham Evangelistic Association have had a significant role in creating SECA ethnicity.

11. Examples include various "superchurches" loosely tied to their denominations, some of which have "television ministries" like those of Charles Stanley, Robert Schuller and D. James Kennedy.

12. It is ironic that SECA's who boycotted movies during their growing up years after World War II become avid loyalists of a former movie star.

13. Other important issues include anti-pluralism, legalism, individualism (Larson 1985), etc. See Flake (1984) for further development.

14. Empirical evidence supports the notion that ethnolinguistic groups have life cycles of their own. The development of pidgin and creole languages seems to be one mark of the origin of such groups, and it is clear that they disappear when the last native speaker dies. Of course, to focus on a people as an "ethnolinguistic community" is to give more attention to linguistic characteristics. In view of the role that language plays in SECA, it seems reasonable to describe it as an ethnolinguistic community, at least tentatively.

Two key concepts are important in distinguishing ethnic groups from social aggregates: talk-work and communicative events. *Talk-work* is the talk that it takes to work and the work that it takes to talk. *Communicative events* are structured differently for homogeneous and heterogeneous communication. Members talk to members in one way and non-members in another (see Larson, 1984).

15. See Gerlach (1969) for evidence of this claim.

16. I am indebted to my son Brett for helping me to see and clarify the discussion of SECA tribalism.

17. While living in Thailand, I frequently heard evangelical missionaries referred to by Thais as "people selling religion."

18. SECA has both secular and sacred work to manage. It sacralizes secular work that supports sacred work in the form of proclamation of the gospel, Christian service and fellowship. It's meager resources must be managed carefully and parlayed into greater and greater investments with a view toward the day when contributions and volunteers will no longer be necessary to get the work done. SECA members supply what SECAs demand: money or life. If one has no money, one gives one's life. To keep one's life for oneself, one gives money. It's a grim picture. Its sacred work really provides an abundance of social activity from Bible Study Fellowship to Athletes in Action, Operation Sonshine, Amsterdam '86, Christian restaurants and discos, all of which are legitimized on the grounds that they are "witnesses" to unbelievers.

19. Like the monkey in the parable, some leaders of SECA colleges need to forsake their simplistic characterizations of *Christian college*, their defensive postures with reference to their budgetdrivenness, to deal therapeutically with their own personal monolingual and mono-cultural myopia, and to open themselves to the possibility of learning from ethnic-minorities about swimming upstream. See Brushaber (1989) as a case in point. Foster (1962), who cites this parable from the work of Adams (1960), Kuhn (1970) and Wallace (1957) provide good starting points.

An Assessment of Christian Commitment and Attitudinal Prejudice among Adults in Various Academic and Church Settings

Michael J. Boivin and Harold W. Darling

Racial Prejudice: A Spiritual Battleground

Robert Coles is reknowned as one of the most respected writers in child psychiatry in the past 20 years, and in a revealing article by Philip Yancey (*Christianity Today*, February 6, 1987) Coles talks about some of the early experiences which had a profound influence on his life and faith. Coles recounts two experiences in particular which altered the course of his spiritual pilgrimage. The first took place when he was a young psychiatrist serving as director of an air force psychiatric unit near Biloxi, Mississippi. One day, he happened to witness a very ugly racial incident which nearly turned to violence, in which a group of Blacks attempted a "swim in" at an all-white beach. Particularly distressing was a conversation Coles overheard afterward by two friends of his, white policemen who Coles had always known to be courteous and gentle individuals, who were considering retaliating against the Blacks with physical violence. The tremendous hate and anger evoked by this attempt among those present caused Coles to wonder at those forces in life that could evoke such darkness in the human spirit.

The second incident took place one day in New Orleans while Coles was driving to an appointment with his psychiatrist as part of an attempt to sort through the *angst* of Coles' own personal life. Because of an unexpected detour, Coles encountered a lower-class industrial district that had been cordoned off by State Troopers because of a racial disturbance. There, at a nearby elementary school, six year old Ruby Bridges, escorted by federal marshals, was attending Frantz School as a result of a federal court order to integrate that school district. Coles watched her arriving at her first day at school, as she and the marshals walked through a mob of white people who were screaming obscenities, threats, and shaking their fists at her (Coles, 1985).

Intrigued by the poise and courage of this young girl, Coles got to know her and her family, meeting with them repeatedly over the next few months. When later asked how she had responded to the angry mob on that terrible day in September, Ruby replied that she simply had prayed that she might be brave and strong, and she prayed that God would forgive them. "Jesus prayed that on the cross," she told Coles; "'forgive them, because they don't know what they're doing'" (Yancey, 1987, p. 17). Out of these visits with Ruby as well as other visits with all manner of children from many situations of poverty and hardship, eventually came the multi-volume series *Children of Crisis* for which Coles won a Pulitzer prize in 1973. Out of this work also came an eventual commitment to Jesus Christ, and to a world view epitomized by Jesus' Sermon on the Mount.

What is especially intriguing about Coles' story is the fact that it was within the context of human prejudice that furrows were plowed in the soil of his life so that the seeds of the gospel of the Kingdom of God could take hold. It was his own confrontation with the human evil and human courage in the midst of racial conflict that Coles was inspired to go beyond traditional psychiatry, and to seek a moral dimension to the human condition.

Psychological Research and Prejudice: No Longer Fashionable

Unfortunately, despite the potential for prejudice as a window into some of the most significant aspects of human psychological and moral well-being, in the last 15 years we have seen a waning of interest among social science researchers in this topic. Figure 1 illustrates this trend by depicting a declining trend since 1969 in the proportion of attitudinal articles in *Psychological Abstracts* pertaining specifically to racial prejudice. This is despite a corresponding increase in the proportion of *Psychological Abstract* citations pertaining to attitudes in general.

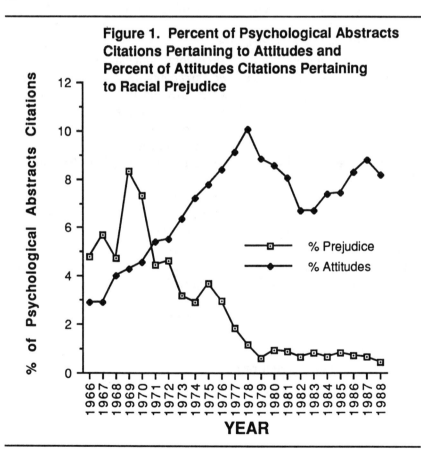

Figure 1. Percent of Psychological Abstracts Citations Pertaining to Attitudes and Percent of Attitudes Citations Pertaining to Racial Prejudice

However, within American society there seems to be a growing sense of racial and ethnic intolerance as witnessed by the recent cultural fad of "Jap-bashing" (Shapiro, 1988) and the chilling wave of racism embodied in the recent cultural phenomenon of youthful skinheads with strong neo-fascist idealogies (Leo, 1988). These more recent trends are in addition to the more traditional raw racism towards Blacks in American society that can always readily be found (e.g., Gup, 1988; Minerbrook, 1988).

On American college and university campuses as well, racism is once again becoming an immediate and difficult concern (e.g., Fields, 1988; Collison, 1988). Clearly, a declining interest in racial prejudice among psychological researchers is not because the issue has been resolved or is no longer of immediate significance within our culture.

Christian Psychology and Prejudice

Within one representative psychology journal that focuses on integration topics, the *Journal of Psychology and Theology* (JPT), fewer articles were published between 1973 and 1987 on such topics as racial prejudice and racial minorities than for the topics of human sexuality, maturity, or morality, to name a few (see Figure 2). In fact, the present authors were involved in both of the only two JPT articles on racial prejudice (Boivin, Darling, & Darling, 1987; Hollister & Boivin, 1987).

As one surveys the various topics for research and theoretical work in JPT (see Comprehensive Index for volumes 1 - 15 for the *Journal of Psychology and Theology* in Volume 16 (1), 1988), one notices that there is a highly individualistic emphasis. In simply reading the various titles and abstracts, one can readily see that whether with respect to Christian maturity, spiritual well-being, compassion, needs assessment, or morality, the primary focus is on the individual person and/or how one responds to other individual persons. Very rarely are these same topics interpreted within the broader context of social justice or reconciliation between estranged social groups, including those of different races.

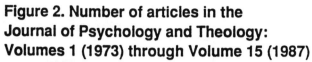

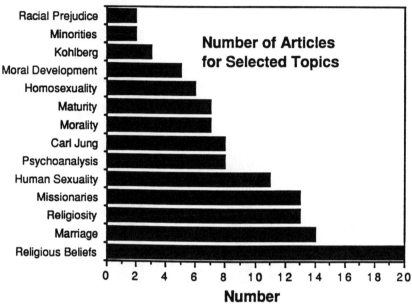

Figure 2. Number of articles in the
Journal of Psychology and Theology:
Volumes 1 (1973) through Volume 15 (1987)

Number of Articles
for Selected Topics

This tendency is also evident when comparing the two most prominent Christian integration journals in psychology (JPT and the *Journal of Psychology and Christianity* (JPC)) with a journal publication that is not an avowedly integration journal, yet also includes a focus on religious issues from a research perspective (the *Journal for the Scientific Study of Religion* (JSSR)). Both integration journals contain substantially more articles on human sexuality than on racial prejudice (see Figure 3), while the opposite is true for JSSR. However, although JSSR has published more articles pertaining to racial prejudice, the proportion of such articles to articles on human sexuality has declined more recently when one examines these proportions by decade (see Figure 4). Apparently, the popularity of attitudinal prejudice as a topic for religious research is waning, in keeping with the decline in the amount of attitudinal prejudice research within psychology in general.

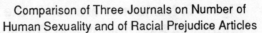

Figure 3

Comparison of Three Journals on Number of
Human Sexuality and of Racial Prejudice Articles

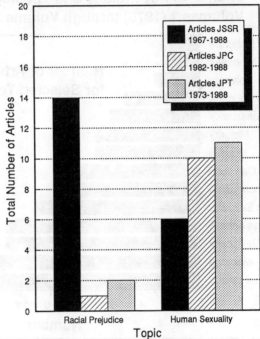

Spiritual Well-being and American Individualism

With the rising interest in educational, psychological, and social assessment have come numerous recent attempts among Christian practitioners to measure religious or spiritual well-being. Some examples are the Spiritual Well-being Scales (Moberg, 1984; Paloutzian & Ellison, 1982), "Nearness to God" and "Fundamentalism" Scales (Broen, 1957; Gorsuch & Smith, 1983), the Shepherd Scale (Bassett et al., 1981), and Character Assessment Scale (Schmidt, 1980). In fact, at the time of this writing Wheaton College (Wheaton, IL) psychologist Richard Butman and his former student Daniel Tangeman are coordinating a comprehensive review and compendium of such measures to be published as a resource volume for practitioners, researchers, pastors, and helping professionals. Anywhere between 70 to 100 instruments have been identified through this project as generally pertaining to the assessment of religiosity and spiritual well-being. Even a cursory review of the related research literature pertaining to this projects reveals, over the past 10 years, this mode of assessment has become of greater interest to integration psychologists, health care professionals, pastors, and professional counselors.

Figure 4   Number of Articles on Human Sexuality and on Racial
              Prejudice in Journal for the Scientific Study of Religion

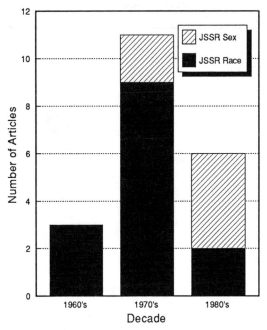

Figure 5 consists of a comparison of the above five religiosity measures in terms of the content of the individual items. For three of the five instruments, most of the questions or items pertain to the respondent's personal beliefs or sense of spiritual well-being (Gorsuch & Smith, 1983; Paloutzian & Ellison, 1983; Moberg, 1984). The Shepherd Scale developed by Bassett et al. (1981) goes beyond the respondent's beliefs and personal spiritual well-being, and includes a Christian "walk" or lifestyle subscale, which include a number of items pertaining to how the respondent treats other individuals. The

Character Assessment Scale developed by Schmidt (1980) is intended as a Biblically-based comprehensive assessment of character, and includes among other things, subscales devoted to one's sexuality and to one's use of money.

Among all five of the instruments in Figure 5, however, not a single item or question pertains to how a respondent feels about or treats members of a different racial group. Nor do any of the items clearly address the sensitivity of the respondent to social justice issues or the extent to which that person is likely to extend a helping hand to a member of a stigmatized social group.

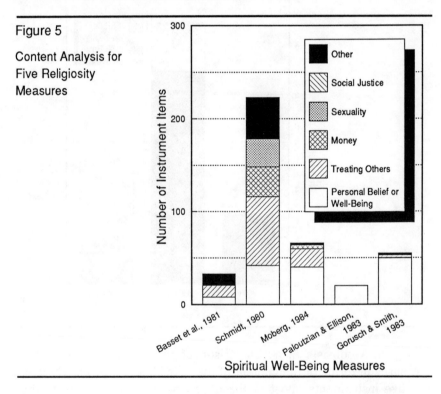

Figure 5

Content Analysis for
Five Religiosity
Measures

To summarize, Christian integration psychologists have not been all that interested in formally exploring attitudinal prejudice, at least when compared to interest in other issues such as human sexuality, religiosity, and moral development, to name a few. Likewise, when conceptualizing the various factors that comprise spiritual well-being and its assessment, how an individual responds within the context of ethnic or racial prejudice is not really considered. Again, the vantage point in our assessment of spiritual and psychological well-being has been one of the individual and how that individual treats other individuals. What is not really considered is how that individual, as a member of a stratum or group, responds to members of distinctly different and possibly estranged racial, social, or economic groups.

Individualism is a prominent value in American society that permeates the social fabric of this culture. Likewise, an individualistic perspective also permeates the efforts of Christian integration psychologists as they endeavor to better understand what it means to be psychologically and spiritually whole.

Religiosity and Prejudice: Some Recent Research

Despite a waning of interest in recent years on the relationship between religiosity and psychological wholeness in the lives of individuals, there has been some recent research which merits consideration. In terms of a brief historical review, in the late 1960's and 1970's a significant topic in attitudinal research was whether being religious contributed to one being more or less prejudiced. Allport and Ross (1967) suggested that in investigating this issue, it was important to make a distinction between individuals who were extrinsically religious and those who were more intrinsically motivated in their religious faith. They concluded that although churchgoers in general tended to be more prejudiced than non-churchgoers, it was the extrinsically religious individuals especially who seemed to be the most prejudiced. Intrinsically religious persons, or those were sincere in their beliefs and did not pursue religion as a means to a social end, also tended to be more racially tolerant (see Boivin, Donkin, & Darling, 1990 for a more thorough review of this research area).

Allport and Ross' conclusion is well taken in that the sincerity and integrity of motives underlying one's religious beliefs most certainly should contribute to the extent to which that faith will reflect psychological and/or social wholeness (including racial tolerance). Still, it would be most reassuring to the evangelical perspective if somehow the distinction between extrinsic versus intrinsic religiosity coincided with the extent to which the Holy Spirit was purported to be at work in the life of the individual. Simply put, can individuals who characterize themselves as "born-again" and faithful to Christ also be characterized as more intrinsically religious and racially tolerant?

Generally, those in contemporary American society who characterize themselves as "born-again" also tend to be more orthodox and conservative in their religious and social views. As a result, attempts to denote such individuals in surveys or interviews often end up focusing primarily on orthodoxy of belief with respect to such issues as the divinity, resurrection, and second coming of Christ, the divine inspiration of the Bible, and personal piety on the part of the respondent.

Unfortunately, in their careful review of the research literature examining the relationship between Christian faith and ethnic prejudice, Gorsuch and Aleshire (1974) essentially concluded that the more orthodox the respondents were in terms of their Christian beliefs and practices, the more attitudinal prejudice they exhibited. Thus, in identifying those who are "truly" Christian, it seems that one must go beyond orthodoxy of belief and social conservatism, especially if one wants to establish the same sort of positive relationship with racial tolerance as is apparent with the notion of intrinsic religiosity.

How then, to define the truly Christian individual? One team of scholars at Roberts Wesleyan College attempted to arrive at a Biblically based and valid instrument to differentiate "the sheep from the goats", and named their instrument the Shepherd Scale (Bassett et al., 1981). The items in their instrument were based on a systematic and exhaustive review of Biblically-based criteria for distinguishing those who follow Christ, and examined both integrity of lifestyle and Christian belief. Furthermore, the construct validation and reliability measures provided by Bassett and his co-workers as well as by Pecnik and Epperson (1985) suggested that in assessing the integrity of a respondent's Christian commitment, this instrument went far beyond its predecessors, many of which often amounted to little more than the Apostles' Creed in Likert format or else a cursory self-report on one's faithfulness in attending religious services.

Hopeful that a valid instrument for assessing integrity of Christian commitment might prove more successful in documenting a significant positive relationship with racial tolerance, Boivin, Darling and Darling (1987) used the Shepherd Scale in conjunction with a respected multi-dimensional measure of racial attitudes (Multifactor Racial Attitudes Inventory (MRAI)—Woodmansee & Cook, 1967). The respondents in this study consisted of a group of predominantly evangelical students at a small Christian liberal arts college, and a group of predominantly non-evangelical college students from a nearby community college. While the use of Shepherd Scale proved effective in distinguishing between the two groups in terms of Christian commitment and lifestyle, there was no clear relationship between Shepherd Scale scores and degree of attitudinal racial tolerance as reflected in the MRAI values.

Table 1 consists of a comparison of the community and Christian college samples for the various measures in the present study. The Christian college sample of students scored significantly higher than their community college counterparts on the Shepherd Belief, Shepherd Walk, Christian Conservatism, and Church Attendance measures. However, no significant differences were apparent for any of the measures of racial tolerance. Rather than strength of Christian commitment, other measures as reported by the respondents in the survey turned out to be better predictors of degree of attitudinal prejudice. These included gender, age, social background, and the extent to which parents, friends and significant others were reported as being prejudiced.

Boivin, Donkin and Darling (1990) was an attempt to extend the findings of Boivin, Darling and Darling (1987) with a sample of adults who were interviewed in a church, as opposed to a college classroom setting. The particular community chosen for the study was a large town in southcentral Michigan which had a population of approximately 10,000 individuals. The Michigan Department of Corrections (MDOC) has located two correctional facilities near this town. Because of recent affirmative action programs by the MDOC, a number of Black correctional officers and staff have been hired in to work in these facilities and have located in this formerly all-white community with their families. Some residents have noted privately that the recent influx of Black families to this community has necessitated a certain degree of adjustment and flexibility for many longtime residents. As such, this particular town seemed like a reasonable setting for exploring the relationship between religiosity and prejudice for adults within a church setting.

Table 1

A comparison of community and Christian college students on measures of Christian commitment and measures of attitudinal racial prejudices

SCALE	Community College (n=40)		Christian College (n=64)		
	M	SD	M	SD	t-score
Shepherd Walk	5.71	7.32	12.59	3.82	-6.13**
Shepherd Belief	6.63	6.01	10.50	1.92	-4.75**
Christian Conservatism	3.51	3.52	6.39	0.97	-6.15**
Christian Self Rating	3.00	2.51	3.64	1.98	1.45
Church Attendance (# per year)	32.80	39.85	98.75	52.80	6.78**
Social Desirability	-5.68	9.41	-6.50	10.00	0.43
Multi-Factor Racial Attitude Inventory					
Total Score	30.70	19.70	31.60	21.70	-0.17
Integration/ segregation	7.97	2.34	6.93	3.04	1.76
Ease in inter-racial contacts	-1.62	5.15	-0.37	5.44	-1.15
Black inferiority	5.59	3.49	6.50	2.24	-1.61
Subtle derogatory beliefs	0.68	4.11	0.23	4.58	0.50
Acceptance in close personal relationships	8.15	2.92	8.52	2.40	-0.68
Local autonomy	1.23	3.45	1.47	4.22	-0.27
Private rights	4.14	3.82	5.08	3.35	-1.29
Acceptance in superior status relationships	8.28	2.83	8.33	2.55	-0.09
Gradualism	-3.56	4.55	-3.35	4.66	-0.21

*$p<0.05$, **$p<0.01$

Perhaps the most telling aspect of the present study was the fact that eight of the churches approached by Donkin (1989) refused to participate in the assessment, despite every effort to work with them in a flexible and sensitive manner. Finally, however, Donkin was able to evaluate a total of 101 individuals at four churches (Free Methodist,

Independent Bible, Nazarene, and Reformed Lutheran) (age: M = 47.2, SD = 15.6). For the sake of comparison, the exact same instrument was used as in the Boivin, Darling, and Darling (1987) study, and consisted not only of the MRAI and Shepherd Scales, but also the Christian Conservatism and Marlowe-Crowne Social Desirability Scales as well as a number of other descriptive social, political, and familial indicators.

The present findings confirmed those of Boivin, Darling and Darling in that racial tolerance and strength of Christian commitment were statistically independent of one another. Figure 6 consists of a scatterplot in which a composite score for Christian commitment (average of Shepherd Belief, Shepherd Walk, Christian Conservatism, and Christian self rating) is plotted as a function of racial tolerance (MRAI total). What is evident from this plot is the fact that in the present study, one cannot predict the degree of racial tolerance (the higher the MRAI total, the more tolerant) on the basis of strength of Christian commitment.

A principal-component factor analysis for the various religiosity and prejudice indicators from the present instrument was performed on the combined samples from the Boivin, Darling, and Darling (1987) and the Boivin, Donkin, and Darling (1990) studies (see Table 2). For these data, the measures of Christian commitment (Shepherd Belief, Shepherd Walk, Christian Conservatism, and Christian Self Rating) were separate and distinct factors from the various measures of racial tolerance.

However, for the adult church sample in the Boivin, Donkin, and Darling study, there was a categorical relationship between overall level of the respondent's attitudinal prejudice and the extent to which the respondent's pastor and friends were perceived as being prejudiced (see Table 3). Respondents who categorized their friends, spouses (boyfriend, girlfriend), or parents as being more prejudiced were themselves more likely to fall into the upper half of the sample in terms of their overall racial prejudice (MRAI total).

Figure 6

The relationship between Christian Commitment and Attitudinal Racial Prejudice (MRAI Total) for adults in a church setting (Donkin, 1979).

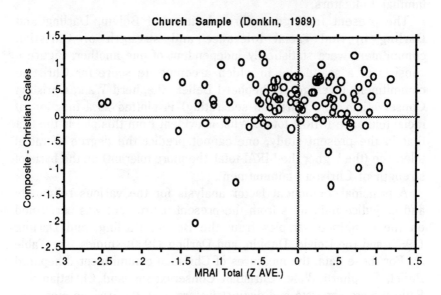

When comparing the sample of church adults from Donkin (1989) to the sample of Christian college students from Boivin et al. (1987), the church adults were significantly higher in terms of their age, Shepherd Walk and Christian Self Rating scores. However, they were significantly lower on the MRAI subscales of Ease in Interracial Contacts and the Private Rights of Blacks (see Table 4), although the church adults exhibited somewhat more attitudinal prejudice with respect to certain MRAI subscale measures. Apparently, the sociological context of the sample (comparing Christian college students to Christian adult non-students in a community in transition in terms of racial composition) is a more significant factor when considering group differences than the expressed degree of Christian commitment (Christian versus non-Christian college students).

Table 2

Principal-Component Factor Analysis for Measures of Christian Commitment and Attitudinal Prejudice for College Students (Boivin, Darling & Darling, 1987) and Church Adults (Donkin, 1989) Samples combined: Orthogonal Rotation Varimax Solution

	Factor 1	Factor 2	Factor 3	Factor 4	Factor 5	Proportion of Scale Variance Accounted For
Shepherd belief	0.86					0.70
Christian conservatism	0.83					0.78
Shepherd walk	0.88					0.69
Christian self rating	0.66					0.72
Church attendance	0.58					0.75
*Acceptance in close personal relationships		0.83				0.80
*Acceptance in superior status		0.82				0.76
*Integration/ segregation		0.55	0.60			0.81
*Black inferiority		0.61				0.77
*Local autonomy			0.86			0.69
*Gradualism			0.73			0.71
*Private rights			0.70			0.76
*Subtle derogatory beliefs			0.46			0.83
Temperature towards Blacks				0.79		0.69
Temperature Towards Whites				0.91		0.52
Ease in interracial contacts					0.63	0.80
Social desirability scale					0.79	0.41
Eigenvalues (before Varimax rotation)	3.15	4.10	1.54	1.40	1.14	
% of total variance	19%	24%	9%	8%	7%	67% total

Note: The criterion for Significant loading on any given factor was ± 0.50. Only factors with Eigenvalues of 1.00 or more were included. The Multi-Factor Racial Attitude Inventory Scales are denoted with an asterisk.

Table 3

For Church Adult Sample (Donkin, 1989), the Interactions between Level of Attitudinal Prejudice (Above Sample Median, Below Sample Median) and Prejudice Ranking of Significant Others (Little or no prejudice, somewhat prejudiced, very prejudiced). Both College Student and Adult Church (Donkin, 1989) samples combined. (Boivin, Darling & Darling, 1987)

Significant Other	Chi-Square	Results
Pastor (or priest)	8.49*	Positive Relationship
Mother	1.91	
Father	3.19	
Friends	9.36*	Positive Relationship
Spouse (boyfriend, girlfriend)	3.45	

p<0.05

To summarize, the findings of Donkin (1989) and Boivin, Donkin, and Darling (1990) support and extend the results of Boivin, Darling and Darling (1987), in that assessed strength of Christian commitment is independent from racial tolerance. There are also some preliminary findings in these studies to suggest that certain social descriptors such as age and perceived degree of prejudice among ones friends might be related to attitudinal prejudice. A study by Hollister and Boivin (1987) provides further evidence to support these notions.

In a study commissioned by the Free Methodist Church of North America, J. Elliot Hollister developed a questionnaire which was intended to evaluate the following: the degree of contact by denominational leaders with members of four different ethnic/racial groups (Blacks, Hispanics, Orientals, Caucasians), approved patterns of social interaction with these groups, and the amount of social distance that the respondents tend to maintain to each group. From the instrument, Hollister and Boivin derived several measures of ethnocentrism for a national sample of Free Methodist students, layleaders and clergy, and noted the descriptive variables which seemed to be most significant in terms of degree of ethnocentrism. The most significant of these was level of education, in which the more educated respondents were less ethnocentric (see Table 5). Occupation was the next most significant factor, in which professionals and pastors were less ethnocentric than non-professionals.

Table 4

A comparison of Christian College Students (Boivin, Darling & Darling, 1987) to Church Adults (Donkin, 1989) on Measures of Christian Commitment and Attitudinal Prejudice.

Scale	Christian College Students (n=60)		Church Adults (n=101)		
	M	SD	M	SD	t-score
Age (years)	19.28	1.65	47.26	16.39	-13.59**
Shepherd Belief	10.50	1.90	10.67	2.05	-0.53
Shepherd Walk	12.59	3.82	14.70	2.66	-4.11**
Christian Conservatism	6.39	0.97	6.22	1.52	0.80
Christian Self Rating	3.64	1.98	5.59	2.08	-5.90**
Church Attendance	98.75	52.60	113.42	60.26	-1.60
Social Desirability	-6.53	10.01	-0.58	10.13	-3.59**
Multi-Factor Racial Attitude Inventory					
Total Score (2 ave.)	0.09	0.55	-0.07	0.73	-1.54
Integration/ segregation	6.93	3.04	6.53	4.40	0.62
Ease in interracial contacts	-2.70	4.25	-0.37	5.44	-2.95**
Black inferiority	6.50	2.24	6.31	2.69	0.47
Subtle derogatory beliefs	0.23	4.58	-0.70	4.53	1.18
Acceptance in close personal relationships	8.52	2.40	8.01	3.31	1.04
Local autonomy	1.47	4.22	2.30	4.90	-1.05
Private rights	5.08	3.35	2.62	4.60	3.66**
Acceptance in superior status relationships	8.33	2.55	8.59	2.29	-0.69
Gradualism	-3.35	4.67	-2.68	4.97	-0.78
Temperature towards Blacks	5.87	2.59	7.52	1.84	-4.42**
Temperature towards Whites	10.47	4.85	13.63	2.36	-5.51**

**p<0.01

One portion of the questionnaire was used to evaluate the amount of social distance that the denominational leaders would maintain with Blacks, Hispanics, or Orientals respectively (i.e., Bogardus social distance scale). In this section, respondents would note their agreement or disagreement to a series of statements which differed in the extent to which they proposed close proximity to members of a different racial group (see Table 6). The denominational leaders consistently agreed with statements of a more general nature maintaining social distance (e.g., "Life is enriched by ethnic/racial diversity", "Free Methodists profit from interethnic/racial diversity") but agreed much less with statements proposing close social proximity (e.g., statements pertaining to interracial dating, marriage, or integration of one's church). Furthermore, the reluctance of the respondents to agree as much with statements proposing a close social proximity with other racial groups was particularly striking when the statements were applied to Blacks.

For example, only 15.8% of the denominational leaders agreed consistently with those statements proposing the closest degree of social proximity with Blacks, whereas 32.8% of the sample agreed when the statements were applied to Hispanics and 30.0 % when the statements were applied to Orientals. In the Hollister and Boivin sample, there was clearly a greater tendency to be exclusivistic towards Blacks than the other racial groups considered.

The above findings are consistent with the conclusions reached by Schuman, Steeh, and Bobo (1985) in their comprehensive review and analysis of nationwide surveys on racial attitudes completed over the past 20 years. As they evaluated attitudinal trends during this time, they found that there has been a generally consistent move among white Americans toward expressing less prejudice and towards viewing integration more favorably. However, at the same time, they are generally not supportive of implementing concrete policies toward integration, particularly when it impacts on their jobs, schools and neighborhoods (closer social proximity). In this respect, the denominational layleaders surveyed in the Hollister and Boivin study are consistent with the sociological trends of the prevalent culture, rather than with the ideals of their Christian faith.

Table 5 (Hollister & Boivin, 1987)

Rank Order Comparisons: Index of Ethnocentrism, Interethnic/Racial Contact, Interethnic/Racial Social Distance Score

Descriptor Categories	N	Index of Ethno-centrism Rank Order $(X)^a$	Interethnic/ Racial Contact Measure Rank Order $(Y)^b$	Interethnic/ Racial Social Distance Score Rank Order $(Z)^c$
Inner-city churches	6	1	26	26
Clergy	73	2	22	24
Conference superintendents	16	3	25	25
Pastors	52	4	17	19
Post-Graduates	89	5	21	20
Racially White only	174	6	14	14
College graduates	25	7	12	22
Professionals occupational	94	8	20	21
Over 100 church membership	89	9	24	18
Young adults	64	10	6	17
Males	131	11	11	3
City & suburban churches	96	12	23	16
Married	138	13	13	15
College seniors	14	14	15	12
Older aged	45	15	19	10
Middle aged	71	16	1	13
Rural & small town church	77	17	7	9
Church membership of 100 or less	90	18	5	7
Singles	37	19	2	11
Females	49	20	10	8
Non-professionals	85	21	16	23
Laymen	103	22	4	6
Racially other than White	6	23	7	5
Some college	54	24	3	4
No college	12	25	18	1
College freshmen	12	26	9	2

Note: Rank number ordered from the least (1) to the most (26) for the Index of Ethnocentrism and the Interethnic/Racial Contact Measure. Rank number ordered from the greatest (1) to the least (26) for the Interethnic/Racial Social Distance Score.
[a]Rho for (X) and $(Y) = -0.6337; p<0.01,$ [b]Rho for (Y) and $(Z) = -0.402; p<0.01,$ [c]Rho for (X) and $(Z) = -0.879; p<.01$

Table 6 (Hollister & Boivin, 1987)

Expressed % of Agreement/Disagreement to Interethnic/Racial Attitude Items

Item No.	Subject	M	SD	Rank Order
32	Interethnic dating	-0.66	1.07	1
29	Interracial dating	-0.57	1.14	2
43	Marriage between ethnically diverse	-0.21	1.06	3
37	Marriage between racially diverse	0.03	1.21	4
44	General church progress in integrating diverse ethnic/racial groups	0.09	0.92	5
33	Seek interethnic/racial	0.58	1.22	6
42	Local church should be more involved in social and civil rights issues	0.58	0.91	6
35	Commitment to desegregation	0.60	1.21	8
34	Denominational endogamy (marriage within denomination)	0.63	1.05	9
38	General Free Methodist Church should be more active in issues of human rights	0.68	0.96	10
31	Local congregation directly involved in help for inner city churches	0.74	0.87	11
30	Recommend workshops to better inform on ethnic/racial issues	0.74	0.87	11
28	Personal need for more information	0.78	0.94	13
45	Local church make facilities available to interethnic/racial groups	0.83	0.90	14
41	I do not consider myself prejudiced	0.92	0.86	15
40	F.M.'s profit fron interethnic/racial exp.	1.04	0.75	16
36	Life is enriched by ethnic/racial diversity	1.13	0.78	17
39	Inner city churches have valuable insights	1.15	0.61	18

Note: Showing agreement/disagreement scores for survey items 28-45, mean item scores and rank order of mean scores from greatest disagreement = 1 to greatest agreement = 18. N=180.

Christians and Racial Tolerance: On the Horns of a Theological Dilemma

The implications from the studies we reviewed above are clear: there is no evidence that simply identifying oneself as a Christian, either in lifestyle or belief, makes a *measurable* difference in terms of racial tolerance. This is irrespective of whether the respondents are college students on a Christian college campus or denominational leaders in a church setting. Although perhaps not surprising, the lack of a clear relationship between strength of Christian commitment and racial tolerance in the above studies is theologically troublesome. After all, theological orthodoxy and sincere commitment to the Christian faith among evangelical Christians is worthless as a salting influence in the society at large unless it inspires social and psychological wholeness. As it stands, however, either this generalized inspired wholeness does not exist as anticipated, or an altogether different approach is needed in conceptualizing racial tolerance, Christian commitment and/or spiritual maturity within this realm of research.

From our perspective, prejudice is deeply ingrained in the American culture. As it persists, it is symptomatic of a diseased state for that culture. This is because prejudice represents a drastic departure from three hallmarks of wholeness; rationality, justice, and human-heartedness (Allport, 1954, 1967).

First, prejudice arises when we are predisposed to react to individuals within a racial situation in a negatively charged emotional state, as did Robert Coles' two police friends. The better alternative would be to reasonably and carefully consider the distinctives of the individuals within the racial encounter.

Second, concerning injustice: desegregation, discrimination and denial of rights to Blacks are all evidence of an unjust system which should stir righteous indignation among believers in Christ. The third, however, of Allport's hallmarks, human-heartedness, strikes at the heart of Christianity. Lack of love, rejection of and contempt for others is the very antithesis of the teachings of Christ. In fact, what is abundantly evident from the gospel accounts of the life of Christ is his tolerance of and compassion for others, whether stigmatized socially (tax collectors and publicans: see Luke 19:5-9, Matthew 9:11, Luke 7:34), ethnically or racially (Samaritans: see John 4:9; Syrophoenicians: see Mark 7:26-29; Romans: see Matthew 8:5-13).

If we follow Christ's example, we will not allow prejudice to limit our fellowship with and our love for those of other races. However, Christians may tend to do so, especially if they somehow perceive such interactions as infringing on things or persons important to them (e.g., losing a job opportunity to a Black due to affirmative action, having one's property values diminished through neighborhood integration, having one's son or daughter date or marry a Black). It is perhaps at these times especially that the words of Christ pose a significant challenge for all of us in that, "For whoever would save his life shall lose it; but whosoever will lose his life for my sake, the same shall save it" (Luke 9:24, KJV).

However, religion, even as expressed within Christianity, can sometimes be used by an individual with the expressed purpose to "save" his life in an emotional and psychological sense, rather than "lose his life for Christ's sake". Allport has discussed at length the two threads that are often woven together into the fabric of religion— brotherhood and bigotry. He admits that there are large numbers of people,

> by virtue of their psychological make-up, (that) require for their economy of living both prejudice and religion. Some are tormented by self-doubt and insecurity. Prejudice enhances their self-esteem; religion provides them a tailored security. Others are guilt-ridden; prejudice provides a scapegoat, and religion relief. Still others live in fear of failure. Prejudice provides an explanation in terms of menacing out-groups; religion provides a heavenly if not terrestrial reward. Thus for many individuals the functional significance of prejudice and religion is identical. One does not cause the other; rather both satisfy the same psychological needs. Multitudes of churchgoers, perhaps *especially in times of social anomie and crisis* (emphasis ours) embrace both supports (Allport, 1967, p.24).

These words are just as true today as they were two decades ago. America's uncertain economic, social, political and military future all contribute to an uneasiness. The 'me' generation, the styles of hair and dress, the intolerance of others different from ourselves and the inclination to be less altruistic in our outlook: these are but the tip of the iceberg in delineating the anxiety and insecurity that are prevalent in our nation. Such traits are also prevalent in the lives of young people on Christian college campuses all over America.

However, while our "psychological makeup" may provide a convenient excuse or rationale, prejudice needs to be squarely faced. Admittedly, it is difficult for us to transcend our traditional practices and concepts. In the Apostle Peter's case it took a miraculous vision from God to make him realize that, "God does not show favoritism, but accepts men from every nation who fear him and do what is right" (Acts 10:34-35, NIV). If those first century Christians had not overcome their prejudice, what we call Christianity today would in all likelihood be just a sect within Judaism and we Gentiles would be outsiders.

In the eighties, we have been lulled into thinking that the civil rights activities and legislation of the sixties have put us on the road to the solution of racism. Forcing Blacks to sit in the back of the bus was outlawed. Separate restrooms and drinking fountains for Blacks and whites were abolished. Blacks were no longer excluded from eating at the restaurant of their choice. Public colleges and universities and even most private institutions of higher learning opened their doors to students irrespective of color.

However, the permanent structures of society, education, housing and the job market continue to work for the benefit of whites and to the detriment of minorities, especially Blacks. Ron Sider (1977, p.11) presented a clear, convincing example of how this structural racism operates.

> Philadelphia Northeast High School was famous for its superb academic standards, its brilliant long-standing athletic triumphs.... [But] the neighborhood began to change; black people moved in and whites began to flee. A new high school became a necessity. An excellent new facility was completed out in the new, all-white 'Greater Northeast' in 1957. It took with it the name and the traditions, all the awards, the powerful alumni, and all the money in the treasury. Teachers were given the option of

transferring; two-thirds [went]. Black students [of] Edison [were left with] a rapidly deteriorating building, substitute teachers, and no traditions. [Its] academic record since has been terrible.... [It has] one claim to uniqueness: more students from Edison High died in Vietnam than from any other high school in America.

Is there a Christian response suitable to the enormity of the problem? A modest attempt follows to answer that question. First, we as Christians must be persuaded that prejudice and racism are sinful. We should be altogether convinced after reading the Sider article just quoted from. The entire article deserves our serious consideration, but for the purposes here, two more illustrations will have to suffice:

> Think of the grandson of a Victorian mine owner who hired ten to fourteen-year old children to work twelve to sixteen hours a day down in the narrow, low, muddy tunnels. The children often died after a few years. But the owner got rich, passed along his wealth to his sons, and they in turn passed it on to his grandsons. The grandson's cultured, affluent life and Oxford education are possible because thousands of small children were literally ground into the dust and mire of the mines. Certainly the grandson is not guilty in the precise way his grandfather was, [but should he not confess:] 'I and my fathers have sinned?'
>
> Or, to come nearer home, think of the 300 years during which the slaves donated their services via long hours of free labor to the rest of American society. They picked the cotton—and received nothing. Everybody in American society—and that includes those Northerners who have tried to plead innocent just as much as the plantation owners—everybody...paid less for their clothes because of the free labor of the slaves. Is there not a signigicant sense in which all of us today can and should say...'My father and I have sinned against Black Americans?' (Sider, 1977, p. 26).

Sider acknowledged that we as evangelicals believe we are called to live lives of separation from the wrongdoings of our sinful culture and society. We have defied, with God's help, the cultural milieu that is so quick to accept sexual misconduct and lying along with the abuse of alcohol and drugs. Thompson, (1971, p.8), writing in *Christianity Today*, declared that it is time to put the two halves of the gospel together.

> I find myself standing in no-man's land. I am dis-turbed...by churchmen who emphasize social action but have little gospel... I am equally disturbed by evangelicals who are gung ho about getting people converted, but who have little social vision and less social action.

Recognizing that in either case there is but half a gospel, he quotes Elton Trueblood (1970, pp. 21, 27):

> Intense social action without a life of devotion produces damaging results, one of which is calculated arrogance... While concentrated attention upon devotion, evangelism and piety may lead us to focus of the love of Christ it may lead us to forget those whom Christ loves.

Christianity is at its best when it is appropriating God's resources in behalf of those in need about us. We are to be instruments through which Christ can accomplish His work and His will in the world. Frank Laubach, one of the great Christians of our century, pictured graphically the stance that the church of Christ should be taking in the world: we are to throw one arm up vertically to receive Christ's love and throw the other arm out horizontally to channel it (Larson, 1965).

Some Positive Recommendations for Change

Once persuaded that prejudice and racism have to be addressed by us as informed evangelicals, we must look for ways to become involved in making wrongs right. It is at this point that Tony Campolo's (1984) notion of "praxis" as a primary means of change is worth considering. In applying this notion, Campolo suggests that our attitudes towards others changes in accordance with our behavior. This is because rational belief systems are always developed by the individual to support convictions already deduced from that person's private experience. As Campolo notes, praxis

> Unlike rationalization, which tries to make what is wrong right,...is a process whereby a person who has discovered what is right through non-rationalistic means endeavors to establish a rational justification for what he or she has come to believe. (p. 48)

Unfortunately, in American education we often assume that it works the other way, and insist on trying to change peoples' attitudes through information and argument in order to achieve attitudinal and behavioral change. With the approach of praxis, on the other hand, it is assumed that the best way to achieve lasting change is to simply begin behaving in a more tolerant manner, presumably by placing oneself into situations which more directly facilitate positive interactions with members of other racial and ethnic groups. Such interactions will gradually bring one's attitudes and feelings into accordance with the behavior (and the ideals which the behavior reflect).

John Perkins (1979), formerly the guiding force in Voice of Calvary, an evangelical 'whole person' ministry in Mississippi, has proposed a three-point strategy which we conceptualize as a first step in praxis.

1) *Relocation*: Move into the black community. Alexander (1976, p. 49), also emphasized the point:

> (Move) to a city neighborhood that is changing racially....The city begins cutting back services. The garbage is collected less than often; holes in the street aren't filled; city offices are moved into more prosperous neighborhoods, money for public transport is rechanneled to suburban commuter lines, etc.
> [So], join neighborhood organizations that are already fighting this kind of oppression. Force yourself to renounce some of the privileges of being white and

middle class. By moving to a changing neighborhood, you will not be working on all those poor Blacks, you will be working beside them (or better yet, under them). Together you will fight city hall. Make your street a neighborhood, a place with some community feeling. If the people on your street don't know each other...they pull their shades. Get to know your neighbors and organize your blocks (to fight crime).

2) *Reconciliation*: Make friends; become part of the healing of the rift between the races. Martin Luther King once contended that, "Men often hate each other because they fear each other; they fear each other because they do not know each other; they do not know each other because they cannot communicate; they cannot communicate because they separated" (Boyd, 1976, p. 410). Jesus' words from the Sermon on the Mount seem appropriate here: "So if you are offering your gift at the altar, and there remember that you brother has something against you, leave your gift there...and go; first be reconciled to your brother and then come and offer your gift" (Matt. 5:23-24, RSV). Jesus' prayer for his disciples—first century and twentieth—was, "that they may be one,... I in them, and you in me, that they may grow complete into one; so that the world may realize that you sent me (John 17:22-23, Phillips). Paul declared that God "has reconciled us to himself through Jesus Christ; and he has made us agents of the reconciliation... We are now Christ's ambassadors" (II Cor. 5:18-20, Phillips). We need to ask ourselves how we can be agents of reconciliation to those disadvantaged Blacks within our sphere of influence.

3) *Redistribution.* Redistribution of skills and resources with the community of need is also needed. Perkins (1979, p. 21) elaborated on this strategy:

> This is a most difficult and threatening step to take. Redistribution is organizing resources within the community, sharing and developing skills people have and mobilizing outside resources to make capital available within the community... This helps them to become responsible for their lives and they begin to minister to moral and spiritual conditions... A major investment

corporation could supply economic resources for holistic Gospel ministry... Individual churches, denominations and Christian organizations (could) invest a percentage of their annual budgets. Evangelical schools could be a part... Individual Christians could take advantage of the opportunity to combine investment and ministry.

Michael Haynes (1969, pp. 2, 5-6) a pastor and legislator in Massachusetts, added his assessment and proposed solutions.

If America is to arrest and heal the rapidly spreading consequences of generations of racism, it has little time in which to act... The evangelical church has been grossly guilty of the sin of omission. In reality, save for scattered tokenistic acts here and there, the...Black man...has been too much a case of 'out of sight, out of mind.'

The evangelical colleges...need to get some black faces on their faculties and staffs, and get more Black students into their schools. They need to provide full and partial scholarships for needy black young marginal Christian men and women... The Christian colleges ought to provide a special remedial program to help prepare mal-educated Blacks for admission.

Here we are, a group of Christian professionals, mental health experts and college professors. How can *we* respond? Most members of the Christian college communities across America probably consider themselves to be racially tolerant and supportive of integration and social justice. However, in all honesty, there are probably not many white Christian college faculty or staff who would be willing to relocate with their families in Black communities in open display of such ideals.

All of us, however, can be *reconcilers*. It may mean going out of our way to make and/or further an acquaintanceship or friendship with a Black person. We may have to take the initiative, be persistent, and risk rejection. The longer range goal, of course, is to be color blind in our relationships; like the young lad whose mother asked, "Does the little boy you were playing with today have a black face? I don't know, Mommy; I'll look tomorrow."

Finally, can we become involved in the *redistribution* of skills and resources? At a recent national meeting of the Christian Association for Psychological Studies, we presented a paper pertaining to the above issues and had an opportunity to ask the Christian psychologists in attendance for our presentation the following question: "To what extent are your time and talents devoted to the service of underprivileged minority groups?" Unfortunately, almost all of us as Christian helping professionals are involved in clinical, counseling, or educational interventions which are not directed towards social or racial groups very different than our own. This "fact of professional life" is not so much the direct result of overt prejudice or an intentional disregard for the needs of other racial groups or the underclass in general. Our professional efforts (which are sociologically self-serving with respect to social class) are simply the end-product of being firmly imbedded within the communities which have nurtured and now employ us.

Parting from our own social communities to seek other social or racial groups potentially in need of our services can be a difficult and threatening endeavor, because it can mean giving up those communities which we find most secure and comfortable. Nevertheless, these are small ways in which we can serve that don't necessitate "becoming sojourners in a foreign land, and among an alien people." To illustrate, one of the authors has personally committed himself for the past eight years to sponsoring a Psychology Club, once a month, at the State Prison of Southern Michigan. However, this psychology activity has also become a forum through which the Gospel of Christ can be shared as it pertains to psychological and social wholeness.

Others within our own campus community are involved at one level or another with such organizations as Jubilee Housing, Voice of Calvary, or Habitat for Humanity. Others of us have linked up with World Impact, Prison Fellowship or Food for the Hungry—and the list goes on. Counseling skills, mechanical skills, tutoring skills; those are good for starters. Donating professional time and expertise to tutoring minority members to better serve their communities—that's another distinct possibility.

Also, there should be a willingness on our parts to be tutored with respect to the cultural distinctives and needs of other racial, ethnic, and social groups. Each of us has a sphere of influence, and surely that can be widened as we allow ourselves to be equipped. As we sensitively seek to have a part in reducing our own prejudice and the nation's racism the prayer of Saul of Tarsus on the Damascus Road might well become our prayer: "Lord, what wilt thou have me to do?" (Acts 9:6, KJV).

A Final Note

In conclusion, to understand the process of Christian growth as reflected in psychological and social wholeness, we need to better understand crucial social environmental influences as reflected in the family and in the church or fellowship community. This will come about as we begin to develop a model of Christian commitment that goes well beyond an emphasis of orthodoxy of belief and personal piety with respect to behaviors traditionally emphasized within the evangelical church. Perhaps, also, it will come about as we more effectively evaluate the integrity of the Christian community and larger culture of which the individual is a part. The present results suggest that the social modeling and value system implemented day-to-day in the social environment will strongly influence the psychological and sociological wholeness of the Christian individual, irrespective of the religious ideals advertised—especially if active steps are not taken to implement those ideals through praxis.

Unfortunately, the alternative to failing to take positive action towards social and psychological growth, is to instead become shaped by a maladaptive and fallen society, the natural extension of a fallen human race. The following words penned by Rene Padilla (1985) sound this warning clearly.

> When the church lets itself be squeezed into the mold of the fallen world, it loses the capacity to see and, even more, to denounce the social evils in its own situation. Like the color-blind person who is able to distinguish certain colors but not others, the worldly church recognizes the personal vices traditionally condemned within its ranks but is unable to see the evil features of its surrounding culture. In my understanding, this is the only way one can explain, for example, how it is possible for North American culture Christianity to infuse racial and class segregation [homogeneous unit principle] into its

strategy for world evangelization. The idea is that people *like* to be with those of their own race and class and that we must therefore plant segregated churches, which will undoubtedly grow faster. (p. 31)

Unfortunately, in such a setting where the church fails to proclaim and live social justice within the full gospel of Christ, "The racist can continue to be a racist; the exploiter can continue to be an exploiter" (Padilla, 1985, p. 32). The end product, is a continued lack of a clear relationship between depth of commitment to Christ within evangelical Christianity, and a general psychological and social wholeness. Simply said, the salt has lost its flavor.

References

Alexander, J.F., (1976). Action against racism: The costly possibility. *The Other Side, 12,* 47-51.

Allport, G.W. (1954). *The nature of prejudice.* New York: Doubleday and Co., Inc.

Allport, G.W. (1967). The religious context of prejudice. *Pastoral Psychology, 18,* 20-30.

Allport, G.W. & Ross, J.M. (1967). Personal religious orientation and prejudice. *Journal of Personality and Social Psychology, 5,* 432-443.

Bassett, R.L., Sadler, R.D., Kobischen, E.E., Skiff, D.M., Merrill, I.J., Atwater, J.J., & Livermore, P.W. (1981). The Shepherd Scale: Separating the sheep from the goats. *Journal of Psychology and Theology, 9,* 335-351.

Boivin, M.J., Darling H.W., & Darling, T.W. (1987). Racial prejudice among Christian and non-Christian college students. *Journal of Psychology and Theology, 15,* 47-56.

Boivin, M. J., Donkin, A. J., & Darling, H. W. (1990). Religiosity and prejudice: A case study in evaluating the construct validity of Christian measures. *Journal of Psychology and Christianity, 9,* 42-56.

Boyd, M. (1976). Blacks and whites in America: Growing farther apart. *Christian Century, 93,* 408-411.

Broen, W.E., Jr., (1957). A factor analytic study of religious attitudes. *Journal of Abnormal and Social Psychology, 54,* 176-79.

Campolo, T. (1984, Spring). Praxis: The revolutionary new principle for crisis counseling. *Youth Worker,* pp. 48-51.

Coles, R. (1985, August). The inexplicable prayers of Ruby Bridges. *Christianity Today,* 17-20.

Collison, M. (1988, September 7). For many freshmen, orientation now includes efforts to promote racial understanding. *The Chronicle of Higher Education*, A29.

Donkin, A.J. (1989). *An assessment of religiosity and prejudice among adults in various church settings.* Unpublished undergraduate honors thesis, Spring Arbor College, Spring Arbor, MI.

Fields, C.M. (1988, July 20). Colleges advised to develop strong procedures to deal with incidents of racial harassment. *The Chronicle of Higher Education*, A11.

Gorsuch, R.L. & Aleshire, D. (1974). Christian faith and ethnic prejudice: A review and interpretation of research. *Journal of the Scientific Study of Religion, 13,* 281-307.

Gorsuch, R.L. and Smith, C.S., (1983). Attributions of responsibility to God: An interaction of religious beliefs and outcomes. *Journal for the Scientific Study of Religion, 22,* (4), 340-52.

Gup, T. (1988, October 17). Racism in the raw in suburban Chicago: Two harrowing tales show how brutal bias can still be. *Time,* 25-26.

Haynes, M.E., (1968). Three minutes to midnight: The evangelical and racism. *Evangelical Missions Quarterly, 5,* (1) 1-6.

Hollister, J.E. & Boivin, M.J. (1987). Ethnocentrism among Free Methodist leaders and students. *Journal of Psychology and Theology, 15,* 57-67.

Larson, B. (1965). *Dare to live now!* Grand Rapids, MI: Zondervans Publishing House.

Leo, J., (1988, January 25). A chilling wave of racism: From L.A. to Boston, the skinheads are on the march. *Time,* 57.

Minerbrook, S., (1988, August 22). A face-off with racism: In a Manhattan train station, grappling with the tricky questions of prejudice and race relations. *U.S. News & World Report,* 57.

Moberg, D.O., (1984). Subjective measures of spiritual well-being. *Review of Religious Research, 25,* (4), 351-59.

Padilla, C.R. (1985). *Mission between the times: Essays on the Kingdom.* Grand Rapids, MI: Eerdmans.

Paloutzian, R.F. and Ellison, C.W., (1982). Loneliness, spiritual well-being and quality of life. In L.A. Peplau and D. Perlman (eds.), *Loneliness: a Sourcebook of Current theory, research and therapy.* New York: Wiley Interscience.

Pecnik, J.A. & Epperson, D.L. (1985). A factor analysis and further validation of the Shepherd Scale. *Journal of Psychology and Theology, 13,* 42-49.

Perkins, J. (1979). Piercing ghetto oppression. *United Evangelical Action, 38,* 18-22.

Schmidt, P.F., (1980). *Manual for use of the Character Assessment Scale* (2nd ed.). Shelbyville, KY: Institute for Character Development.

Schuman, H., Steeh, C., and Bobo, L., (1985). *Racial attitudes in America: Trends and interpretations.* Boston: Harvard University Press.

Shapiro, L., (1988, May 23). When is a joke not a joke? Shouts and swastikas are getting the last laugh. *Newsweek,* 78.

Sider, R. (1977). Corporate guilt and institutionalized racism. *United Evangelical Action, 36,* 11-12; 26-28.

Thompson, C. (1971). Social reform: An evangelical imperative. *Christianity Today, 15,* 8-12.

Trueblood, E. (1970). *The new man for our time.* New York: Harper and row.

Yancey, P. (1987, February). The crayon man. *Christianity Today,* 14-20.

Woodmansee, J.J. & Cook, S.W. (1967). Dimensions of verbal racial attitudes: Their identification and measurement. *Journal of Personality and Social Psychology, 7,* 240-250.

Acknowledgements

Portions of this work were presented in a talk entitled "An assessment of religiosity and prejudice among adults in various church settings", at the annual national meeting of the Christian Association for Psychological Studies, April 29, 1989 in Philadelphia, PA.

The efforts of the Spring Arbor College library staff, and in particular the bibliographic research contributed by Karen Parsons and Marilyn Starr, are very much appreciated. Elaine Courter assisted very capably in table and manuscript word processing. The assistance provided by the research efforts of Spring Arbor College graduates Amy Donkin and Laura Mackenzie were of great help in the preparation of this work.

Ethnic-Minority Faculty in Evangelical Christian Colleges: Models in Search of an Identity

Tony M. Wong and Kenneth Polite

Issues related to the negative impact of ethnic-minority student underrepresentation has been documented and discussed elsewhere in this volume. However, issues and implications related to the experience of the ethnic-minority faculty member have been relatively neglected in the general literature. Such concerns are particularly important in light of the fact that an often proposed factor in enhancing the multicultural environment of educational institutions is the recruitment of ethnic-minority faculty to serve, ostensibly, as successful role models.

The purpose of this chapter is to introduce some critical issues of concern that are relevant and unique to the experience of the ethnic-minority faculty member. Another purpose is to initiate dialogue and research in an area in which there has been relatively little systematic analysis conducted. For that reason, much of the present discussion will be rather tentative and should be most appropriately viewed as a proposal for further discussion and investigation. Emphasis will be placed on those factors that adversely impact the success of the faculty member's function as a role model to ethnic-minority students.

Throughout this discussion, the terms *ethnic-minority* and *ethnic-majority* will be used instead of *minority* and *white*. except when referring to the work of others, in order to describe the relevant subgroups on relatively equivalent dimensions and in order to avoid terms with possible perjorative connotations (cf. Lee & Rice, Chapter 3, on the term *ethnicity*.).

The Ethnic-Minority Faculty Member: Assimilation vs. Isolation

A commonly proposed strategy towards enhancing the multi-cultural environment of educational institutions is to recruit ethnic-minority faculty members in hopes that they would become influential role models for ethnic-minority students. Theoretically, this is an attractive strategy. The addition of ethnic-minority faculty would increase the ethnic and cultural diversity of the campus and would concomitantly provide scholars with whom ethnic-minority students can relate and identify. Thus, the intellectual and social climate becomes more conducive to successful learning among the ethnic-minority students, and recruitment and retention of this target group is enhanced. Unfortunately, the promise of this strategy has remained largely unfulfilled due to the erroneous assumption that ethnic-minority faculty are well-prepared and well-supported in their efforts to become successful and respected educators.

Issues and concerns unique to ethnic-minority faculty members need to be addressed before they can become successful models for ethnic-minority students. Waggaman (1983), in an examination of faculty recruiting and retention in American higher education, noted that black educators tended to leave their faculty positions for different reasons than their white colleagues. The cause of this difference appeared to be related to certain tensions and anxieties inherent in being black in a white institution. In our efforts to address the needs of the ethnic-minority students, it often forgotten that the ethnic-minority educator is also subject to ethnic insensitivity and other factors which hamper personal and professional growth and progress. Unless more attention is focused on such issues, institutions of higher education will either risk losing ethnic-minority faculty members or they will retain dissatisfied ones. In either case, the whole process of increasing multi-ethnic and multi-cultural diversity through providing successful role models for students is undermined.

One area of concern is that of representation. While ethnic-minority students have been historically underrepresented in Christian colleges, the lack of ethnic-minority faculty has been even more acute (e.g., Nieves, 1985). For example, at Biola University, although the ethnic-minority student enrollment for 1989-1990 is 25.8% of the total enrollment (highest proportion in the Christian College Coalition), the number of ethnic-minority faculty members account for only 8.1% of the total full-time faculty. Although the base rate of ethnic-minority students and teachers may be higher than that of most Coalition colleges due to Biola's proximity to a major metropolitan area (Los Angeles), the discrepancy in representation between students and faculty appear to reflect the basic trend. That is, in most cases there are numerically and proportionally more ethnic-minority students than there are ethnic-minority faculty members. There are two major implications related to this discrepancy that affect the ethnic-minority educator's role as a model for ethnic-minority students.

First, tremendous demands will be placed on the ethnic-minority educator's time and energy if she attempts to fulfill the expectation of being an effective role model. In addition to the formal duties required of most college faculty (i.e., teaching, research, advisement), the ethnic-minority professor might be expected to spend extra time addressing the needs of the underserved student population through such activities as additional advisement, serving on special faculty committees, and other contributions of personal resources that are not usually required or expected of ethnic-majority faculty. Because these activities are not usually part of the formal job description, and thus is not taken into account in terms of compensation or faculty load, the ethnic-minority educator is often caught in a dilemma of choosing between serving the specific needs of the ethnic-minority student community or serving her own professional development and advancement by concentrating on the formal requirements of her position.

The second major implication of the discrepancy between the respective proportions of ethnic-minority students and faculty members is the relative ethnic isolation that the faculty member experiences on campus. In most Christian colleges, the ethnic-minority professor is a relative rarity. Even in cases where there are more than one or two faculty members with an ethnic-minority background, when specific ethnic identification is taken into account, it is clear that the individual professors are at high risk for isolation. For example, at Biola University, although 8.1% of the full-time faculty are identified as ethnic minorities, only 1.6% are of an African-American background. Moreover, the latter figure represents two individuals, only one of who has his teaching responsibilities in the undergraduate program! Although the remaining 6.5% represents eight faculty members of Asian descent, this group can also be broken down into more specific identification. For example, only one out this group is an individual of Japanese-American descent. When age, academic rank, and other factors are taken into account, it becomes eminently clear that most ethnic-minority educators are hard-pressed to find a natural peer group to whom she can relate. The general situation among the Christian colleges as a whole appears even more acute when one takes into account that Biola University, the institution used as an example above, has a higher number and proportion of ethnic-minority faculty than the average Christian College Coalition school.

The ethnic-minority faculty member who has difficulty finding a true peer on campus really is faced with two choices, neither of which is truly desirable or healthy: to assimilate into the majority culture of the institution and to deny or sacrifice her own ethnic identity in the process, or to remain in relative social isolation. It is clear that the latter choice is ultimately unhealthy and self-destructive. However, many social scientists have noted that social withdrawal is one consequence of persons who perceive themselves as victims of racial prejudice (e.g., Allport, 1954). As to the former choice, while some assimilation is both healthy and necessary for multiethnic and multicultural integration, unless some reciprocality is involved in the process, the ultimate end is truly more capitulation than assimilation. This route, in the opinion of the present authors, is the one that most ethnic-minority faculty members in Christian colleges are prone to take. However, this option also eventually puts the ethnic-minority educator at high risk for social withdrawal and isolation, as his ethnicity is highly salient (especially in light of the small number of ethnic-minorities on most Christian college campuses), and this saliency creates an experience that is different than that of non-minority colleagues.

In the remainder of this chapter, the experiences that are unique to the ethnic-minority professor will be discussed in the context of social psychological research and theory on prejudice, discrimination, and interracial interaction. It will be argued that sufficient evidence exists suggesting that ethnic-minority educators are vulnerable to certain discriminatory factors that impede their professional development, thus undermining their expected function as compelling role models for ethnic-minority students.

The Ultimate Attribution Error in Interracial Interactions

The *fundamental attribution error* is a frequently used social psychological concept describing the tendency to prefer internal, dispositional explanations of behavior over external, situational explanations (e.g., Lippa, 1990; Myers, 1990). In other words, we are likely to ignore the power of social roles and other situational factors in explaining behaviors. In a classic experiment that is often cited as support for the fundamental attribution error, Ross, Amabile, and Steinmetz (1977) had pairs of college students play a quiz game in which one student was randomly designated as the "quiz master," and the other student was the "contestant." The quiz masters were asked to generate questions on topics with which they were familiar in order to be used as quiz items for the contestants. Despite the tremendous advantage that the quiz masters had in utilizing their own idiosyncratic wealth of knowledge within the game context, the contestants rated the quiz masters as possessing more general knowledge than themselves. Other experiments have found that this tendency to favor internal explanations of behavior appears to be stronger when describing another person's actions rather than one's own behaviors. This is commonly called the *actor-observer* hypothesis or effect (e.g., Jones & Nisbett, 1972).

Pettigrew (1979) extended the basic notion of the fundamental attribution error to explain intergroup phenomena. This notion of an *ultimate attribution error* describes the tendency to grant the benefit of the doubt to members of one's own group and not towards members of another group. Thus, while socially undesirable behaviors of in-group members are attributed to external, situational factors, those same behaviors of out-group members are explained by internal, dispositional factors. For example, as Myers (1990) noted, the shove that is perceived by Whites as mere "horsing around" when done by a fellow White man becomes a "violent gesture" when done by a Black. On the other hand, as part of Pettigrew's proposed theory of the ultimate attribution error, positive behaviors of out-group members are usually dismissed by in-group members by one or more of the following attributions: (a) as a "special case" or an "exceptional case" (e.g., "He is articulate and witty, not like other Chinese!"); (b) as due to luck or special advantage (e.g., "She must have been hired at that prestigious law firm because of some affirmative action policy."); (c) as due to high motivation and effort (e.g., "That Hispanic is a credit to his race, he's really worked hard to get into medical school."), and; (d) as due to situational demands (e.g., "Of course that Black man didn't get violent, not with that security guard looking on!").

The concept of an ultimate attribution error suitably describes a variety of disturbing experiences that are often reported by ethnic-minority faculty. One example is the experience that majority students do not allow or tolerate as much latitude with their ethnic-minority professors than with their ethnic-majority professors. Thus, these students are much less forgiving of perceived negative behaviors by ethnic-minority faculty (e.g., a poor lecture, lack of organization, etc.) than by ethnic-majority faculty. Moreover, according to attribution theory, these behaviors by the ethnic-minority faculty are more likely to be attributed to internal, dispositional factors (e.g., "He can't teach.") rather than to external, situational factors (e.g., "He must have had a busy week.").

If ethnic-minority professors are indeed victims of the ultimate attribution error, this might be reflected in student evaluations of teacher performance. More specifically, these evaluations may un-fairly discriminate against ethnic-minority professors relative to ethnic-majority faculty if students hold the former group to a more stringent standard. This has powerful implications, as student evaluations of teaching performance are commonly used criteria in higher education for promotion and tenure consideration. This is also especially relevant in evangelical Christian colleges, which are usually small institutions with heavy emphasis on teaching rather than on research. Unfortunately, systematic research on the effects of ethnicity of student and teacher on evaluations of teacher effectiveness is virtually non-existent. For example, in preparation of a preliminary study of the effects of perceived ethnicity on teacher evaluation, Wong & Grace (1990) found no articles cross-referenced under race or ethnicity and teacher evaluation when two major social science computer data bases were used (PSYCINFO and Sociological Abstracts).

Although there is a lack of published research examining possible discriminatory factors affecting student evaluations of teaching effectiveness, there is much informal data suggesting that many ethnic-minority faculty members feel that their teaching performance is judged unfairly and may be susceptible to a type of ultimate attribution error. An example of this was reported to one of the present authors by an ethnic-minority colleague from another evangelical Christian college. Suffering a severe personal tragedy (loss of a parent) during the course of an academic term, this professor was disappointed and hurt to find that her teaching performance for that particular period was harshly criticized with no apparent acknowledgement of her personal distress. This was especially surprising to her in light of the fact that the students were distinctly aware of the professor's loss. In other words, these students were attributing the ethnic-minority professor's erratic performance more to dispositional factors rather than to some rather salient situational factors.

While, as in the case of the individual mentioned above, many ethnic-minority faculty members are rather convinced that evaluations of teaching performance are unfairly biased against them, they are usually unsuccessful in garnering any sympathy. This is primarily because of two reasons. First, as mentioned previously, the ethnic-minority faculty member is severely underrepresented in the evangelical Christian colleges. So, she is unlikely to find a colleague of similar background with whom she can share these experiences. Secondly, ethnic-minority faculty members are not only vulnerable to the ultimate attribution error by their students, but also by their ethnic-majority colleagues! That is, the ethnic-minority educator's complaints may be perceived as attempts to explain away dispositionally based shortcomings with complaints about prejudice. The result is that her experience, which she encounters as particularly genuine, is not affirmed by the very group from whom she expects and desires support. Tragically, the ethnic-minority faculty member not only feels socially isolated and alienated from ethnic-majority colleagues, but is also at professional and economic risk because of the reliance on an assumed equitable evaluation process for the purposes of promotion and/or advancement.

Illusory Correlations: The Bases of Stereotypes

Stereotypes typically involve a correlation between a person's ethnicity and some trait or characteristic. For example, a ethnic-majority college student, upon seeing an unfamiliar African-American on campus, may wonder if he is on one of the athletic teams. Or, it is assumed that the quiet Asian-American coed will be "setting the curve" in the advanced calculus class. One way to understand stereotyping is through the concept of an illusory correlation: a false impression created by the co-occurence of two rather distinctive, or salient, events. Since ethnic-minorities are particularly salient in evangelical Christian colleges because of their relative scarcity, they are especially vulnerable to being stereotyped. This would be especially true with socially undesirable or negative behaviors, which tend to be the more salient or distinctive events.

Social science research has documented the tendency to form illusory correlations. For example, Hamilton & Gifford (1976) conducted an experiment in which subjects were shown a series of slides on which various people were described as having performed something either desirable or undesirable. The people were also described as belonging to one of two different groups. Although members of one group were presented less frequently than members of the other group, the proportion of desirable to undesirable behaviors (9:4) associated with each group was identical. Nevertheless, the subjects overestimated the frequency with which the smaller or "minority" group behaved undesirably.

Because ethnic-minority faculty members are one of the more salient groups on the evangelical Christian college campus, it would not be surprising to find that they would be particularly prone to being stereotyped, especially in relation to the more distinctive negative behaviors or characteristics. Asian professors would be avoided or ridiculed for their predicted inability to articulate eloquently. African-American teachers would be suspect in their ability to grapple with abstract theoretical issues. Similarly, the Asian-American teacher might be quickly asked to give a special scholarly lecture, but not to give an inspirational message during the student chapel hour. The African-American professor, in the meantime, would be happily invited to deliver that fiery sermon, but not to lecture on recent advances in scientific technology. Wong & Grace (1990), in their study of perceived ethnicity and teacher evaluations, found some qualitative evidence of stereotyping of ethnic-minority teachers. In a follow-up questionnaire in which they were asked to choose among having an Asian-American professor, a Black-American professor, a Caucasian-American professor, or letting a computer decide, fewer student subjects chose the Asian-American alternative than any other available category. A number of subjects wrote that they were hesitant to have the Asian-American professor because they were concerned with language problems. This is interesting in light of the fact that the qualifier American was used, and no other information was made available to the subjects other than ethnic identity. While this data should be interpreted with caution because of the low base rates involved and because many subjects did not explain their choices, its consistency with a commonly observed stereotype is striking.

Note that stereotyping and the concept of an ultimate attribution error are not orthogonal. Stereotyping not only often involves the illusory correlation of one salient event (e.g., Asian) with another (e.g., poor English), but also the attribution of that event to something dispositional (e.g., "Asians are not good speakers/teachers.") rather than situational (e.g., "She's having difficulty because English is not her first language.").

A subtle form of stereotyping is positive stereotyping, where positive or desirable characteristics are attributed to a particular ethnic group. An example of this is the myth of Asian-Americans as the model minority group. This refers to the impression that Asian-Americans have achieved phenomenal educational and economic success in our society. However, as Suzuki (1989) notes, "one damaging repercussion from the media's model minority characterization of Asian Americans is the perception by many educators that Asians are 'outwhiting whites' and, therefore, have no serious problems or needs." This is a concern that is especially relevant to the present discussion, as some college administrations may overlook Asian-American faculty members as a group needing equitable treatment. Related to this, Chan (1989) argues that while in some cases Asian-American faculty in American universities may have reputational power (recognition for scholarly work), they seldom have collegial (e.g., heads of major committees) and/or administrative power (formal positions of authority within the university structure).

The tragic consequence of stereotyping, whether positive or negative, is that the unique qualities and needs of the individual are not affirmed or are minimized. Individual characteristics are ignored for the convenient sake of swift categorization based on limited experience. As in the case of the ultimate attribution error, ethnic-minority faculty may be stereotyped by ethnic-majority students as well as by their ethnic-majority colleagues. Stifled and restricted by narrow-band illusory correlations, she struggles with issues of personal and professional fulfillment. Again, these issues not only impact ethnic-minority faculty at a psychosocial level, but also at more concrete levels including academic status.

Self-Fulfilling Prophecies: A Vicious Cycle

One of the major consequences of the relative dearth of ethnic-minority faculty in evangelical Christian colleges is the lack of an opportunity to develop true multicultural and multiethnic understanding. Because of this, it is often difficult for ethnic-majority faculty and their ethnic-minority colleagues to know how to comfortably interact with one another. The salience of ethnicity, though often denied, is almost never ignored. Often, the experience of the ethnic-minority professor is that she is somehow treated differently by her ethnic-majority students and colleagues relative to other ethnic-minority professors. The stage is set then, for stilted faculty-faculty and faculty-student interactions.

Word, Zanna, & Cooper (1974) conducted a pair of experiments to examine the effects of nonverbal behaviors on interracial interaction. In the first experiment, naive White male college subjects were asked to interview trained White and Black job applicants. Interviewer behavior was assessed and it was determined that the Black applicants received less immediacy, as measured by physical distance between interviewer and interviewee, than the White job candidates. In addition, the White interviewers spent 25% less time and made more speech errors with Black as compared to White job candidates. In the second experiment, confederate interviewers were trained to treat job applicant subjects either as the White applicants were treated in the first experiment (Immediate condition), or as the Black applicants were treated (Nonimmediate condition). Subsequent ratings by independent judges revealed that subjects in the Nonimmediate condition were judged to be significantly less adequate for the job than subjects in the Immediate condition. Also, the Nonimmediate subjects were also judged to be less calm and composed than the Immediate subjects. Moreover, the Nonimmediate subjects appeared to reciprocate with less immediate behaviors, as they sat further away from the interviewers than their Immediate counterparts. Finally, the Nonimmediate subjects rated their interviewer as less friendly and less adequate than did the Immediate applicants.

The results of the Word et al. (1974) experiments were significant from a number of aspects. First, the results from the first experiment suggest that race or ethnicity is a salient variable that could elicit unfavorable nonverbal communications from ethnic-majority persons. Thus, empirical support exists for the notion that ethnicity can be a stigmatizing trait in our society. Secondly, the second experiment suggests that negative nonverbal behaviors of the type that occurred in the first experiment can in turn influence the performance and attitudes of the victims of those behaviors. Taken together, the results from both experiments give evidence of the vicious cycle nature of self-fulfilling prophecies: Ethnicity, as a salient factor, elicits negative expectations and concomitant unfavorable nonverbal behaviors, which in turn provokes negative behaviors that reinforce the original biases. Note also that the victims of this self-fulfilling prophecy cycle tend to have lower regard for the perpetrators.

The implications of the Word et al. study and others like it for interracial interactions in evangelical Christian colleges are both obvious and powerful. The probability that the salience of ethnic-minority educators on these campuses would provoke uncomfortable nonverbal communications from the ethnic-majority community is most likely very high. Jenkins (1987) listed a variety of ways by which ethnic-majority faculty may communicate uneasiness or differential expectations to ethnic-minority students. An unexamined, although equally plausible, phenomenon is that ethnic-majority students often nonverbally communicate uneasiness to ethnic-minority faculty. These behaviors might then provoke poorer teaching performance from the ethnic-minority faculty member, which in turns becomes attributed dispositionally on teaching evaluations. The same type of process might also occur in intercollegial interactions which similarly leads to undesirable impressions that are attributed dispositionally and are reflected on peer evaluations. Thus, significant hindrances are placed on the ethnic-minority educator's attempts to advance professionally.

The self-fulfilling prophecy cycle can also hamper the ethnic-minority educator's social relationships with her professional colleagues. While she can seek social supports outside the work environment, this can be an especially frustrating position to be in, as informal social networking is one important source of learning and information that aids in professional growth and advancement. The faculty member who is not well-connected nor highly visible in the academic community has a lower probability of being selected for faculty committees and/or other positions that might enhance her academic status or lead to administrative positions.

Being on the wrong end of a self-fulfilling prophecy cycle is an experience that is well known to many ethnic-minority faculty members. Negative nonverbal communications are by their very nature difficult to describe and objectify, criteria that ethnic-majority colleagues often desire in attempting to understand the ethnic-minority educator's protestations. This fact, along with the typical absence of peers with similar background, leaves the ethnic-minority professor with virtually nobody with whom she can share her experiences. Note also that this is another instance in which the ethnic-minority faculty member is at risk for professional and social isolation, a frustrating condition which can ultimately lead to long-term dissatisfaction and ineffectiveness.

Conclusions and Recommendations

Both anecdotal and empirical evidence has been presented to support the view that ethnic-minority faculty members in evangelical Christian colleges, because of their relatively low representation and resulting salience, are particularly vulnerable to rather subtle but powerful prejudicial factors that tend to undermine their long-term satisfaction and effectiveness as educators. Of particularly relevant concern here is that these discriminatory factors also tend to undermine the ethnic-minority professor's expected role as an influential role-model for ethnic-minority students.

Three concepts that have been routinely used in social psychology to explain prejudice were discussed as being relevant to understanding the plight of the ethnic-minority educator. These concepts (i.e., the ultimate attribution error, illusory correlations, and self-fulfilling prophecies), although discussed as discrete factors, in reality operate interactively to inhibit her social and professional progress. Other heuristic mechanisms than those mentioned above can be employed to explain prejudicial behavior, but the ultimate phenomenological effect upon its victims are the same: they are trivialized by the perpetrators and are driven further towards isolation.

It should be noted that most of the cognitive errors foundational to prejudice and discrimination are quite subtle in operation and are usually committed without much awareness. However, it is precisely for this reason that such problems persist and create its own vicious cycle. That is, because ethnic-majority persons are often unaware of any intentional effort to be prejudicial, they have difficulty understanding the concerns of ethnic-minority persons and thus taking some responsibility for their behaviors. Feeling misunderstood and having the reality of her phenomenological experience denied by others, the ethnic-minority person becomes frustrated and begins to withdraw from those who she feels are not supportive of her struggles. Thus, interpersonal as well as intrapersonal tension develops and either grows or remains unresolved until active attempts are made to deal with the problem appropriately.

Because the actual prevalence of racial or ethnic discrimination in evangelical Christian colleges at the faculty level has not been systematically studied, one may question whether it is indeed a prominent problem in that setting. This issue can be addressed in several ways. Even if the subjective impressions of ethnic-minority faculty members of these Christian colleges can be legitimately ignored (which they cannot be), the objective demographics cannot be denied. That ethnic-minority faculty members are severely underrepresented at most of these institutions is rather obvious and is indicative of discrimination or neglect at some level. Also, unless active and persistent attempts are made to increase multiethnic and multicultural understanding, there is no reason to expect that the degree of interracial tension and discrimination should be any less in evangelical Christian college settings relative to society as a whole. Crosby, Bromley, & Saxe (1980), in a review of unobtrusive studies of antiblack racism among white Americans, found that antiblack prejudice was still strong. However, this finding was obvious only in those research studies that used actual behavioral measures rather than the less sensitive attitudinal measures. In other words, what appears to be true in actual experience was supported by that review: people may not feel or think that they are prejudiced, but their behaviors reveal that discrimination is prevalent.

Based on the previous discussion, it is clear that the evangelical Christian colleges must address the needs and concerns of its ethnic-minority faculty members if they are to be successful in creating true multiethnic communities. As Waggaman (1983) notes in addressing the issue of retention of black faculty in higher education, "It seems clear that to recruit black faculty to a white institution creates a responsibility to help them adapt to the white institution. The department chair must work to root out racist institutional practices, in addition to supplying guidance and assistance to new minority faculty." Without such efforts, ethnic-minority faculty members are likely to become disillusioned and either be relatively isolated members of the college community, or decide to leave. In either case, they become poor role-models for the ethnic-minority students.

The following is a list of suggestions for improving the professional and social climate for ethnic-minority faculty members at evangelical Christian colleges:

1. **Develop a strategic plan for recruiting ethnic-minority faculty** - if ethnic-minority faculty are to be role models for ethnic-minority students, then there should be attempts to achieve similar proportions between the two groups. In addition, recruiting of faculty should be active and aggressive (seeking one that fits the job description) rather than passive (waiting for the right person to apply).

2. **Encourage rather than discourage fellowship and/or meetings of ethnic-minority educators** - as mentioned before, because they are usually so few in number at a given institution, the ethnic-minority faculty member is prone to feel isolated and discouraged. It is eminently helpful to be able share experiences with those of similar background.

3. **Consider the development of mentoring programs for junior-level ethnic-minority faculty members** - this is especially critical in light of the fact that much of what contributes to professional development in the academic setting (e.g., developing a research program, enhancing teaching skills, etc.) is learned informally through collegial interaction. Unfortunately, because of factors mentioned previously, the young ethnic-minority professor may have less access to this informal network. Therefore, having a more senior-level mentor to assist her professional development might be helpful.

4. **Offer ethnic-sensitivity training to ethnic-majority faculty** - in order to break the vicious cycle of self-fulfilling prophecies, ethnic-majority faculty need to be aware and understand at some level the experiences of the ethnic-minority colleague. Having a well-trained and experienced leader to facilitate this process could go a long way towards dealing with interracial tension. In some cases, just having ethnic-majority persons

acknowledge that there is a problem would help alleviate the concerns of an ethnic-minority colleague in a meaningful way.

5. **If absent, introduce courses on cross-cultural or ethnic-minority issues into the curriculum** - this is especially important because this could help the ethnic-majority student to be more sensitive in how she relates to ethnic-minority students as well as faculty. This would also help students of all ethnic backgrounds, minority and majority, to appreciate their own and other's unique backgrounds.

6. **Evaluate promotion and tenure procedures to ensure equitable treatment across groups** - this would include, but would not be limited to, procedures like the teacher evaluation process, which may be inherently biased against ethnic-minority teachers. The issue of equitable faculty load in light of informal job requirements would be included here.

7. **Support scholarly activity on ethnic-minority issues** - demographic and research data on many issues relevant to ethnic-minorities in evangelical Christian colleges, including those mentioned in this chapter, are lacking and are needed in order to facilitate future program development.

8. **Seek consultation from ethnic-minority faculty on institutional policy and other major issues** - it is important that ethnic-minority faculty feel that they are equal partners in building the character of the institution. They can also provide insight into ethnic-minority perspectives on major policy and policy changes.

9. **Provide opportunities for ethnic-minority faculty to develop collegial and administrative power** - it is important that participation in and leadership of important faculty committees and other bodies are not limited to ethnic-majority faculty.

While this list of suggestions is clearly not exhaustive, it does provide examples of interventions which will address some of the concerns of ethnic-minority faculty. Hopefully, by utilizing some of these suggestions or other similar ones, evangelical Christian colleges can continue to move toward celebrating and and affirming diversity within the unity. Without decisive, proactive steps toward resolving the aforementioned issues, ethnic-minority faculty members will indeed remain models in search of an identity.

Authors' Note:

The authors have decided to use "she" and "her" as the generic pronouns in this chapter wherever appropriate. Appreciation is expressed to Dr. Christopher Grace for his helpful comments on the social psychological issues discussed. Thanks also to Wayne Chute, registrar at Biola University, for providing some of the demographic data.

References

Allport, G. (1954). *The nature of prejudice.* Cambridge, Mass.: Addison-Wesley.

Chan, S. (1989, November). Beyond affirmative action. *Change*, 48-51.

Crosby, F., Bromley, S., & Saxe, L. (1980). Recent unobtrusive studies of black and white discrimination and prejudice: A literature review. *Psychological Bulletin, 87*, 546-563.

Hamilton, D. L., & Gifford, R. K. (1976). Illusory correlation in interpersonal perception: A cognitive basis of stereotypic judgements. *Journal of Experimental Social Psychology, 12*, 392-407.

Jenkins, C.A. (1987). Educating for equity: Challenges, choices, and changes. *Faculty Dialogue, 9*, 53-68.

Jones, E. E., & Nisbett, R. E. (1972). The actor and observer: Divergent perception of the causes of behavior. In E. Jones, D. Kanouse, H. Kelley, R. Nisbett, S. Valins, & B. Weiner (Eds.), *Attribution: Perceiving the causes of behavior.* Morristown, NJ: General Learning Press.

Lippa, R. A. (1990). *Introduction to social psychology.* Belmont, Calif.: Wadsworth.

Myers, D. G. (1990). *Social psychology* (3rd ed.). New York: McGraw-Hill.

Nieves, A. L. (1985, November). Urban minorities and Christian higher education. *Urban Mission*, 20-28.

Pettigrew, T. F. (1979). The ultimate attribution error: Extending Allport's cognitive analysis of prejudice. *Personality and Social Psychology Bulletin, 5*, 461-476.

Ross, L. D., Amabile, T. M., & Steinmetz, J. L. (1977). Social roles, social control, and biases in social-perception processes. *Journal of Personality and Social Psychology, 35,* 485-494.

Suzuki, B. H. (1989, November). Asian Americans as the "model minority." *Change,* 13-19.

Waggaman, J. S. (1983). *Faculty recruitment, retention, and fair employment: Obligations and opportunities* (Higher Education Research Report No. 2). Washington DC: Association for the Study of Higher Education.

Wong, T. M., & Grace, C. (1990, August). Effects of perceived ethnicity on speaker/teacher ratings. Paper presented at the convention of the American Psychological Association, Boston.

Word, C. O., Zanna, M. P., & Cooper, J. (1974). The nonverbal mediation of self-fulfilling prophecies in interracial interaction. *Journal of Experimental Social Psychology, 10,* 109-120.

EDUCATING FOR EQUITY: ISSUES AND STRATEGIES FOR EFFECTIVE MULTICULTURAL INSTRUCTION

Carol A. Jenkins and Deborah Bainer

Ethnic and minority diversity on university campuses continues to increase. As Christian educators, we recognize that equitable treatment for all students is our responsibility, but often we do not know which attitudes and behaviors may be misunderstood by ethnic and/or minority students. This discussion seeks to (1) identify specific issues which may help us develop more effective strategies for bringing about and maintaining equity in the classroom; and (2) help us understand that educating for equity in the midst of diversity is not one of passive avoidance, but rather of active risk-taking, peacemaking and reconciliation.

Educating for Equity and Justice

Should Christian education emphasize knowledge or action? Christian education in modern Western societies has never been content merely with "knowledge for knowledge's sake". Its aims have always included changes in behavior and actions toward a better world. However, working out the tension, or balance, between knowledge and right action has never been easy.

In every historical context Christian educators have had to work at two dimensions of the knowledge/action problem. On the one hand, how did their strategies of education for equity and justice affect the knowledge-action issue? On the other hand, how did the ethical issues that demanded Christian action as they emerged in that situation influence the "curriculum" of their education? For example, how did ethical issues and perceptions of equity, cultural diversity, historical accuracy, differential expectations, differential interaction, and limited English proficiency influence the conceptualization and development of curriculum?

The challenge to Christian educators, then, consists of continually identifying emergent issues of diversity and developing the best possible educational processes to enable the Christian community to contribute to "setting things right". Or to restate the question, how can Christian education more effectively help people discern and participate in responding to the issues of diversity on our campus?

There are five basic assumptions which we make concerning the challenge of educating for equity in the midst of diversity: (1) our society today is dangerously unjust and unpeaceful; (2) our society does not have to be that way; (3) philosophically and pragmatically neither God nor most human beings want our society to be that way; (4) our Christian tradition gives us a vision of how our society could and should be as well as guidance about how to move toward that vision; and (5) as Christian educators we can have a modest but significant part in bringing about meaningful equity in the classroom. That is our challenge. Our question is how!

A biblical approach requires theological and ethical coherence if our students, as well as colleagues, are to care for each other. Educating for equity and justice should encompass four components of ethical decision-making: (1) exploring the biblical-theological vision expressed in Scripture (teaching a liberating hermeneutic); (2) analyzing realities of the human-social situation that enhance or block the vision of equity and justice (awareness and analysis of the realities that impinge on us and others); (3) identifying specific choices and action opportunities that approximate the vision (developing habits of advocacy to accompany acts of service, and to approach issues in ways that develop prophetic consciousness); and (4) clarifying middle range norms (social values and goals) at stake in, and served by, specific actions (engaging in the task of contextual social ethics— exploring the social philosophy and values served by specific issues and evaluating in light of biblical thought) (Seifert, 1983).

Educating for equity needs to encompass all four components and explore each in depth through a continuous cycle of awareness, analysis, action and reflection. Our objective as equity educators should be to develop the university's capability in these four components.

Individual Perceptions of Equity

As a mechanism of understanding forces and patterns influencing human behavior, C. Wright Mills (1961) introduced a model of biography which attempted to link individual experience to social phenomena in order to enrich an understanding of both personal problems and social structure. With an understanding of Mills' "sociological imagination" and recalling the "educating for equity and justice" components, let us give an example of a way we have engaged in education for equity with groups of adult educators. First, we ask them to share with one another in groups of seven or eight two tasks: (1) Describe an experience in your life when you were most indignant because you saw something that you thought was wrong; (2) Describe an experience in your life when you were most pleased because you saw something that you thought was right. The participants take an hour for that sharing and then write summaries of their examples on newsprint and post them around the room—the angry ones together and the excited ones together. During a break they walk around and read each other's summaries, trying to see where any patterns emerge when they look at all of them together.

The second step comes when we ask each of them to think about why they classified some as wrong, and others as right. What criteria did they use for their judgment? Then we ask the question "Where did you get those criteria?" Or, perhaps better, "Where do you get them?" After pondering that a little while, we discuss their answers and put them up on newsprint. Often one of the sad moments for us as

Christian educators comes when we see not what they put up, but what they leave out! The biblical and theological references named are usually restricted to the simple and familiar ones. Not much grounding on which to build an ethic for today's world! Nor is there much evidence of either social analysis or the use of ethical principles in their judgments and decisions.

In addition, C. Wright Mills' (1961) "sociological imagination" is useful in opening up two lines for further development: the hermeneutical circle between the present situation and the tradition, especially the Bible, and the dialectic between the personal and the political in students' lives. It also leads into social analysis and makes possible critical consciousness. For example, asking students to write a position paper analyzing a perceived social injustice, integrating appropriate biblical/theological reflection and building a strategy for action should demonstrate the extent of understanding of the linkages of individual experience to social phenomena and personal problems to structural explanations.

This pedagogical action has some real advantages. It starts where people are. It uses what "operational" theology they already know. It can go beyond the cognitive when the most disturbing or exciting events with their emotional memories are recalled. It builds a community of sharing when it gets below the ordinary, urbane, polite discourse and cumulatively frees persons to experience mutual learning. It exposes some of the gross social sins that sometimes form the basis for righteous indignation and provides the context for personal pain and joy.

All of these positive values a good instructor can enjoy and build upon by using sensitivity along with specialized theological and ethical knowledge to enrich, challenge and enhance the learning process. But it is only a very modest first step, for it lacks the power to transform persons or structures. It does not go far enough, however, to fulfill either of the two goals necessary for Christian education for equity: (1) helping students see what God is doing and wanting done among people in this world, and (2) helping students work with God to get it done. The process may help us and others clarify, but it does not yet commit us as instruments to be used by God to fulfill the prayer Christians pray: "Your kingdom come. Your will be done on earth as it is in heaven," or the much more concrete, "Give us this day our daily bread," when the "us" is the whole human community, not just those seated at my table!

In order to help us see more effectively, and to develop a more critical consciousness and useful social analysis, we need to learn from and with those who are not what some people call "your kind of people". We must get beyond the ordinary social groupings if we are to discern cognitively what God sees as injustice and what God wants done for justice and peace.

For example, regardless of their backgrounds, virtually all students will have had exposure to racial prejudice and stereotypes in the form of jokes or humor. As an exercise, have students make a written record of jokes with which they are familiar that involve racial, ethnic, or gender elements. Students can read the jokes individually in class, or you can collect them and read them aloud to the class. Then conduct a miniature content analysis, analyzing the jokes on the basis of consistent themes and recurring stereotypes and characterizations. Be sure to include a wide range of racial and ethnic groups and be sure to collect jokes from minority students about Anglo ethnic groups and from women about men. Encourage members of the class to vocalize how these jokes tend to contribute to an ideology of racism, sexism, and even ethnocentrism. Are there any jokes that focus on positive aspects of minorities? What negative ingredients are implied by the jokes? How do these ingredients relate to processes of stereotyping? (Davidson, 1987).

If we are to use our imaginations to bring together and enliven our theory and practice, we need to share a radical heterogeneity so as to achieve some relative liberation from the ideological cocoon within which we are constantly nurtured. We need some affirmative action guidelines in our Christian education.

Ideological Cocoons

Think of how great a portion of our time and energy is spent with people very much like ourselves. Our university makes it difficult for it to be otherwise. Our work structures and processes continue to push us further toward private living often reinforcing a near cocoon existence. Yes, continuity of a structured community is necessary for our development and maintenance as individual selves but that combination of continuity and homogeneity has its underside—namely it traps us in cocoons where it is difficult to sense our common humanity working together to preserve it.

That "cocoon" as we call it is a way of understanding ideology and its enormous educating power over us all, for we are all educators in a system which is part of a larger system. If we include support staff as well as teachers, administrators and students, three of every ten persons in the U.S. population participate directly in this system. Overall, some $230 billion will be spent on education this year. We are a part of it! We belong to it! We live in it, and we live off of it! Its day-to-day influence on our lives is incalculable. Its momentum is massive.

The point for us here and now is that this educational system tends to reproduce the injustices in this society. Pierre Bourdieu and Claude Passeron (1977) have analyzed that reproductive function in France. But the same reproduction occurs here, and in all capitalistic countries. In fact, Basil Bernstein (1970) suggests that there are three stabilities evident in every school system in every culture we know or have known: (1) the system separates mental from manual labor, and gives privilege to the mental; (2) the system exercises symbolic control in the society; and (3) while access to the system may be more or less widespread and open, acquisition of power through it is always limited and controlled.

As educators we profit from and perpetuate those stabilities. If racism is one of the structured features of our society—and it is—then the educational system helps reproduce it. If sexism is a factor in our society—and it is—then schools help reproduce it. If cultural domination by the powerful is a characteristic of our society—and it is—then the educational system helps reproduce it. If class advantage of the rich over the poor is structured into our society—and it is—then schools help reproduce it. If a preferred language is structured into our society—and it is—then schools help reproduce it. We need to understand more adequately how our own structures, in particular Christian structures, tend to reproduce injustice.

The Relationship of Christian Higher Education to a Diversified Campus Community

Through intense critical inquiry, historic empirical studies of diversity (Stark, et al., 1971; Tyler, 1965; Berger, 1961) have contributed in an important way to the changing role of Christianity in American minority relations and conflict resolution, for they have at least cut the intellectual ground out from under "theological" and "biblical" rationalizations for separatism and discrimination. Today, no person in the Christian community with any intelligence can take seriously old arguments about the inferiority of minorities.

In spite of this, the changes in the Christian college or university have been largely ideological and action does not yet, for the most part, kept pace with the theological emphases on the universalism of God's love, individual's natural rights as revealed in the natural law, and brotherhood.

It has been only of recent that increasing student diversity in the classroom has heightened an awareness of our relative inability to be effective communicators. Extensive studies of many cultures (Condon and Yousef, 1988; Ainsworth, 1986; Banks, 1983; Astin, 1982; Good, 1981; Kaplan, 1970) have also demonstrated that while all peoples have broadly similar capacities and face the same problems of living, they are subject in each situation to differing natural conditions and have hence developed diverse ways of meeting problems. No longer can the Christian professor meaningfully interact with peoples of diversity without a willingness to learn as well as teach. There must be ample time for students and professors to test each other out, to estimate reactions, and to familiarize themselves with the communication styles of other people(s) (Phillips and Ericksen, 1970).

Perhaps the greatest problem in the Christian college or university then is that they are conservative institutions in possession of a revolutionary gospel; selective groups founded upon inclusive theology. A re-examination of the infrastructure of Christian institutions would give much ground for hoping that universities which are Christian will move as a reforming force in the current crisis of increasing student diversity on American campuses.

As non-minorities learn more about minority cultures—how they are integrated, their historical and evolutional development, process of cultural change, and the nurturing of a learning environment which is distinctly biblical—Christian colleges and universities can become increasingly useful in the understanding and direction of intergroup relations within the academic community.

Application: Minority Students and Faculty Members

It will be argued that if we are willing to assume that a college education is not restricted to mere acquisition of facts or skills, but rather encompasses personal development, examination of values, learning to think creatively and analytically, and improving communication skills, then attention is warranted to instructional strategies that expand student/student and student/professor involvement in academically appropriate ways.

For example, learning, achievement and retention appear to be socially-rooted phenomena (Astin, 1982; Tinto, 1982). Several retention studies (Noel 1978; Astin, 1982; University of Pittsburgh Retention Report 1980; McCroskey and Sheahan, 1978) have concluded that students tend to persevere on those campuses where they feel they are a part of the community. Noel (1978) recommends that universities establish and maintain a supportive campus climate, which he terms a "staying" environment. The University of Pittsburgh Retention Report (1980) exhorts faculty "to assume responsibilities beyond those of providing solid classroom instruction: they must help students build self-confidence; they must seek ways to interact with students; they must be willing to serve, formally or informally in an advising capacity." Furthermore, informal interviews of alumni at a small midwestern Christian College (Jenkins, 1981) showed that the single most important thing that students felt they had gotten out of college was not something they had learned in a course or their preparation for employment but the relationship that they had formed with a faculty member.

Apparently, in a climate of psychological safety students will feel more comfortable about "showing their ignorance" or displaying their knowledge, more willing to share experiences and expertise, and to disagree with the point of view of the professor (Kelley and Thibaut, 1954).

In discussing the concept of psychological safety, Benjamin (1978) states that the class climate affects the student's sense of belonging and whether or not they look forward to class, participate, drop the class, or leave college altogether. A safe and friendly climate increases participation levels and class attendance.

If these statements are true for majority students, then it is especially true for minority students, many of whom are attempting to function in an alien (and from their perspective) often hostile environment. Many times the responsibility for establishing strong faculty/student relationships with minority students falls to minority faculty and administrators. Although most minority academicians are more than cognizant of their role-model function for both minority and majority students, it is impossible for them to bear this responsibility alone, for one very obvious reason: they represent only a negligible percentage of the total faculty at most predominalty Anglo and male-dominated institutions. Given certain choices of majors and their concommitant course requirements, some minority students may never be taught by a minority faculty member during their tenure at most Christian colleges and universities. Consequently, the primary responsibility for teaching minority students continues to reside with predominantly male-Anglo tenured faculty members.

Since the arrival of significant numbers of diverse minority students to predominantly Anglo Christian institutions of higher learning, countless educators and private persons have been concerned about the academic performance of these students. Research conducted during the past fifteen years has been rather consistent in identifying a variety of factors that influence the academic success of minority students. Those factors which are most often cited fall into distinct categories: prior educational background and achievement, environmental and familial support, level of student motivation and commitment, high teacher expectations of student achievement, as well as a pleasant institutional environment (Berube, 1984; Jenkins, 1969).

It is clear that the quality of early education (i.e., the exposure to intellectual content and the development of academic skills) is critically important to the success of minority students at the University (Weiss, 1985). Nevertheless, a significant number of minority students lack appropriate skills in the areas of numerical and verbal literacy, analytical reading, and problem-solving. Furthermore, they have often not been exposed to meaningful coursework in the laboratory sciences, foreign languages, English writing, and mathematics. This lack of exposure, coupled with inadequate skills, acts as an inhibiting factor in college-level course selection, decisions related to choice of majors, and ultimately flexibility of career options.

It is well known that educational attainment is strongly correlated with socioeconomic status. "Not only does one's education affect occupational and income life chances, but the education of parents has a bearing on the education and socioeconomic position of the offspring" (Lieberson, 1980). Since many minority students are often the first persons in their families to attend college, they do not have the firmly established environmental and familial support structure that is common to many of their Anglo counterparts (Berube, 1984). Even the most well meaning friends and family members are often not in the position to provide the helpful insights and much needed encouragement that is based on personal collegiate experience. Consequently, minority students are frequently forced to "go it alone."

Perhaps the most prevalent assumption, in a society which values the 'rugged individual' and the 'Horatio Alger myth,' is that the ability of individual minority students to succeed is directly related to their level of motivation and commitment to the educational enterprise. Yet, when one closely and realistically examines the complex of issues (e.g., inferior prior education, the lack of environmental and familial support, and the built-in institutional hindrances) that mitigate against the role of the individual, it is obvious that the responsibility for success or failure does not reside primarily with the individual. In fact, research with pre-college students suggests that 75-80 percent of academic achievement can be directly attributed to context variables: culture and home environment, familial support, primary language, values and beliefs. Of the approximately 20 percent of academic achievement directly related to schooling, however, the strongest single variable is the teacher (Brookover, 1979). Given the external barriers that have been described above, there are probably few minority students who would be able to succeed if left completely to their own resources. If not the individual student, then who plays the crucial role in insuring that minority students are academically successful?

Technically, because of contractual obligations, expertise, and power the professor has major responsibility for the outcome of a particular course. Yet college students, as adults, share a significant responsibility for creating a successful learning experience (Billson, 1986).

Two assumptions must be continually challenged: (1) equal educational opportunity produces equal educational attainment and increased economic opportunity for all classes; and (2) the deterministic notion implicit in the equal access-equal results formula that the meanings of mainstream culture are necessarily internalized by students. Students no longer passively accept those meanings (e.g., meritoratic achievement) even when they recognize that doing so would be in their best interest (Weiss, 1985) because their practices are attempts to deal with a variety of conflicting attitudes and dispositions that pervade their marginal situation.

Members of minority groups have less chance of finishing high school or attending college than whites do. In 1985, 12.2 percent of whites aged 25 to 34 had not completed high school; the comparable figures for Blacks and Hispanics were 20.3 percent and 41.5 percent, respectively. The greatest difference is in attainment of a college diploma plus graduate training. In 1985, among Americans aged 25 to 29, only 11.5 percent of blacks and 11 percent of Hispanics had had four years of college or more, compared to 22.2 percent of all people in this age group (Statistical Abstracts, 1987).

If minority students are to succeed academically, it is imperative that the interaction between students and faculty members be positive, encouraging, and, in general, conducive to academic growth. This is a difficult task in a society that has often so isolated and alienated racial groups that faculty members are frequently unaware of behaviors and attitudes that have a strikingly negative impact on their minority students (despite their good intentions).

A university with interest in and commitment to the academic success of diverse students must assist its majority faculty members in developing pedagogy appropriate to the affective and cognitive needs of all students, as well as an awareness of the ways in which their relationships with minority students could be strengthened. Moreover, there must be a willingness to institutionalize curricular modifications, academic support services, and, in general, a campus ambience that is conducive to furthering academic excellence. In short, it is the responsibility, both moral and intellectual, of Christian colleges and universities to (1) initiate faculty development in pedagogical skills that will provide equal access to learning in the classroom; (2) weave minority students into the essential fabric of the institution; and (3) meaningfully integrate minority scholarship into the curriculum. A Christian university or college which wishes to be viewed as egalitarian has a responsibility to provide equal access to high quality education for all of its constituents.

Common Instructional Problems in Multicultural Classrooms

Research suggests that a major factor contributing to the lack of achievement among minority students is ineffective teaching. Brown (1986) argues that this does not mean that "poor" teaching is being practiced, but rather that classroom teaching is "ineffective" in impacting particular groups in multicultural classrooms. Sadly, many faculty members are not aware of the behaviors which they exhibit which are offensive to or ineffective with minority students. Following is a listing of faculty behaviors reported by minority students (Hall, 1982 adapted) which tend to communicate uneasiness and differential expectations.

Faculty Behaviors Reported By Minority Students Which May Communicate Uneasiness and Differential Expectations
1. Avoiding eye contact with minority students while making eye contact with majority students.
2. Ignoring minority students while recognizing majority students. This behavior includes ignoring comments by minorities or not showing any recognition of their contribution.
3. Calling directly on majority students but not minority students.
4. Coaching majority students more than minority students in working toward a fuller answer by probing for additional elaboration or explanation.
5. Interrupting minority students more when they do respond.

6. Waiting longer for and responding more extensively to the comments of majority students. Also using a tone that communicates more interest with majority students and a patronizing or impatient tone with minorities.
7. Offering little guidance and criticism of the work minority students produce.
8. Attributing the success of minority students to luck or factors other than ability.
9. Maintaining physical distance by assuming a posture of attentiveness when majority students speak and habitually choosing a location nearer majority students.
10. Making seemingly helpful comments which imply that minorities are not as competent as majority students.
11. Ignoring the cultural contributions of minorities and using examples in such a way as to reinforce a stereotyped and negative view of minorities.
12. Reacting to comments or questions articulated in a minority language style as if it is inherently of less value.

Effects of These Behaviors

Minority students tend to verify that these faculty behaviors have adverse effects on their affective and cognitive development. Among other effects, Hall (1982) observed that minority students tend to report the following concerning effects of faculty behaviors:

1. Discourages classroom participation.
2. Discourages students from seeking help outside of class.
3. Leads students to drop or avoid certain classes, to switch majors or subspecialities within majors, and in some cases to leave a given institution.
4. Minimizes the development of collegial relationships with faculty that are important for future professional growth.
5. Undermines confidence.
6. "Dampens" career aspirations.

It is imperative to understand educational equity to be strongly related to maximizing opportunities for the educational success of all students in the classroom (Davidson and Davidson, 1989). The teacher has a role in creating and maintaining educational equity at the classroom level. The disequilibrium that often exists between lecturing about the significant effects of non-verbal behavior and mentoring bias-free behavior needs to be minimized. Creating a "community of learners" environment is very appropriate.

Continually analyzing the results of classroom behavior is also necessary in order to make certain that opportunities lead to successful educational results for the diversity of students enrolling in our classes (Davidson and Davidson, 1989).

Recommendations for Creating a Learning Environment that is More Conducive to the Participation of Minority Students:

Multicultural teaching is an exciting, important and sophisticated model of instruction. The sophistication pertains to the wide range of "instructional" decisions which a professor needs to make in order to create a comprehensive multicultural curriculum. Davidson and Davidson, (1989) propose a typology of multicultural education which emphasizes the professor's role in creating educational equity at the classroom level. Although all four types of multicultural teaching tend to overlap, the model is an attempt, in behavioral terms. to create a clearer conceptual-ization of "multicultural teaching" at the class-room level.

It has been suggested that the aspect of the total college/university environment which, with minimal modification, can maximally impact minority student achievement is faculty instructional strategies and teaching styles. Brown (1986) asserts that subtle adjustments in classroom delivery can produce incredible gains in the academic achievement of minority students. Specifically, although the faculty cannot force students to learn, they can increase the probability that students in multicultural classrooms will learn by manipulating factors in the learning environment.

Student motivation and student/teacher interactions have already been identified as variables related to minority student learning. These two variables are easily manipulated by subtle changes in teaching style that have been shown to increase learning in multicultural classrooms. Motivation recognizes that all students are capable of learning, but that they learn for different reasons and in

Figure 1
A Typology of Multicultural Planning and Teaching
(adapted from Davidson & Davidson, 1989)

TYPE	AIM/OBJECTIVE	METHOD	GOAL/OUTCOME
I	create a collaborative/ supportive learning environment	cooperative learning strategy	multiability curriculum
II	foster (1) intercultural, inter-group and inter-ethnic understanding and comaraderie with- in classroom; (2) multicultural appreciation, tolerance, and sensitivity in the community and larger culture	multiperspective teaching of history/current events cooperative learning	affective goals w/in American context in general immediate class-room context in particular "in praise of diversity"
III	place the teacher in a position to collect/use knowledge of student's family and cultural background to provide sensitive, sensible instruction	parent/teacher conferences (K-12); manifest cultural sensitivity; elicit family cultural knowledge; develop parent/teacher teamwork	"our success will be your child's success"
IV	develop culturally literate individuals	systematically provide studies with indepth, comparative knowledge, of a variety of domestic and international ethnic groups and cultures	transmission and acquisition of cultural knowledge, geographical forces domestic and international

different ways. Thus motivation in multicultural classrooms involves issues of learning styles and perceived relevance. With respect to student/teacher interactions in multicultural classrooms, it is essential to recognize that, because interactions affect learning outcomes, these interactions must be thoughtfully determined rather than random.

Motivating Students in Multicultural Classrooms

Just as the way in which individuals learn is as individual as fingerprints, so does motivation vary within multicultural classrooms. What motivates one individual or group may have no observable effect on others. Educators and psychologists have long recognized that a key to student motivation is creating interest in the course or topic. Creating interest in a multicultural classroom provides a challenge for the instructor because of the varied backgrounds and perceived needs among students.

For example, Anglo students have been shown to be motivated by moderately novel stimuli or approaches to classroom instruction. Instructional strategies as simple as changing the seating arrangement, beginning a lecture with a personal or humorous story, adding color and varied type styles to overhead transparencies, using a role play, discussion, or film instead of lecturing, or adding dramatics create interest among Anglo students. These novel approaches, however, often intimidate or complicate the learning experience for minority students.

Interest is also linked to student perceptions of relevance and purposefulness of the course or topic (Biehler and Snowman, 1986). These perceptions of relevance vary across cultural groups in the multicultural classroom. For white, middle class students in higher education, for example, strong familial support began early in life. These achievement-oriented students are motivated by the realization that a course is a necessary requirement for their degree or that it may help them on qualifying exams for graduate school or professional credentials. For Black Americans of African descent or Hispanic students, however, this perception of deferred relevance is often not sufficient motivation to achieve. Early in the course, minority students must be shown how the course relates to the real, immediate world in which they live. In order to be perceived as relevant and purposeful, the course must recognize and address the needs of the minority students and must provide frequent applications in order to validate the subject matter.

Too often, instructors fail to recognize the immediate and perceived needs of the students in a diverse classroom. There often exists a disparity between the needs perceived by the instructor and those perceived and experienced by the students. As a result, instructors are often ineffective in motivating students to achieve. An example of this disparity arises from personal observation and experience teaching high school science in a rural Appalachian community. Early in a unit on latitude, longitude and mapping, it was discovered that more than half of the students in the class could not read a road map. The teacher announced that the unit would be halted in order to address this skill. "Why do we need to know how to read a road map?" the students honestly questioned. The teacher countered that they would need to be able to read a map in order to go places. The students politely informed the teacher that they had all the roads in the county memorized. Further, they had no interest or need to go anywhere outside the county, so had no need for map-reading skills. Because the well-meaning teacher and the students differed in their perception of the relevance, student motivation for the ensuing unit was low!

Learning experiences must have meaning for all of the students in the class. Teaching in a diverse classroom means that the instructor must present multiple purposes for the course and topics under study. Even though large classroom enrollments often preclude individualized instruction, a renewed understanding of differing minority student motivation and learning styles necessitates conscious efforts to vary pedagogical strategies. To successfully motivate all the individuals and cultural groups in the class, the course must also be viewed as meeting the specific needs of students, both immediate and deferred.

Student/Teacher Interactions in Multicultural Classrooms

Student/teacher interactions have been extensively researched (Good, 1981; Brophy and Good, 1979; Baptiste and Baptiste, 1979). From this research, two patterns are evident. First, teachers tend to hold differing expectations for students in their classrooms. Further, teachers tend to interact with students in ways that often convey their expectations of student achievement. These expectations have a significant impact on present performance, even if that level of achievement is different from the student's past performance record. Good (1981) found a causal relationship between teacher expectations and student achievement.

Second, teachers tend to demonstrate differential treatment toward students for whom they hold high and low expectations. Research further suggests that teachers are less likely to plan and direct instruction at students not expected to make significant academic gains. That is, differing expectations tend to lead to differential treatment in the classroom. Students of whom little is expected are taught less effectively than are students who are expected to achieve (Biehler and Snowman, 1986; Good, 1981; Woolfolk and McCune-Nicolich, 1980).

Teaching has been described as interaction that induces learning. If the quality of classroom teaching is linked to the quality of interaction, it is important for instructors to be able to understand and manipulate student/teacher interactions in the classroom. Further, because nonverbal communication is often more powerful and significant than verbal interaction, teachers need to be able to identify and interpret classroom interactions at both levels.

Ironically, instructors are often unaware of the attitudes which tend to lead to differing expectations and treatments. The following fictionalized but real situations illustrate this lack of awareness.

> An economics professor who has never used an example that refers to minorities, especially American Blacks of African descent or Hispanics, in his class introduces the topic of unemployment and poverty. He then asks a minority student to provide relevant background information and illustrations to support his assertion. The student, who comes from a well-to-do family, responds that she cannot provide such data. The instructor believes that the student is being insolent and disagreeable. The instructor is obviously unaware of the stereotypes that are at the root of his assumptions and behaviors.

> A Bible professor with an average class size of 200 has chosen to utilize computer assisted grading to facilitate testing and evaluation. Enrolled in the class are 23 older students, predominantly female, who have returned to

school after working an average of six years. These students need to express their understanding of the material covered beyond objective-oriented testing but find the professor unresponsive to their request for alternate testing strategies. The professor is perhaps unaware of the very diverse development and culturally socialized learning styles of the learners enrolled in his class.

A history professor receives a term paper from a Hispanic student in one of her courses. It is a good paper, but it does have some flaws which, if corrected, would make this an excellent paper. The professor gives the student a "B" and neglects to mention the paper's shortcomings because it is overall a "good" paper in its present form. It is interesting to note that the professor generally believes that stringent criticism results in improved work. She acts on this belief with her majority students, but she apparently believes unconsciously that "good" work is more than sufficient for Hispanic students.

One way that instructors relate their expectations to students is through oral and written comments. According to Brown (1986) at all levels of schooling, especially with minority students, teacher interactions reinforce behavior or socialization more than academics. The result, according to Brown (1986), is that minority students think the business of schooling is pleasing the professor, not academics. Subtle changes in teacher interaction behaviors can change the focus to learning. Teacher comments should emphasize the link between behavior or socialization and academic achievement. Links between the format, content and thought quality of the effort should be pointed out. Finally, a link should be made to immediate student benefits.

The following examples contrast teacher interaction that emphasizes behavior with feedback that stresses academics as the true business of schooling:

"Your writing style is improving."	*versus*	"Your writing style is improving. It is clear to see your idea develop and build throughout the paper because of your varied sentence structure."
"All papers must be in on time."	*versus*	"All papers must be in on time. Having reacted to the author's ideas will provide you with a good basis of comparison as we read another author's point of view next week."

Because the key to communication in the classroom is mutual intelligibility, student/teacher interactions are complicated when students or instructors have limited English proficiency. When students have poor writing or speaking skills, it is difficult to assess their progress in the classroom. The resulting frustration felt by the instructor is generally subtly communicated to the students, which further compounds the communication process.

Limited English Proficiency

Students with limited oral proficiency often hesitate to participate orally in class, especially if they suspect that their contribution will be judged for language conformity rather than for content. The teacher's reaction further aggravates the problem, causing the student to withdraw from learning activities and to view the teacher and the class as a source of humiliation. According to Brown (1986), when students have thus withdrawn, it is nearly impossible to further involve them in the learning process.

Subtle changes in teacher behavior, however, can create a learning environment in the college/university classroom which is more conducive to the participation of minority students. Perhaps most important, an atmosphere of mutual respect must be fostered in which it is "safe" to respond. Following is a list of teacher behaviors which tend to communicate respect for all students during classroom interactions.

1. Pay particular attention to classroom interaction patterns during the first few weeks of class, and make a special effort to draw minorities into discussion during that time.

2. Respond to minority and majority students in similar ways when they make comparable contributions to class discussion by developing those comments, crediting the comments to their author, and coaching both minority and majority students for additional information or further thoughts.
3. Be careful to ask minority and majority students qualitatively similar questions and give minorities and majorities an equal amount of time to respond after asking a question.
4. Make eye contact with minority as well as majority students after the instructor asks a question to invite a response.
5. Assume an attentive posture when responding to questions from minorities or when listening to their comments.
6. Notice patterns of interruption to determine if minority students tend to be interrupted more than majority students either by themselves or by other students. Intervene when communication patterns among students tend to shut out minorities. (Hall, 1982 adapted).

In a classroom environment characterized by effective instruction, much of this respect is communicated nonverbally by the instructor. In his investigation of effective schooling with Alaskan Native students, Scollon (1981) found that effective teachers were "tuned in" to nonverbal student rhythms during conversation. The hand, eye, and body movements of the listener were timed to coincide with the movements and speech of the speaker. The author concluded that this unconscious rhythm led to effective communication among Native Alaskans and limited the effectiveness of classroom interaction between students and "outsider" teachers. Scollon posits that the key for classroom interaction for non-native teachers is a positive attitude toward the students which makes it easier for teachers to tune in to student nonverbal communication behaviors. It is important, then, that instructors in any multicultural classroom first examine their own attitudes toward verbal and nonverbal language style and evaluate whether the language style of a minority student's comment, question or response consciously affects their own perception of its importance or validity.

Subtle changes in teacher behavior are also essential in interacting with students who have limited written English proficiency. Considerable frustration results when instructors fail to recognize that patterns of organization in speech and writing vary across cultures. Condon and Yousef (1988) report that cultural differences are readily apparant in routine theme papers written by students. These differences are attributable to cultural and personal factors such as persuasive purpose and speaker-audience relationships. The dominant Anglo-American syle, for example, approximates the organization of a debate. In this directive style, the presenter's position is stated with confidence, the opponent's position is presented as incorrect, supporting evidence is presented, and a conclusion reaffirms the truth of the presenter's position. The style exhibited by students whose cultural context seeks consensus shows a different organizational pattern with less strength of conviction. To the Anglo instructor, this style seems to be cautious, tentative, tolerant or even complimentary of disparate opinions, and incomplete in making a point. Condon and Yousef (1988) suggest that this style may be carefully organized so as not to come to a central point or conclusion, as expected by most college/university instructors.

Kaplan (1970) notes marked differences between the "logic" or style of writing and building a position between native English writers and foreign-student writers. He summarizes by way of diagrams:

Figure 2.
Differences in Writing Logic

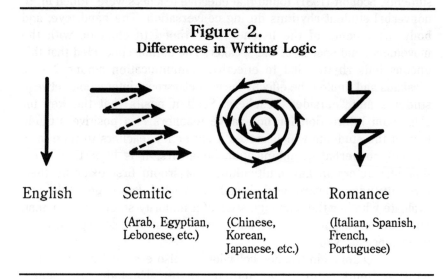

English	Semitic	Oriental	Romance
	(Arab, Egyptian, Lebonese, etc.)	(Chinese, Korean, Japanese, etc.)	(Italian, Spanish, French, Portuguese)

According to Kaplan (1970), problems in written communication in minority classrooms emerge at the level of the paragraph. That is, while the individual sentences in a paper may appear to be "good English", minority students who have not mastered the syntax of standard English may still write bad paragraphs or bad papers unless they also master the logic of English. According to Davidson and Davidson (1989), students with limited English proficiency tend to conceptualize paragraphs in terms of length rather than in terms of meaning with interrelated components. The resulting paragraph generally contains a series of run-on sentences, fragments, and disregard for capitalization and punctuation.

It may be necessary to instruct students from certain countries, such as Japan, that the writing process in English involves a different set of assumptions from the ones with which they are accustomed to working.

Instructors may encourage more meaningful writing by shifting the focus away from paper length. Instead of asking students to respond in one paragraph, it may be easier for minority students to write eight to twelve sentences on a given topic. Directions for writing a paper, then, should stress that the assignment should be six to eight paragraphs in length, with an introductory paragraph, one paragraph to develop and support each idea, followed by a summary paragraph. This enables students to focus on interrelated units of thought and tends to eliminate many mechanical problems.

Beyond understanding the stylistic differences in multicultural classrooms, instructors need to affirm these cultural styles. When it is important that the directive English style be used, those standards should be clearly stated. The required style should be modeled and contrasted to the minority group's style, and instructors should be sure that students understand the structure of the expected style of writing for the assignment. The use of outlines and drafts before the final paper enable the instructor to coach the student in the expected style throughout the writing process, and thus tend to eliminate much of the frustration related to writing proficiency in multicultural classrooms.

Another aspect of building a climate of mutual respect in the classroom is personal involvement in the culture and lives of students, especially minority students. It is essential that instructors attempt to understand the worldview of minority students. This means going beyond the traditional "culture" components and expressions such as food, art forms, music, dance, and literature to understanding the perspectives and values which minority students hold. It is vital to understand the minority student's perspective of time, family, competition and orientation toward nature. Scollon (1981) found that teachers who were effective in teaching cross-culturally went beyond attempting to understand the culture of the students by allowing themselves be known as *persons*. They gave students an idea from where they were coming , what they like and don't like, their interests, and information about their family, and their own worldview. This process, of course, requires personal interaction outside of the framework of the traditional classroom. In classrooms where students have limited English proficiency, instructors must also employ different ways to check for student understanding of the course content, especially if minority students hesitate to participate in class. When successful minority students at one Christian university were asked if they understood the content of their courses, they estimated that their comprehension was limited to 25 percent of the content presented (Bainer, 1988). Following are instructional strategies which tend to facilitate communication of content and checking for understanding in multicultural classrooms.

1. Rather than asking if there are any questions at the end of a class session, check for student understanding throughout the lesson. Nonverbal checks or signals work effectively. Students can signal their level of understanding with cards, their pencils or fingers. The instructor can then gauge if the main points of the lecture were communicated effectively by asking students to submit anonymous feedback cards at the end of the session summarizing the main points from the lesson and any questions that they have.
2. Using the Preview Method students with limited English proficiency are able to preview the main points of the lesson in their primary language. In a classroom with students whose primary language is Spanish, for example, the main points of the lesson would be presented in Spanish as well as English, the body of the lesson in English, and a summary in Spanish as well as English. Alternately, the lesson can be presented in the students' primary language prior to class, and in English

during the class session. It is important, of course, for limited English proficiency students to attend both sessions in order to build their communication skills.
3. Strategies of "sheltered instruction" are important in multicultural classrooms. In sheltered instruction, the instructor uses a variety of instructional modifications to make the content more comprehensible. For example, the instructor speaks more slowly and uses shorter sentences. Key words are reentered and defined, and main points are presented in writing as well as verbally to facilitate note taking. Pictures, no matter how sketchy, are helpful in communicating directions. Sheltered instruction includes using an abundance of visuals and manipulatives. Frequently checking for understanding by asking students to restate main points in their own words or in their primary language involves other limited English proficiency students in a peer checking system. Lessons should also be interactive to enable students to practice their communication skills.

Facilitating Change

A primary obstacle to significant change in many educational systems is that educational institutions often reflect a built-in tendency to resist change. To some extent this is a useful quality for schools do tend to conserve values of preference rather than yielding to educational fads. Nevertheless, there are times when reevaluation and adjustment is necessitated.

Changing everyday classroom behavior that expresses devalued and limited views of minorities is a difficult challenge—especially because much of the differential treatment that may occur in classroom and related interaction is inadvertent, and often below the level of consciousness of both faculty and students. However, although this kind of change is elusive and difficult, it is already underway on our campuses, and directions for future changes need to be chartered by ongoing dialog and research.

We need to acknowledge that many faculty on our campus have already recognized the importance of classroom language, and are attempting to identify and to change language that excludes or disparages minorities. Perhaps leaders of faculty development could aid professors who want to become more aware of their own subtle behaviors that may discourage minority college students. Many of the strategies discussed are also useful in identifying behaviors that express attitudes and perceptions based on diversity. Indeed the impact of diversity on interactions in the university and society is becoming a major focus for research on many fronts, both within and outside academe.

The results of culturally relevent education cannot but help contribute to social participation and community solidarity on campus. After all, Christianity is, in the main, a response to the need to have a mechanism for allaying anxieties created by our inability to predict and understand events that do not apparantly conform to expectations.

In Christian higher education, knowledge of processes of learning often permits understanding behavior of others more sufficiently thus enhancing better interpersonal relations. Particularly important is the recognition that when people of diversity react differently they do not do so from stupidity or maliciousness. Getting to know people of diversity is a necessary prelude to understanding and respect, but such knowledge alone does not resolve our differences or insure our liking people whose ways are alien to us (Brown, 1986).

The intellectual recognizes that all needs cannot be met immediately, but a start can be made...even if on a basis that can be criticized as somewhat inadequate. The real task of the university is to begin to bridge the credibility gap that exists between peoples of diversity and the predominantly Anglo, male-dominated Christian university. The university can do this by attempting to understand the concerns of minority students and begin to deal with them directly.

The greatest of life's resources lies mainly in the power to meet contemporary challenges. Why are we so resistant to change? Why is change so difficult for each of us? We find a clue in the fact that Jesus likened us to sheep (stubborn, hostile and self-willed) and, if this is true, perhaps this may be one of the reasons we have difficulty with change. We can begin to understand what our problem is as seen through His eyes. But whether we are basically innovators or reactionaries, there is no possibility for growth without change. To live is to change. To be alive is to be dynamic and adaptable.

Educating for equity means that we not only want our students to be warm and loving—we want them to be knowledgeable and competent. We think it is the same in the field of Christian influence. God is sovereign particularly in the field of Christian influence and persuasion. He doesn't need us and could influence people directly if it so pleased Him. But for whatever reason, God has chosen us as His ambassadors, usually making his appeal to people through us. We can be humanly competent as we seek to persuade, or we can butcher the job. God can overrule our bumbling efforts, but it is irresponsible to expect God to do so if we haven't taken the trouble to discover the best possible means of influence. As Christian influencers for equity it behooves us to learn these principles so that we will be cooperating with the Holy Spirit rather than working against Him.

The Christian higher education can be the answer for minority students' needs if the Christian college and university can and are willing to become a powerful force in the area of intergroup relations. The university must have courage to set the example for and lead others to a biblical understanding and model for equitable and just behavior in intergroup relations. At this juncture, it is necessary to remember that "every social problem affecting multitudes of people is also a problem for each individual member of those multitudes" (Moberg, 1968).

We must be ever remindful that peacemaking efforts in the midst of diversity is not one of passive avoidance, but rather of active reconciliation.

Where do we go from here? Do whatever is necessary, but do so that we may remain one!

References

Ainsworth, C.L. (January 1986). "The college classroom: Changing climates and cultures." Paper presented at the Regional Conference on University Teaching, Las Cruces, N.M. (ED 281 411).

Astin, A.W. (1982). *Minorities in American higher education: Recent trends, current prospects, and recommendations*. San Francisco: Jossey-Bass.

Bainer, D.L. (1988). Student interviews. LaMirada, CA: Biola University.

Banks, J.A. (1983). Multiethnic education and the quest for equality. *Phi Delta Kappan, 64* (8). 582-585.

Benjamin, A. (1978). *Behavior in small groups*. Boston: Houghton Mifflin.

Baptiste, H. & Baptiste, M. (1979). *Developing the multicultural process in classroom instruction: Competencies for teachers*. Washington, D.C.: University Press of America.

Berger, P. (1961). *The noise of solemn assemblies*. New York: Doubleday.

Bernstein, B. (1970). Social class, language and socialization. In *Class, codes and control*, Vol (1): Theoretical Studies Toward A Sociology of Education. Boston: Routledge and Kegan Paul.

Berube, M. R. (1984). *Education and poverty: Effective schooling in the United States and Cuba*. Westport, CT: Greenwood Press.

Biehler, R. F. & Snowman, J. (1986). *Psychology applied to teaching*. Boston: Houghton-Mifflin.

Billson, J. (July 1986). The small classroom as a small group: Some implications for teaching and learning. *Teaching Sociology 14*, 143-151.

Bourdieu, P. & Passeron, C. (1977). *Reproduction in education, society and culture*. Richard Nice, Trans. London: Sage Publications.

Brookover, W. (1979). *School social systems and student achievement*. New York: Praeger.

Brophy, J. E. & Good, T.L.. (October, 1979) Analyzing classroom interactions: A more powerful alternative. *Educational Technology, 21, 26.*

Brown, T. J. (1986). *Teaching minorities more effectively: A model for educators*. New York: University Press of America.

Condon, J. C. & Yousef, F. (1988). *An introduction to intercultural communications*. New York: Macmillan.

Davidson, C. (July 1987). Ethnic jokes: An introduction to race and nationality. *Teaching Sociology, 15,* 296-302.

Davidson, L. & Davidson, P. (1989). *Supervising with a multicultural perspective: Adding a new dimension to clinical supervision in a preservice program*. San Luis Obispo, CA: California Polytechnic State University.

Good, T. L. (April 1981). Teacher expectations and student perceptions: A decade of research. *Educational Leadership, 38,* 415-422.

Hall, R. M. (1982). The classroom climate: A chilly one for women? *Project on the Status and Education of Women*. Washington, D.C.: Association of American Colleges.

Jenkins, C. (1969). *The black student and the Christian college*. Master's Thesis. Chicago Graduate School of Theology. Chicago, Illinois. Unpublished.

Jenkins, C. (1981). Alumni interviews. Hillsboro, KS: Tabor College.

Kaplan, R. B. (1970). Cultural thought patterns in inter-cultural education. *Language Learning, 16,* 1-20.

Kelley, H. & Thibaut, J. (1954). Experimental studies of group problem solving and process. In G. Lindzey, *Handbook of Social Psychology* Vol II. Reading, MA: Addison-Wesley.

Lieberson, S. (1980). *A piece of the pie: Black and white immigrants since 1980.* Berkeley, CA: University of California Press.

McCroskey, J., & Sheahan, M. (1978) Communication apprehension, social preference, and social behavior in a college environment. *Communication Quarterly, 26* (2), 41-45.

Mills, C. W. (1961). *The sociological imagination.* New York: Grove Press.

Moberg, D. O. (Fall, 1968). Some practical steps toward evangelical social involvement. *The Gordon Review,* 128-136.

Noel, J. (1978). *Reducing the dropout rate.* San Francisco: Jossey-Bass.

Phillips, G. & Ericksen, E. (1970). *Interpersonal dynamics in the small group.* New York: Random House.

Scollon, R. (1981). *Teachers' questions about Alaska native education.* Fairbanks, Alaska: University of Alaska Center for Cross Cultural Studies. (ED 238661).

Seifert, H. (1983). New patterns of social education. In D. T. Hessel, A whole ministry of social education. *Religious Education, 78* (4). 545.

Stark, R., & Foster, B., Glock, C., Quinley, H. (1971). *Wayward shepherds: Prejudice and the Protestant Clergy.* New York: Harper and Row.

Statistical Abstracts. (1987). *Statistical Abstracts of the United States.* Washington, D.C.: U.S. Bureau of the Census.

The Retention Committee (University of Pittsburgh). (1980). *A Report to the Provost.* .

Tinto, V. (1982). Limits of theory and practice in student attrition. *Journal of Higher Education, 53* (6), 687-701.

Tyler, L. E. (1965). *The psychology of human differences*, 3rd edition. New York: Appleton-Century-Crofts.

Weiss, L. (1985). *Between two worlds: Black students and an urban community college.* Boston: Routledge and Kegan Paul.

Woolfolk, A. E. & McCune-Nicolich, L. (1980). *Educational Psychology for Teachers.* Englewood, NJ: Prentice-Hall.

Multiculturalizing the Curricula at Evangelical Christian Colleges

Abraham Davis, Jr.

The proposition of this chapter is that the evangelical Christian college curricula should continually be ethnically and culturally integrated. It is not my intention to indict colleges of institutional, systemic or individual racism, but rather my purpose is to share practical recommendations with examples and reasons in an effort to encourage curriculum designers and teachers to integrate ethnically their respective curricula *continually*.

The constituency and order of this chapter will consist of rationales and recommendations interspersed with reasons and examples or models. The connotation of the terms examples and models are used interchangeably in various contexts of this chapter; also rationale, recommendations, and reasons will not always be sharply delineated, for they will be variously influenced and distributed by the foci and arrangement of the respective resources from which quotations and paraphrases will come. With these observations and qualifications, topical divisions will be imposed upon this writing for the convenience of the reader, commencing with an extended rationale for multiculturalizing the evangelical college curricula.

Rationale for Multiculturalizing the Curricula

The State of Evangelical Colleges

Allen (1985) has pointed out that "the majority of evangelical colleges have few, if any, minority representatives on the faculty" (p. 65). He further observed that "resembling other predominately white institutions of higher education in this society, the evangelical college has minimized or ignored minority participation in establishing or reforming its social structure in the direction of racial and cultural pluralism" (p. 67). Thus the evangelical colleges are ignorantly insensitive to the contributions and deeper needs of minorities. Thus "the rationale for altering the white ethnocentric subculture endemic to the evangelical college has spiritual, cultural, and practical aspects" (p. 70). These "aspects" imply the inclusion of other than Euro-American perspectives in the academic curricula.

Jenkins (1987) sought "to identify specific issues which may help us develop more effective strategies for bringing about and maintaining equity in the classroom." Among these "specific issues" and "strategies" is the intellectual and moral responsibility of the "Christian colleges and universities [not only] to weave minority students into the essential fabric of the institution [but to] *meaningfully integrate minority scholarship into curriculum*" (p. 62) (Emphasis mine). Further, Jenkins notes the practice of "ignoring the cultural contributions of minorities and using examples in such a way as to reinforce a stereotyped and negative view of minorities" (p. 63). Related to this negative observation is the positive recommendation to "become aware of contributions by minorities in your area and use examples when appropriate" (p. 64).

Despite the lack of sustained effort, there are three evangelical Christian colleges which have attempted to multiculturalize their curricula.

Messiah College. In my library I have a typewritten speech manuscript by a white student at Messiah College in Pennsylvania presented in 1979 on "Racism in the Curriculum at Messiah" (Anonymous, 1979). First off, the student describes the results of some interviews he did with some white faculty members at Messiah. Then, after briefly reviewing racism at other colleges, he offers "some specific recommendations for improving the [curricular] situation at Messiah and any other school that faces this same problem." Two of his recommendations were (1) that more emphasis be given to minorities (by means of) special lectures and lecturers and (2) that college events consistently reflect the presence of Black and other minority students on campus.

In interviewing a Messiah professor, the student reported that the professor acknowledged living "in a white-oriented society" in which he and the students "learn about the great masters in literature, art, music, and history... without ever learning about minorities who contributed something in one of the previously mentioned fields."

Were that student of 1979 to follow up on the curricular situation at Messiah College by examining its 1988-1990 Catalog, he would find Interdepartmental Courses categorized as (1) Cross-Cultural Studies, (2) Golden Ages of China and India, (3) Africa and the Arab World, and (4) Africa Through Literature. Under Cross-Cultural Studies, the student would find eight courses which may be used to fulfill the language requirement for the Bachelor of Arts degree and the cross-cultural requirement for the Bachelor of Science degree. In addition to the cross-cultural study tours in England, Greece, Newfoundland, and Israel, non-white cross-cultural studies are individually described as "Study Tour of Navajos," "Study Tour of Guatemala," "Studies of the Puerto Rican," and "Studies of the Black American" (Messiah College, 1988).

These cross-cultural courses and a few non-white faculty indicate an awareness of ethnocentrism and efforts to combat some manifestations of it in the curriculum and faculty composition. However, the lack of ethnic integration of the mainstream courses "in literature, art, music, and history" as observed by the Messiah's professor is another question for discussion and implementation.

Goshen College. Similar to the multicultural offerings at Messiah College are those described in 1988-90 Catalog of Goshen College in Indiana. But, it is clear that Goshen is more *demanding* in its international study. For example, the distinctive and innovative Study-Service Term which requires students to spend a semester immersed in another culture has received national recognition. The benefits of this program according to studies have shown that (1) "students leave Goshen College with better communication, language, world history and intercultural skills than most American college graduates" and (2) "they are able to build connections and have a vision that is not just national but global" (p.8). In terms of extensiveness, if not uniqueness, Goshen has a Department of Hispanic Ministries designed to train leaders for Hispanic congregations. Thus, its course in "Church History and the Reformation" deliberately considers the Hispanic dimension or perspective.

In the History and Political Science Department a number of cross-cultural courses are offered: African, African-American, and Latin American histories along with minority rights and international politics. With all of these specific cross-cultural offerings my hope *still* is that ethnic integration extend to the mainstream courses of literature, art, history, and others where the contributors and events fit into the chronological and topical schema.

Calvin College. Another evangelical liberal arts college who is making some deliberate efforts toward minimizing ethnocentrism is Calvin College in Michigan. Unlike Messiah and Goshen, Calvin's awareness is not apparent in its catalogued course offerings to date, but it is manifested in a rather uniquely written *Comprehensive Plan* (1985). This *Plan* "plots out a course that will make Calvin the multicultural community here envisioned. The vision is of a Christian community that celebrates cultural diversity and is shaped by the biblical vision of the kingdom of God" (p. 4).

One of the four critical areas identified and described in the document is "Curriculum" with its anticipated goal "that Calvin graduates will know and appreciate cultures other than those dominant in North America and Western Europe, and that they will be prepared to interact effectively with people from cultures other than their own" (p. 3). The primary strategy is for the college to establish "a distribution requirement of a set number of approved courses in multicultural studies to be completed by all students who graduate from Calvin" (p. 23).

Rationale Reflected in Personal Experience

In teaching and lecturing in secular colleges and universities, I have not been an alien or distant spectator. I commenced teaching in 1956 at a secular "Black" college, South Carolina State College, and retired in 1988 as a visiting professor at "White" evangelical college,

Calvin College. Although I have taught and lectured at other secular schools such as Indiana University, James Madison University in Virginia, the University of New York at Albany, I have spent most of my thirty-two years of teaching at evangelical colleges including Messiah College, Houghton College in New York, Eastern Mennonite College in Virginia, and Calvin College—all of which are *still* prevailingly white, not only in population but also in curricula and pedagogy.

By design my expressed purpose and approach to this chapter are to be positive and encouraging to my colleagues as stated in my introduction and exemplified throughout to the conclusion. However, I must confess degrees of pain and discouragement, for after approximately a quarter of a century as a tactful teacher and an active rhetorician in a number evangelical collegiate contexts and thirty years after the Supreme Court desegregation ruling, I am still observing and concluding that the evangelical mainstream "curricula and pedagogy" are still "prevailingly white."

Although I have been a college lecturer and practicing rhetorician in evangelical colleges since 1961, my first article on this intercultural subject published in 1974 was "Ethnic Integration: An Appeal To Evangelical Liberal Arts Educators" (Davis, 1974). Using the Native American and African-American as examples in the article, even *then* as a rather *new* advocate, I expressed my difficulty perceiving an "intellectually and ethically liberal arts education that studies American history, American rhetoric, American art, music, and drama solely from *one* ethnic perspective" (p. 48). This pedagogical practice seems all the more invalid in the light of Dr. Paul G. Hiebert's anthropological observation of current "cultural pluralism" in this country (Hiebert, 1983) and in the light of the abundance of noteworthy contributions and achievements of American ethnic-minorities.

Back then and now I make the claim that "honest academic administrators—especially Christian ones—ought to ethnically integrate their curricula so as to convey to their students the full range of American achievement" (p. 48). And to neglect to work diligently at this integration or to avoid it by adding specific ethnic courses as electives is most inadequate, if not irresponsible; for such electives may be an effort to avoid the rigor of putting ethnic works into the formal mainstream of American studies. To keep them out is to perpetuate racism and stereotypes in the study of American rhetoric, music, science, technology, history and other disciplines.

In the conclusion of my article I observe that "failure to implement ethnic integration throughout the curricula not only academically and psychologically injures the minority students, but also perpetuates ignorance among the majority students, even those who may graduate with honors from 'prestige' schools under the delusion of being liberally educated in American studies. Christian teachers and scholars should no longer be guilty of perpetuating this sin" (p. 48). Even if a professor in his ethnocentric education has not been formally exposed to Native American and African-American literature, history, drama, music, science and technology; he need not deprive his/her students of these and other significant American compositions and contributions. Useful and excellent bibliographies, anthologies, multi-media materials, and well qualified resource persons and scholars are available for occasional lectures and workshops. Therefore, white professors and students can by themselves become more liberally educated in American studies by continually studying non-white contributors and achievers in a manner which chronologically and topically integrate them into and with their own heritage and models.

Rationale Reflected in Popular Media
    Based upon a report released by the Joint Center for Political Studies, an article appeared in *The Washington Post* (Williams, 1985) titled "Support for Desegregation Declines." This reverting was the conclusion from the Center's observations of public school educational systems thirty years after the Supreme Court's landmark ruling. Nevertheless the Center further observes that there is "compelling evidence that desegregation works if it is done well." What is relevant to our subject is the perception regarding curriculum renovation, for the report said, "desegregation can be a 'catalyst for educational changes' that benefit all students, such as the reevaluation of curriculum" in addition to new training programs for teachers and administrators.

    The non-religious African-American popular *Jet* magazine also reports in May of 1989, that "hundreds of students on college campuses across the U.S. recently participated in National Black Student Action Day as part of a nation wide call for Black studies requirements and for other remedies to what students say are persistent patterns of bias on campus, including Harvard, Duke, Northwestern, Penn State, and LaSalle universities (May 15, 1989).

It is grievous to read articles and studies of active racism and passive or rationalized ethnocentrism in evangelical colleges in the 1980's. Some titles or captions *alone* indicate this trend—articles such as "Can Christian Colleges Mix With Minorities?" in *Christianity Today* (Niklaus, 1981) and "Racism With a Smile" (Gross, 1985) in InterVarsity's *His* magazine. Reports of this kind of prejudical behavior emanating from secular, humanistic institutions in 1989, even *beyond* the South, is not surprising; but they are especially grievous when evident in evangelical institutions of higher learning professing to be Biblically influenced and Christocentric. Despite this prevailing characteristic in curricula, the thrust of this chapter endeavors to be *positive* in recommendations, reasons, and models or examples.

Before proceeding from rationale to recommendation, I would summon one more academic witness from a source or reference describes as "indispensable to anyone Black or white concerned with the contemporary education crisis." It is a book written in the late 1960's that advocated *then* what this chapter urges *now* in the 1990's. Under part three on "The University Scene" of *What Black Educators Are Saying*, the Dean of the Graduate School of the University of North Carolina, Dr. Darwin T. Turner (1970), reminded educators that "Afro-American" is but *one example* of American ethnicities. Turner, therefore, recommends not only that the college "should offer subjects and materials of interest to students of Afro-American ancestry," but likewise "to those of non-Afro-Americans," and that "a course or two" focusing on *specific* minority studies "is not sufficient" (p. 96).

As an example in discussing a practical approach, Dr. Turner saw in 1968 "the need for courses in the history of art, literature, and music of Africans and Afro-Americans" (p. 96). He claimed *then*, as I do now, that "current curricula frequently include the philosophical ideas of Descartes, Berkeley, Rousseau, Voltaire, Locke, Paine, Kant..., but room should be made for the philosophical ideas of Thoureau, King, and Malcolm X" (p. 97). Turner discouraged the claim of "color blindness" for the planners and revisers of the curriculum, be they Black or white. He also suggested that "attempts should be made—especially in the humanities and social sciences—to devise material which are significant to the needs and relative to the interests of the students." This latter suggestion by Dr. Turner is only an excerpt of one of six which he proposed not "as solutions, but as hypotheses to be tested. Ultimately, of course, the success of these or any other suggestions depends upon faculty and administration who are imaginative and concerned." (p. 103)

Rather than indulging in the painful analysis of racism or ethnocentrism in culturally diverse America, let us repent and begin with the practice of using "positive ethnic models" *continually* (Davis, 1984). Whether token or superficial with hypothetical or real examples, it is hoped that the limited recommendations, reasons, and models cited in this chapter may serve as stimuli and motivation for the continual multiculturalizing of collegiate curricula—not merely for pedagogical variety, but because of necessity at this late date *still* characterized by ethnocentrism in our multi-ethnic and multicultural society and world.

Recommendations for Multiculturalizing the Curricula

At the outset of this section on recommendations, I must admit that while I am urgently advocating the ethnic integration of *all* mainstream disciplines, I am well aware that examples for some are more readily available than for others like mathematics and botany. I am also aware that the examples that follow in art, science and technology, history, literature, rhetoric, and Christian missions are comparably infinitesimal. Nevertheless, I plead here for the *continual* use of positive ethnic models and illustrations with the hope that they will serve as samples, stimulating and heuristic.

Art

As an aid for ethnically integrating the curriculum in American art, I recommend a comprehensive pictorial and written survey of 63 artists and their works—paintings, sculptures, graphics and crafts—

in book form titled *Two Centuries of Black American Art* (Driskell, 1976). Despite this title, the assertion in the introduction is that "Black is neither a true color nor an entirely apt word...for this exhibition...(because) so many earlier artists did not reflect 'the black experience' in their subject matter" (p. 9). Their portraits of whites, their Biblical scenes, landscapes and still life have affinities with and should be seen as part of "the mainstream of American Art" (p. 9). This art should fit into the chronological and topical arrangement of any American art course, instead of being ignored or isolated as a "primitive" detachment without serious academic consideration.

Science and Technology

The U.S. Department of Energy's Office of Public Affairs, not considered an academic institution, promotes and demonstrates the concept of "models" in its attractive publication of *Black Contributors To Science and Energy Technology* (1979). The modeling concept and purpose are explicitly and concisely articulated as follows: "These researchers may well serve as models for children who have had little opportunity to learn of Black contributors to science and technology, and as motivation for students who are uncertain about continuing their studies or selecting professions" (p. 1). This booklet consists of twenty-four Black male and female researchers accompanied with respective biographical and pictorial information arranged for facility in viewing, reading, and referencing.

If this non-academic Office of Public Affairs saw this need and made this effort for children and students, it is ironic that academic institutions of higher learning are not making similar continual and concentrated efforts to multiculturalize their curricula in science and technology.

History

Dr. Daphyne Saunders, Professor of Business Law at James Madison University emphasized the need for "History of All Americans" (1985). Her observation was that America is a history of its people—"all of its people". Her analogical argument is that all children in the American public schools were "required to pledge allegiance to the red, white and blue; yet, the history of the red, black and brown people of this country were left out of the textbooks... Black Americans and all citizens of this country need to know their history" (p. 6). Because "red, yellow, brown, black and white" all played a part in America, U.S. history text books should by now *continually* reflect and represent such multicultural contributions to education, the fine arts, government, technology, and literature.

A dramatic example of a white professor at a white university endeavoring to multiculturalize his American History course was reported in the *Medford Mail Tribune* of Oregon college in February of 1972. The caption reads, "SOC (Southern Oregon College) Professor Puts U.S. History In Focus With View of Minorities' Roles." The report identifies by name and picture Dr. William J. Gaboury expressing his concern "that American history as it has been taught in the past—has in reality been 'White American History' and thus has limited and distorted the historical perspective." This observation and practice in and of itself seems to be intellectually and ethically compelling enough to motivate a conscientious teacher to take some corrective action with his/her American history curriculum, however token and superficial it may be. Professor Gaboury taught at Southern Oregon University since 1966, but not until 1971 did he set out to "'restructure' his American History survey classes so they would tell more completely the role played by minority ethnic groups in the nation's development."

The principal impetus and profound motivation for Dr. Gaboury's endeavor for the ethnic integration of his history course occurred while he was doing a year of post-graduate study in Chicago as a Danforth Fellow. During this year he took courses in Black studies at the University of Chicago with Professor John Hope Franklin, the noted Black historian. He realistically perceived his course restructuring as simply a beginning to a much larger task. His major challenge was to try to put together into "one piece...the diverse experiences of the many ethnic groups as they have affected—and continue to affect—the nation's history." Gaboury claimed that without ethnic inclusions, "American history becomes incomplete history, which only creates myths, or is valid for only some groups." His ethnic inclusions were Native Americans, African-Americans, Asian-Americans, and other minority groups with the contention "that unless American history is understood from the viewpoints of those ethnic groups—as well as from the white Americans of European ancestry," the nation as well as the individual will be unable to function rationally in dealing with social problems. He also argued that if "history books leave out the important role played by this country's minority ethnic groups, then a part of the nation's 'memory' becomes a blank or a 'distortion.'" In fact, some citizens' knowledge of American history is based on myths, myths such as the Jacksonian democracy dealing justly with Native Americans and Lincoln's belief in the equality of African-Americans.

The news report on Dr. Gaboury concluded with his thesis regarding the ethnic integration of his curriculum that may apply to other American studies. The thesis is that America is "the story of all the people—rich and poor, Black and White, business and labor men and women, young and old." The challenge is to decide what new emphasis should be given to the contributions of the minority groups in comprehending the essence of America.

I know of another white professor, this time at Eastern Mennonite College, who also makes an effort to multiculturalize his American history course. Along with continually having non-white resource persons to lecture and/or interact with his students, he used a text titled *Red, White and Black: The Peoples of Early America* by Gary B. Nash (1974). The book is described as a "remarkable study of pre-revolutionary America... revealed as vastly more complex than merely the story of how Western Europeans carried their societal structures to America and then declared and fought for independence. It is rather a study of three major cultures—European, Native American and African." These "cultural interactions shaped the course of our history, and continues to do so through current times."

In the "Foreword" of the text, Leon Litwack as editor notes that Nash departs from the traditional approach to early American history commencing with centuries before Plymouth Rock, Roanoke Island, and Christopher Columbus's voyage. Litwack claims that "by the time the Europeans managed to find their way to the old 'New World,' a diversity of native cultures had existed for thousands of years"; thus the ethnocentric focus of traditional history is challenged. Nash then "views the Europeanization of the New World as only one crucial stage in the evolution of colonial society."

This pre-Columbus and pre-revolutionary perspective reminds me of another commendable American history book from another ethnic perspective titled *Before The Mayflower* (Bennett, 1984) which respectfully considers the experiences and contributions of Native Americans, European-Americans, and African-Americans.

Literature

In the general field of literature—prose and poetry—Native Americans, Hispanic, Asian-American, African-American, and other minorities have produced or created a number of works on universal themes as well as on truncated cultural and ethnic experiences. In the process of integrating them into the curricular mainstream, traditional literary criteria may be used in the evaluation and selection of works for the collegiate syllabus.

The *Norton Anthology of Poetry* (Eastman, et al., 1970) short edition included two poems by Paul Laurence Dunbar (1872-1906) and a few by four other African-American poets including the Poet Laureate of Illinois, Gwendolyn Brooks. But an anthology titled *Speaking For Ourselves* (Faderman & Bradshaw, 1969) reflected a more deliberate effort at ethnic integration or multiculturalization. It claimed to be "a new kind of anthology for college students" with the purpose of introducing "American writers of different ethnic backgrounds... whose writing, on the whole, has been neglected in the study of American literature." The genres are stories, poems, and plays by ethnic-minority writers classified as "Oriental," "Jewish American," "Hispanic American," "Indian American," "Negro American," "European," and "Near-Eastern" according to the table of contents. Dr. Nick Aaron Ford (1971) suggests that the poems in standard English by Paul Laurence Dunbar "deserve the right to be judged on their merit as the work of any other English speaking poet is judged, without condescension" (p. 44).

The honored Native American writer Natachee Scott Momaday has edited an anthology of works by *American Indian Authors* (1972). With the claim that "Indians contribution to American literature as a whole has been unique", and thus this volume and others like *American Indian Prose and Poetry* (Astrov, 1962), should be seriously critiqued and integrated into the mainstream curriculum.

Rhetoric: Ancient and Modern

A concise Aristotelian definition of rhetoric is defined as the art of *both* written and spoken discourse. As a visiting professor at Calvin College teaching advanced rhetoric with an ancient, classical base of schemes, tropes, Socratic apology, and Aristotelian logic; I attempted to multiculturalize this course—not thoroughly, perhaps super-ficially—but I took at least a small step toward eliminating ethnocentrism. My creative effort toward this objective, for example, was reflected in examination questions comparing the canons of classical rhetoric explicit in "Socrates Apology" with those that may be identified in the persuasive discourses of Dr. Martin Luther King, Jr., or to identify and discuss aspects of Aristotelean logic implicit or explicit in Malcolm X's discourses as an active modern African-American rhetorician during the 1960's.

Among one of the written papers and class presentations I required was a cross-cultural field study involving dialogue with two or three different non-white persons or groups with distinctive cultural characteristics. Similar multi-ethnic and cross-cultural references, examples, and assignments were also appropriately and topically distributed throughout my basic level oral and written courses.

In all of my cross-cultural curricular endeavors, I have tried to prepare my students to avoid "dangerous communication blunders"[1] by citing and discussing principles, examples, suggestions or recommendations articulated in such references as follows:

(1) *Transracial Communication* (Smith, 1973)
(2) *Interracial Communication* (Rich, 1974)
(3) *Understanding Intercultural Communication* (Samovar, Porter, and Jain, 1981)
(4) *Communicating With Strangers* (Gudykunst and Kim, 1984).

Based upon numerous studies, this latter reference is the most comprehensive discussion. In particular, there is an excellent review of the "functions and dysfunctions of ethnocentrism."

From these four textbooks and others like them, one may define, extract, and apply fundamentals of cross-cultural communication such as "active listening," "honesty," "availability," "a climate of trust," "a willingness to share," and *"linguistic regularity."* Linguistic regularity as described by Smith (1973) is characterized by frequency of conversation: that is, "the more times persons of different racial or ethnic backgrounds spend in communication with each other, the less difficulty each has in unaffected perception of the other" (p. 57).

Christian Missions

For decades evangelical colleges have emphasized missions in their chapel assemblies, classrooms, and curricula. As a student in a Bible school in Lancaster, Pennsylvania and in an evangelical liberal arts college in Houghton, New York, I listened to numerous missionaries, attended numerous missionary conferences, and had to take a course in the History of Missions. Later, as a faculty member in five different evangelical colleges, I again listened to missionary testimonies, reports, and appeals. Now as a retired professor, I recall that in all of those contexts and curricula, ethnocentrism prevailed. My recollections of this perennial condition was so dramatically disturbed by my discovery of significant minority contributions or achievements that I wrote the following essay for personal relief.

The Myth of the "Dark Continent"

When I was a teenager and high schooler, I thought of Africa as a jungle of naked and half-naked spear-throwing head hunters and cannibals. I knew nothing of the great kings of Africa[2] such as Hannibal born 247 B.C. who became one of the greatest generals of all time and led Carthage to great prosperity and prestige. I knew nothing of King Mansa KanKan Mussa of 1312 A.D. (1312-1337) who as a scholar gained the respect of scholars and traders throughout Europe. And I knew nothing of Affonso I, King of the Kongo (1506 - 1540 A.D.) who encouraged his people to adopt Christianity, established one of the most modern school systems in Black Africa, and later became one of the first Black rulers to resist the slave trade.

Lerone Bennett, who is the senior editor of *Ebony* and author of *Before the Mayflower* (1984), reports that "a series of revolutionary discoveries have spurred a radical re-evaluation of African men and women from whose loins sprang one out of every ten Americans". And thus, "Africa, long considered the

Dark Continent, is now regarded as the placed where mankind first received light!" (p. 3).

Beyond the rather secular findings reported in the preceeding testimony, I discovered more pertinent information for ethnically integrating the curriculum of Christian missions. Trulson (1977) reports that "the earliest American missionary was a Black man" and "that the foundation of Methodist missionary work was laid by a Negro preacher to the American Indians." An additional reference regarding the study of missions from a non-white perspective is a book titled *Lott Carey* (Fitts, 1978), as a documented history with a "Selected Bibliography." It purports to "provide substantial information regarding the growth and development of the Christian mission enterprise." Its design is "to aid students, pastors, missionaries and the general reader in an appraisal of the role of Black Americans in the world wide advance of Christian missions" (p. 5). Finally, this book reports the advance of the Lott Carey Baptist Foreign Missionary Convention not only into Africa, including South Africa, but also into Russia and India.

These two records of missionary achievements or activity and others like them from *other* ethnicities should be integrated and studied in the "History of Missions" course or in the discipline of missiology. Students should be encouraged or required to research and report such achievements for their own learning and that of the entire class or study group, even if no minorities are enrolled or present.

The Continual Use of Positive Ethnic Models

The continual use of positive ethnic models or examples and illustrations is presented in this concluding section of this chapter as both a recommendation and a strategy.

As a Recommendation

The concept of "models" in science and technology is suggested and promoted by the U.S. Department of Energy Office of Public Affairs (1979). The term "models" is described in the "Introduction" of its booklet which consists of twenty-four pictures with accompanying biographical sketches of African-American males and females. My persistence in advocating the *continual* use of *positive* models—hypothetical and real, token and thorough—is supported by the observation of Dr. Paul G. Hiebert (1983):

> That we face cultural pluralism when we go abroad is obvious. That we face it at home is becoming more and more apparent; for example more people of Mexican and Vietnames backgrounds live in Los Angeles than in any other city except Mexico City and Ho Chi Minh city respectively. (p. 8)

In addition to Dr. Heibert's observation, other current and historical reports continually remind us that the world in general and America in particular are *multi-ethnic* and *multicultural*. In fact, most of the peoples of the world are non-white. Therefore, logically and probably ethically our models or examples, curricula, methodologies, and even criteria of what is "good" esthetically should reflect *continually* and positively *something* of this ethnic and cultural pluralism.

As a Strategy

The *continual* use of these ethnic models or examples and illustrations in all disciplines becomes a *strategy* when (1) the models and illustrations are restricted to the *positive* ones and (2) they are *made hypothetical* in the absence of real or existential ones—even when no ethnic achiever or contributor can be found. The use of the hypothetical model or illustration may be similar to the use of the parable by Jesus, as reported repeatedly in the four Gospels.

The emphasis on the *positiveness* of the models and illustrations as a significant aspect of the strategy is justified as a means of combating negative stereotypes. Citing negative examples would reinforce existing prejudicial stereotypes. Gudykunst and Kim (1984) discuss and document in detail the "dysfunctions of ethnocentrism" or the misperceptions of members of out-groups maintenance of perjorative stereotypes.

Over the past several years, I have collected over a hundred examples of positive ethnic models. Whatever the discipline, one can probably find more of such positive models or examples from miscellaneous sources ranging from newspaper reports to authentic histories of a field which point out the contributions of women and ethnic-minorities. The constant search for these models will in some fields, tax your time and creativity in applying them; nevertheless the current national and international pluralism and the present prevailing ethnocentrism should motivate academicians to pursue this necessary and urgent task relentlessly.

Of course, *students themselves* can *continually* try to incorporate ethnic-minority contributions into the mainstream of their collegiate majors by means of research papers, art projects, verbal presentations, musical and theatrical performances *whenever* and *however* they appropriately can. This suggestion is for all students, but especially applicable to those who will be the teachers and administrators of the future.

Reasons for the Continual Use of Positive Ethnic Models

Comparably compelling and practical are the following five reasons for the *continual* use of these models and examples taken from my article titled "Positive Ethnic Models" (Davis, 1984). My hope is that the following reasons will be stimulating and heuristic:

1. These models and illustrations can more realistically represent the constituency of our pluralistic and multicultural society and world.
2. They may be models or illustrations (concrete, abstract, historical, factual, or hypothetical) with which the ethnic-minorities can readily and intimately identify.
3. They may aid in refuting negative stereotyping and unsound generalizing. For example, a number of African-Americans sing opera at the Metropolitan Opera.
4. They may be motivating and enhancing of one's self image and/or ethnic pride or cultural heritage.
5. They may aid in changing one's prejudicial and ethnocentric attitude and behavior in accepting and appreciating others who are ethnically and culturally different.

An example of such a profound change resultant from a multicultural exposure and participation is the compelling testimony of the attitudinal and behavioral transformation of the late Malcolm X as a former militant ethnocentric and anti-white African-American. According to his *Autobiography* (1965), he attributed his change and "broadened ... scope" to his pilgrimage to "the Holy World" [Mecca] where he "experienced" and "witnessed" "brotherhood between all men of all nationalities and complexions" (p. 362). He further testified that "in two weeks in the Holy Land," he saw what he "never had seen in thirty-nine years in America" (p. 362).

Repeatedly Malcolm X reports his observations of manifestations of "true brotherhood" practiced "by people of all colors and races" (pp. 339-362). From his multi-ethnic observations, perceptions, and personal participation, he claimed that he was "forced to re-arrange much of [his] thought patterns previously held" (p. 340) and that his "attitude was changed by what [he] experienced and witnessed there" (p. 362). Most comprehensive of his "broadened" vision and phenomenal transformation is Malcolm X's admission that since he "learned the *truth* in Mecca," his "dearest friends" had come to include "all kinds — some Christians, Jews, Buddhists, Hindus, agnostics, and even atheists!. Some of my friends are moderates, conservatives, extremists—some are even Uncle Toms! My friends today are black, brown, red, yellow, and *white!*" (p. 375).

Conclusion

With a growing number of journal articles and books written on the subject (e.g. Columbo et al., 1989; Verberg, 1988), I in this chapter, do not presume to lecture my colleagues on the method of multi-culturalizing their respective curricula. Therefore, what I have endeavored to share are the sources and methods that I have found useful in immediately and longitudinally sensitizing most, if not all, of the collegiate curricula, ranging from missiology to science and technology.

Finally, for both students and professors regarding the objective of multiculturalizing the college curricula, I beseech you to join me in the operational practice and philosophy that however "simplistic" or "token," *"Something is better than nothing,"* and proverbially, "A journey of a thousand miles must begin with a single step."

References

Allen, H. (1985). Racial minorities and evangelical colleges: Thoughts and reflections of a minority social scientist. *Faculty Dialogue,* No. 4, 65-78.

Anonymous, (1979). *Racism in the curriculum at Messiah.* Unpublished manuscript by a student for a speech class at Messiah College in Grantham, PA.

Astrov. M. (1962). *American Indian prose and poetry.* New York: Capricorn Books.

Bennett, L. (1984). *Before The Mayflower,* 5th Edition. New York: Penguin Books.

Calvin College Minority Concerns Task Force, (1985). *The comprehensive plan.* Grand Rapids, MI: Calvin College.

Columbo, G., Cullen, R., & Lisle, B. (1989). *Rereading America: Cultural contexts for critical thinking and writing.* New York: St. Martins.

Davis, A. (1974). Ethnic integration: An appeal to evangelical liberal arts educators. *The Other Side,* Sept.-Oct., 19.

Davis, A. (1984). Positive Ethnic Models. Eastern Mennonite College and Seminary *Bulletin,* Spring, 11.

Driskell, D.C. (1976). *Two centuries of Black-American art.* New York: Alfred A. Knopf.

Eastman, A.M., et. al. (Eds.) (1970). *The Norton anthology of poetry.* New York: W.W. Norton and Company, Inc.

Faderman, L. & Bradshaw, B. (Eds.) (1969). *Speaking for ourselves: American ethnic writing.* Glenview, IL: Scott, Foresman and Company,

Fitts, L. (1978). *Lott Carey: First Black missionary to Africa.* Valley Forge, PA: Judson Press

Ford, N.A. (1971). *Black insights: Significant literature by Black-Americans 1760 to the Present.* Waltham, MA: Ginn And Company.

Goshen College *Catalog,* (1988-90). Goshen, Indiana.

Gross, B. (1985). Racism with a smile. *His,* February, 1-4.

Gudykunst, W.B. & Kim, Y.Y. (1984). *Communicating with strangers: An approach to intercultural communication.* New York: Random House.

Hiebert, P.G. (1983). Culture shock possible here. *Daily News-Record,* November 12.

Jenkins, C.A. (1987). Educating for equity: Challenges, choices, and changes. *Faculty Dialogue,* No. 9, 53-68.

Malcolm X with the assistance of Alex Haley (1965). *The Autobiography of Malcolm X.* New York: Grove Press, Inc.

Messiah College *Catalog,* LXX, 1988-1990. Grantham, Pennsylvania,

Momaday, N.S. (Ed.) (1972). *American Indian authors.* Boston: Houghton Mifflin Company.

Nash, G.B. (1974). *Red, white, and black: The peoples of early America.* Englewood Cliffs, NJ: Prentice-Hall, Inc.

Niklaus, R.L. (1981). Can Christian colleges mix with minorities? *Christianity Today,* November 6, 44-47.

Rich, A.L. (1974). *Interracial communication.* New York: Harper and Row.

Samovar, L.A., Porter, R.E., & Jain, N.C. (1981). *Understanding intercultural communication*. Belmont, CA: Wadsworth.

Saunders, D. (1985). History of all Americans emphasized. James Madison University *News*, February 14, 6.

Smith. A.L. (1973). *Transracial communication*. Englewood Cliffs, NJ: Prentice-Hall, Inc.

Trulson, R. (1977). The Black missionaries. *His*, June, 1.

Turner, D.T. (1970). The Afro-American college in American higher education. In N. Wright (Ed.), *What Black Educators Are Saying*. New York: Hawthorn Book, Inc.

U.S. Department of Energy Office of Public Affairs (1979). *Black Contributors To Science and Energy Technology*. Washington, D.C.

Verburg, C.J. (1988). *Ourselves among others: Cross-cultural readings for writers*. New York: St. Martins.

Williams, J. (1985). Support for desegregation declines. *The Washington Post*, January 19, A7.

Footnotes

1. Here is an anonymous list of 23 "dangerous communication blunders" that I have found useful:

1. Do you assume that it is *easy* to say what you really mean to say?
2. Do you assume that you don't have to be really *concerned* with saying it right?
3. Do you assume that if the *listener* misunderstands you, it is somehow his fault rather than your own?
4. Do you talk about yourself, your experiences, your ideas, every chance you get?
5. Do you become impatient or angry when others do not agree with you?
6. Do you say: "I don't know what it is—she has always been nice to me—but I just don't like her."
7. Do you say: I don't like him and I'll find a *reason* for it yet!"
8. Do you interrupt others and change the subject to one that interests you?
9. Do you argue instead of discussing differences of opinion?
10. Do you read or walk away while others talk to you?
11. Do you talk repeatedly about "the good old days"?
12. Do you monopolize the conversation?
13. Are you quick to contradict others?
14. Do you walk around with a chip on your shoulder and take every criticism as a personal affront?
15. Do you show you are suspicious of the motives of others?
16. Do you listen impatiently when someone tells you her opinion?
17. Do you show you feelings are hurt if you are asked to change something you have done?
18. Do you try to force your opinions on others?
19. Do you show that you are not interested in new ideas?
20. Do you give the kiss of death to the other person's idea?
21. Are you a cynic? an authority on all the reasons why a thing can't be done?
22. Do you forget that to *move* people in the right direction you must *touch* their feelings and *reach* their hearts?

23. Do you assume the words hold the same meaning for your hearers as they do for you?

2. "The Great Kings and Queens of Africa" is available from Anheuser-Busch, Inc., St. Louis, MO 63118.

Berea College:
A Commitment to
Interracial Education
within a Christian Context

Andrew Baskin

Founded in the turbulent years before the Civil War, Berea College in Kentucky is "dedicated to justice and racial equality." A non-denominational Christian institution, its purposes are stated in its Great Commitments. "Suggested...in the 1950's, formulated in 1962 and formally adopted as revised in 1969" (Self-Study, 1983-1984), these purposes are:

> To provide an educational opportunity primarily for students from Appalachia who have high ability but limited economic resources.
> To provide an education of high quality with a liberal arts foundation and outlook.
> To stimulate understanding of the Christian faith and to emphasize the Christian ethic and the motive of service to mankind.
> To demonstrate through the labor program that work, manual and mental, has dignity.

>   To promote ideals of brotherhood, equality, democracy, with particular emphasis on interracial education.
>
>   To maintain on our campus and to encourage in our students a way of life characterized by plain living, pride in labor well done, zest for learning, high personal standards, and concern for the welfare of others.
>
>   To serve the Southern Appalachian region primarily through education but also by other appropriate services (p. 1).

These commitments are the foundation of Berea College; its reasons for existence. Even though all Bereans presumably agree with these idealistic goals, the nagging question is how do you achieve them?

This essay will focus upon how Bereans have tried to achieve these commitments, especially the efforts to balance its commitment to interracial education with its commitment to Appalachia within a nondenominational Christian context. The major questions that Bereans have faced are: Should there be Black oriented courses and activities? Do these activities emphasize our differences as human beings instead of our similarities? How do these activities "stimulate understanding of the Christian faith and...emphasize the Christian ethic and the motive of service to mankind?" How many Black students and faculty and staff are necessary in order to achieve the commitment to interracial education? To ascertain the success of the Berea College community in answering these questions, one must review the history of the institution, a history of at least six distinct stages. In this essay I will review each stage and discuss the implementation of the interracial commitment of Berea College.

The First Stage: Black and White Together

Berea came into existence because of political and religious reasons. The political reasons were provided by a local political leader, Cassius Clay, who invited the religious leader, John G. Fee, to Madison County, Kentucky in order to establish an anti-slavery settlement (Ellis, Everman, and Sears, 1985, p. 105). The son of a slaveowner, Fee "called for immediate uncompensated emancipation of all slaves; he demanded that Christians refuse to commune with slaveholders because slavery itself was sinful--in fact, it was in John Wesley's words, 'the sum of all villainies.'" Besides organizing several anti-slavery churches, Fee also wanted "to have a good school here in central Kentucky, which would be to Kentucky what Oberlin is to Ohio, Anti-slavery, Anti-caste, Anti-rum, Anti-secret societies, Anti-sin." He felt that "we have here a very healthful county far more than Oberlin ever was. Why can we not have such a school here." Some would have probably replied to Fee's question by stating that the reason was obvious: Madison County was a slavery county. For example, in 1860 there were 1,881 slaveholding families who owned a total of 6,118 slaves. Notwithstanding this fact, Fee set out to build the school of his dreams in Madison County: one that was anti-caste, antisectarian, open to the poor, and encouraging manual labor.

Although Clay and Fee eventually parted company because of their differences over the gradual (Clay) or immediate (Fee) termination of slavery, they were still working towards a common goal of creating and building a college when a one-room school was built near the Fee homestead in 1855. By July, 1859 the first articles of incorporation for Berea College had been adopted, but because the leaders of the community were forced to leave the state of Kentucky in December 1859, the document was not recorded at the Madison County county seat of Richmond until 1866. The second by-law of the constitution declared that the college "shall be under an influence strictly Christian, and as such, opposed to sectarianism, slaveholding, caste, and every other wrong institution or practice" (Nelson, 1974). In a letter to Rev. J.A. Rogers, the first principal, Fee declared that "opposition to caste meant the co-education of the (so-called) 'races.'" A promotional leaflet asking for donations emphasized that the school was "open to all of good moral character" (Ellis, et al., 1985, p. 210). Thus, at this time Berea College was not set up to serve any specific area, group of people or denomination. As stated in the first bylaw: "The purpose of the Colllege shall be to furnish the facilities for a thorough education to all persons of good moral character (Peck & Smith, 1982, p. 13). To many, all persons of good moral character included Negroes.

Before the Civil War, in the winter of 1858-1859, a school organi-zation/club, the Dialectic Society, discussed long and earnestly the question of whether Negroes should be admitted to the school, if any applied (Hall & Heckman, 1980, p.331). According to President E. Henry Fairchild, the first president of Berea College, "the question was not embarrassed by legal considerations, for there was no law of Kentucky forbidding education to free colored persons, or even to a slave, with his master's consent." Because the leaders of the anti-slavery community of Berea were escorted out of the county for their radical beliefs, the definitive answer to the question had to wait until their return at the conclusion of the Civil War.

The first constitution recorded in 1866 did not mention that the different divisions of Berea College were supposed to serve any particular race or region; however, the first catalog in 1867 mentioned two groups of people: the recently emancipated Negroes and "the White people of eastern Kentucky and similar regions in adjoining states." Fee stated: "We had then no sufficient precedent to guide, and no theory to maintain, save that it is always safe to do right, follow Christ...The incorporation of the principle of impartial conduct to all, an institution for the public good, was to the founders of Berea College the only course [for] Christians..." (Nelson, 1974, p. 15). In his inaugural address, the first president, E. Henry Fairchild, stated: "We are aware that this feature of the school fails to meet the approbation of many of our fellow citizens," but he did not "doubt that in the end this characteristic...will be most highly approved and popular." He also stated "that Negroes are to have and ought to have, the same civil and political rights as white men, and the sooner and more thoroughly both classes adapt themselves to this idea, the better for all." On March 6, 1866, 43 white students were enrolled in the institution; 18 left when four black students enrolled at the school (Ellis, et al., 1985, p. 211).

Not only did the founders of Berea College integrate the student body, but they also integrated the board of trustees. One of the trustees in 1866 was former slave and soldier Rev. Gabriel Burdett, a friend of John G. Fee. Like Burdett, other Blacks followed Fee to the town of Berea from Camp Nelson, a Union camp located in Jessamine County, Kentucky. They followed Fee because "he had determined that Berea would be the place where black people could own property of their own. He did not wish to promote a system of racially segregated ownership, however, but insisted on a kind of 'interspersion,' with blacks and whites being interspersed about the country's side and in the town." He said, "friends of the colored man will...so arrange sale of lots as to have them in the community so as to have for them schools and churches. Someone may say 'let the colored man alone–let him find his own way'–why not then dispense with educational efforts for him? I do not propose to feed him but put an axe and land within his reach and let him work out his salvation–help him to a home."(Ellis, et al., 1985, p. 219)

As stated earlier, the goal was to educate Negroes and Whites in the same environment. In evaluating the success of efforts to achieve this goal, Fee stated, "Now there is a generation of men and women educated to the principles of justice & mercy of righteousness, who now stand firm against the tendencies of conservatism & Rebelism." To work, this scheme required integration on all levels, even interracial dating. Even though different interpretations have developed about its meaning, a 1872 Board of Trustees resolution did not prohibit social relations "between the races [as long as both parties were discrete]...under existing circumstances" (Burnside, 1986, p.12). Thus, in the first phase of the institution's history there may have not been any Black Studies courses, but there was a commitment to educating Blacks and Whites in the same environment. This commitment was rooted in the founding fathers belief that as Christians, they could do no less. It was a commitment that continued to exist during the two year tenure of the second president, Reverend William B. Stewart. In fact, if the composition of the student body can be used as a criterion for judging the success of this experiment, then Berea was extremely successful. For most years before 1892 there were more Black students than Whites enrolled at the school, although in the college division there were more White students. However, during the second stage of Berea's history, the story was different.

The Second Stage: A Change in Emphasis

The third president of Berea was William Goodell Frost, the grandson of the abolitionist William Goodell. "After his retirement...[Frost] wrote that he was not sure that he would ever have come to Berea 'if it had not been for [his] ancestral and personal interest in befriending the colored race'" (Peck & Smith, 1982, p. 68). However, soon after arriving at Berea, it was obvious that he had a different idea about the commitment to interracial education, or as it was known then—co-education of the races, the education of blacks and whites in the same environment. When he arrived in Kentucky from a faculty position at Oberlin College in Ohio, Frost found an institution in financial trouble. There was an "air of dilapidation about the place, the vacant rooms in the dormitories, and the empty seats in the classes and the Chapel." Many of the original donors to the school had died and the commitment to interracial education was not the commitment that interested many of their descendants; these new donors were more interested in the commitment to serving the Southern Appalachian region. Thus, Frost saw his task to be to find enough financial support in order to continue "the peculiar work of Berea." In a letter in 1892 Frost stated how he wanted to accomplish this objective:

> [a] By actually elevating to the level of cultured manhood as many members of the race [Negroes] as possible. But many other schools are doing this work. Berea's peculiar opportunity is, [b] to do this in connection with the education of white students, thus teaching the races to live and work together, and [c] to afford an object lesson to the whole country, making it possible for advocates of justice everywhere to say 'There is Berea with hundreds of white and colored students working together in friendly relations on the soil of slavery'...We must get more students, and especially more white students (Peck & Smith, 1982, p. 6).

To obtain more white students, Frost implemented a policy to base the racial composition of the student body upon the racial composition of the state of Kentucky. Thus, the student body was to be composed of six Whites students for every Black student. This goal was to be reached not by decreasing the number of Black students but by increasing the number of White students. (In 1884, there were 184 Black students out of a total enrollment of 354; in 1904, the total enrollment was 961 of which 157 were Black) Frost felt that his plan was consistent with the earlier actions of Fee and others. In a speech in 1895 Frost stated, "We have tried our simple plan for twenty-nine years, and the evil consequences have not come; and our way is the way of the Christian world at large." To Frost, a shift in emphasis did not mean that he was not committed to interracial education.

In 1907 Frost clearly admitted this shift in emphasis: "in my own time we frankly shifted emphasis, appealing more for the mountaineers" (Nelson, 1974, p. 25). In fairness to Frost, some observers believe that this shift began during the administration of President Fairchild who gave loving care to his Negro students, but paid an increasing measure of attention to the people of the hills (Peck & Smith, 1982, p. 66). By 1902, as Frost stated in his annual report, "this College now stands before the public as the representative school for the mountains, as Hampton and Tuskegee stands as the representative institutions for the colored people." In the opinion of one observer, this action was necessary because "the sons and daughters upon whom the curse of slavery weighed more heavily than on any other class, [was] the White Mountaineers of Kentucky...For this class neither the state and national governments, nor the benevolent societies of the United States had made provision" (Ellis, et al., 1985, p. 223). In 1911, a statement was added to Article II of the school's constitution recognizing the Southern mountain area as Berea's special field (Peck & Smith, 1982, p. 79).

Even though the effort to educate White mountaineers was motivated by his Christian beliefs, scholars and even his contemporaries, have disagreed about Frost's commitment to interracial education. Frost was interested "in breaking down caste", but expected his "colored students...[to] be of a superior quality." Segregation, not integration, was emphasized on campus. For example, one of his first official acts was to have the Board of Trustees rescind its resolution of 1872 pertaining to interracial dating on campus. Later, he remarked that students "did the proper thing" by separating themselves by race in their eating and living habits" (Nelson, 1974, p. 19). In regards to hiring a Black professor he stated, "A professorship is not the best place in which to demonstrate the powers of the Negro... We shall do [him] poor service...if for the sake of having colored professors we lose our chance to instruct mountain youth." He received support for this position from a member of the Board of Trustees, Rev. William E. Barton, who wrote:

> It is much for a Mountain boy to overcome generations of prejudices and meet colored people on a level; it is too much to expect that now they will not be deterred if a colored man, unless he be a giant in intellectual and moral

qualities, be set over them...Both as a matter of principle
and of expediency, it appears to me unwise to appoint at
this turn a colored professor. (Burnside, 1986, p. 22)

The viewpoint of one of the founding fathers was clear--Frost was
betraying the thoughts and actions of those founders. In 1899 John G.
Fee said,

Let me say that the unique work of Berea College is not
'effacing sectional lines'...and helping white people (the
contemporary ancestors in the southern mountains) [as
Frost had declared] but effacing the barbarous spirit of
caste between colored and white at home. Let the friends of
Berea College demand faithfulness to the original design
of the college....Much more is being done to bring in white
students than colored. This the colored know and feel....
(Nelson, 1974, p.23)

One "colored person" that agreed with Fee was J. S. Hathaway, a
Berea graduate who eventually became the principal at the State
College for Negroes for nine years [Kentucky State University]. In a
newspaper article Hathaway wrote,

The management is pursuing an interpretation of the
design and mission of Berea College in conformity with
the prevailing sentiment, and not the spirit and principles of the college...We believe President Frost is conscientious in his convictions; that he has the good of the
colored people at heart (from his standpoint of what is for
their good) but those convictions are based on false
conceptions of religious obligation (Nelson, 1974, p. 21).

On January 12, 1904, this discussion about the intent of President
Frost became a moot issue. On that day, Representative Carl Day (D) of
Breathitt County, a mountain county, introduced a bill in the
Kentucky House of Representatives which is commonly known as the
Day Law. The purpose of this legislation was to deal with Berea
College—an institution that Day called "a stench in the nostrils of all
good Kentuckians." The Day law made it "unlawful for any person,

corporation, or association of persons to maintain or operate any college, school, or institution where persons of the White and Negro races are both received as pupils for instruction" (Peck & Smith, 1982, p.51). Since there was only one college, school, or institution in the state that attempted to educate Blacks and Whites in the same environment, it was clear that this law applied specifically to Berea.

Initially, in reaction to the Day Law, Frost considered moving the school to Ohio or West Virginia. However, he was dissuaded from pursuing this option. But, the leaders of Berea did fight enactment of the law. Frost was in the forefront of this futile struggle. His rationale was simple: "Now it is my judgment that we ought to fight such a law to the very end. I do not see how we can possibly exist under it. Berea's foundation was laid and its chief endowment given by people who understood and approved our position." The fight ended on November 9, 1908 when the Supreme Court of the United States ruled that the Day law was constitutional. In its ruling the court stated:

> The right to teach white and Negro children in a private school at the time is not a property right. Besides, appellant Berea College as a corporation created by this State had no natural right to teach at all. Its right to teach is such as the State sees fit to give it. The State may withhold it altogether or qualify it (Peck & Smith, 1982, p. 53).

After the ruling by the court, the Board of Trustees decided that Berea would become an all-White institution. The Board also decided to use $200,000 of its endowment and to raise $200,000 in order to establish a school to educate Negroes. Located near Louisville, this institution was incorporated in 1910 as Lincoln Institute. Thus, with the court's ruling, the second phase of Berea's history came to an end. During its duration, the number of Black students had decreased from approximately 50% to 0. Granted, outside forces played a crucial role in this process, but in the opinion of many observers, President Frost was leading the school in the direction desired by these outside forces. The only difference was that his method would have taken longer. He was a Christian, but his Christianity was different from that of individuals like John G. Fee. Frost was primarily interested in the number of White students enrolled at the school. As he wrote in his 1895 report: "The people who contribute money to Berea rather than to

Hampton or Atlanta are interested in it as a mixed school, and measure its success by the number of white students." Thus, to these philanthropists a mixed school meant that the number of Black students had to match a realistic national proportion. They would accept a ratio of seven Whites to one Black, but not a one to one ratio. Seemingly, that was also how Frost measured the success of the institution.

Unfortunately, Frost went even farther than the Day Law required. He barred Negroes from the nondenominational Church of Christian Union, which was affiliated with the college, even though one of the founders was Black and was still alive. He also had the names of Black graduates stricken from the roles of the Alumni Association (Brown, 1989).

The Third Stage: An All-White Institution

The third phase of Berea's history was from 1908 to 1950. Because of the Day law, Berea in these years was an all-white institution dedicated to educating students from the Southern Appalachian region. However, the College did find ways to continue and enhance contact between the races, especially during the administration of William J. Hutchins, the College's fourth president, who annually scheduled one important Negro speaker or musical aggregation. For example, in 1934 Charlotte Hawkins Brown, President of Palmer Institute in North Carolina delivered a lecture at Berea. She informed the students that "the Negro did not want to be white," and did not desire intermarriage, because "slavery had produced a sufficient supply of mulattoes for their children's children if they want light-colored mates." (Berea College Archives).

In 1940, the fifth president, Francis Hutchins (William's son), initiated a series of interracial conferences and summer programs for Berea students to meet and to interact with Negro college students. This period of history concluded in 1950 when Jesse H. Lawrence, the only black representative in the General Assembly of Kentucky, introduced an amendment to the Day law " to allow the co-education of white and Negro students in public or private schools above the high school level provided the governing authorities of the institution, corporation, group or body so elect, and provided that an equal, complete and accredited course is not available at the Kentucky State College for Negroes" (Peck & Smith, 1982, p. 60). The amendment was approved and in the fall of 1950, Berea College re-opened its doors to Black students, an action which initiated the fourth phase of the school's history.

The Fourth Stage: The Return

This fourth phase lasted until 1967. During this era the most important commitment was still the one to Appalachia. For example, in 1950, the Board of Trustees empowered the administration "to admit such Negro students from within this mountain region whom it finds thoroughly qualified, coming completely within provisions of the Kentucky law, and whom in its judgment it appears we should serve" (Peck & Smith, 1982, p. 61). Thus, the Black students were suppose to possess the same characteristics as their White counterparts, that is, they had to be residents of the Southern Appalachian Mountains region. As a result, until the end of the 1960s, the number of Black students enrolled at Berea increased very slowly . In the opinion of Elisabeth Peck, the low number was caused by "the small number of Negroes resident in the southern mountains; the poorer educational opportunities for Negroes in elementary and secondary work; and Berea's policy of admitting Negro applicants most likely to do college work well."

Not withstanding the qualifiers of Peck, Berea was primarily an institution dedicated to educating White mountain students. To be successful, Black students would have to accept this fact and adjust accordingly. There would not be any Black oriented courses or activities. The Black students that would be the most successful would be those that did not openly exhibit any characteristics of their culture or heritage. As stated by Kenneth Stampp, they were to be Whites with Black masks. However, subsequent events were to force change upon the institution.

This change was initiated by Black students with the tacit support of some White members of the faculty and administration. On November 26, 1967, 18 Black students submitted a petition which stated: "We, the Black Students of Berea College, are in support of the initiation [sic] of a Negro History course in the academic curriculum on this campus." As any student of American History is aware, beginning in the late 1960s, Black students were no longer satisfied with being Black imitations of their White brothers and sisters, they wanted their own culture and heritage remembered and taught. The Black students at Berea College were no different. This change in attitude marked the end of the fourth phase of the school's history and the initiation of the fifth phase.

The Fifth Stage: The Black Revolution

In many ways, the fifth phase was the most difficult phase for the leaders of the college. First, there was the problem of the attitude of the White students. In January 1969, four students (two White and two Black) submitted the results of a survey in which they compared the racial attitudes of white students at Berea College to Allport's profile of the prejudicial person and the environment which is most likely to produce a prejudiced person. They concluded that the "typical" (White) Berea College student fit Allport's description of a prejudiced person (Blacks 1924-1970). Unfortunately, the students did not examine the attitudes of Black students to determine if they would have fit Allport's profile.

A second problem involved the Black students. Like their counterparts at other colleges and universitites, they had entered the Black Revolution. No longer were they Negroes; they were Black or Afro-American. They wore African clothing. Their hairstyles were natural. They wanted black dormitories or at least, all Black floors or suites. And, as stated above, they demanded the introduction of Black studies courses. In the Fall Term of 1968, Berea College responded to their demand or request by offering History 373, Negro History, for the first time. However, a problem existed – who was going to teach the course?

The individual selected for this task was Dr. Richard Drake, a member of the History department, who felt that he was "well-prepared in the field." However, the Black students wanted a Black person to teach the course, but not just any Black. This was also one of Drake's concerns. He wrote, "Many 'scholars'...have become sufficiently 'middle class'–Honky perhaps--that they've lost contact with the Black Student group" (Drake, April 26, 1968). In another letter, Drake wrote:

Ideally, perhaps, we should have hired a properly qualified Negro to teach the course–this was the request of the Black Students...But because of the nature of this whole matter, I'm the wrong color so far as many in this course will be concerned...In any event, it would not have been satisfactory for us to hire just any qualified Negro for such a course. The tendency today for white institutions to hire qualified Negroes just because they are academically qualified sometimes created, in our time at least, a situation wholly unacceptable to the needs and requests of the Black Students. Such a Negro, all too often, is a person who has accommodated himself to the white, middle-class structure, and is more out of touch with the modern Black Student than the concerned white liberal. I have found precisely this situation in my search for materials for this Negro History course. Out of necessity and with great fear and trembling, I have already committed myself to John Hope Franklin's *From Slavery to Freedom*. I have found my Negro students, rejecting Franklin's 'accommodating' bias. (July 26, 1968)

Despite the complaints of the Black students, in Drake's opinion, students, both Black and White, responded well to the course (Nov. 16, 1968).

Still, the Black students found other ways to express their concern. On November 7, 1968, approximately 50 students, predominately Black, walked out of a campus wide symposium. In the opinion of one of the students,

I feel that Berea College is not living up to its ideals of racial equality. Most of my fellow white students are not getting an interracial education because of the small number of blacks that they come in contact with. People cannot understand other people if they are not exposed to their thoughts and ideas. This is shown best by the fact that only six percent of the student body is black, there are no black instructors, no blacks in the administration, and very few black chapel speakers. Improvements in these areas would aid greatly in the broadening the perspective

of both black and white students--particularly white
(*Citizen,* Nov. 14, 1968).

This action was perceived in different ways. Dr. Drake saw the
walkout as "skillfully run, and in the best of taste really." Dr. Louis
Smith, Dean of Berea College, stated, "I think it was in very poor taste.
We have been trying and will continue to try to find qualified Negro
teachers. The Negro teachers that we have written seem to feel that they
can be of more value to their race by teaching in all-Negro schools." He
also expressed the belief that the college's "first commitment is to the
underprivileged youth of the Appalachian Mountains and this is the
main reason for the small percentage of Negro students." (*Citizen,* Nov.
14, 1968)

Thus, during the fifth phase of Berea's history, the college offered its
first Black Studies course, an action that was caused by pressure
initiated by Black students. However, in the opinion of Drake, the
History department was glad to respond to this pressure "because most
of us feel that Negro history is a legitimate field—in part created by a
Berea graduate, Carter G. Woodson–and partly too because of Berea's
commitment to bi-racial education" (Drake, July 26, 1968). Notwithstanding this fact, Black students were not satisfied. They also wanted
Black faculty, not only to serve as role models, but also to help educate
the "typical" White students, a group that fit Allport's description of a
prejudiced people. Ironically, within three years of hiring its first
Black administrator, Berea College faced its worst racial incident in its
entire history.

Before obtaining the services of a Black American on a full-time
basis, the College arranged for an individual to teach on a part-time
basis, Dr. Joseph Taylor, a member of the Sociology Department at
Indiana University-Indianapolis. Arranged by Drake to provide
assistance in the Negro History course, this individual scheduled
three two-day visits. (Eventually, he became a member of the Board of
Trustees.) In addition, a committee composed of students and faculty
known as the Negro Studies Committee was formed in 1968. Its task
was to examine the curriculum and to suggest ways to examine the
racial issue in America. The members of the committee reached
agreement on the following basic principles as a guide for its work:

A. As a nation, as Christian, as a college, we face a crisis. We must begin with the recognition that this crisis arises, not from rioting and violence, but from the fact that God made of one blood and man has divided.

B. Berea's religious and educational commitments make it imperative that racism in all its forms be attacked by Christian witness and exposed by scientific analysis.

C. Whatever Berea is now doing in this regard is surely not sufficient for the time and the place.

D. Although problems are not solved by programs, neither are they solved without them. The importance of developing curricular and extracurricular programs must not be minimized nor their implementation disparaged simply because, by themselves, they do not fulfill Berea's commitment. (Report of the Negro Studies Committee, p. 2)

Besides the addition of relevant courses, the committee recommended that all General Education be re-examined to be sure that race and prejudice were receiving adequate attention, that College assemblies be utilized as important avenues of communication, that the Audio-Visual Services holdings of materials related to Negro Studies be examined and expanded and that library materials should be adequate for general reading. Despite these and other recommendations, the Black students did not trust the committee because of its composition (see the Black Consultants Folder). As a result, the institution hired a consultant to visit Berea and to evaluate its efforts to achieve its commitment to interracial education.

The consultant was Ralph J. Bryson, the Chairperson of English at Alabama State University. In many ways, his recommendations were similar to those of the Negro Studies Committee. For example, he recommended the addition of Black Studies courses, the integration of Black Studies in the present course offerings, a concerted effort to recruit Black faculty and more extracurricular activities geared to the interests of Black students. One new recommendation was the establishment of a chair in honor of Carter G. Woodson, the Father of

Negro History who was an alumnus of Berea College (Black Consultants Folder).

Despite the recommendations of the committee and Dr. Bryson, at the beginning of the 1969 Fall Term no one could have predicted the problem that would confront the leaders of Berea College in December of 1971. In 1969 the Admissions Office initiated an aggressive admissions effort to recruit more Black students. The success of the initiative was mainly because of the efforts of "a young black admissions counselor." During the 1968-69 academic year, 70 Black Americans were enrolled at Berea; in 1969-70, this total increased to 120 (Black Consultants Folder). Another new face for the 1969-70 school year was "a young black counselor in the advising office," the individual around whom the incident in 1971 would revolve. However, the first major incident occurred on March 3, 1970.

On that night three Black students were harassed by some of the local citizens, a common happening in Berea at that time. Not only did the White students at the college have to adjust to more Black students, but the local White citizens had to make the same adjustment. (Berea was no longer the integrated city or town of John G. Fee which was the most integrated town or city in Kentucky in 1900, it had become a segregated community. In fact, the local Blacks lived in four distinct Black communities on the out-skirts of the town.) Instead of arresting the local citizens for harassing the students, the police arrested the three Black students for carrying a concealed weapon, "a big stick." The next day, the Black students staged a sit-in in Lincoln Hall, the administration building, in particular, the President's Office (Blacks 1924-1970). Eventually, the charges were dropped against the students by the local authorities. Despite the seriousness of this incident, the one that would shake the foundations of the college would occur in December of 1971.

The president of Berea College who was forced to deal with this controversy was Willis D. Weatherford, the sixth individual to occupy that office. Because his father had been a member of the Berea College Board of Trustees for nearly five decades, there was no doubt that Dr. Weatherford was familiar with the history of the institution when he assumed the position in 1967. As can be quickly surmised from the information mentioned above, one of the problems he would encounter during his early years as president was the protest of Black students for more Black students, courses, and faculty. Also, as mentioned previously, by 1970, the college was attempting to fulfill the demands. There were at least five courses on "the books which might be called Black Studies" courses (Blacks 1924-1970). The number of Black students had increased. There were at least two Blacks on the professional staff. However, there was one deficiency--no full-time Black faculty. This situation changed in the Fall Term of 1971.

For that term, the institution hired two Black faculty members and a Black campus minister. The faculty were in History and Spanish. Thus, some could and would argue that trouble occurred when the racial climate should have been at its best. Unfortunately, despite this viewpoint, trouble did occur.

The immediate cause of the trouble was when the Black counselor hired in 1969 was informed that he would not be re-hired after the conclusion of the 1971-72 academic year. The reason given was "that the students of the college had lost confidence in his performance of duties as a counselor." Another factor in the disturbance was, in the opinion of the counselor, "when a white male student who had written a letter 'full of lies about me' and 'pulled out and flourished' a switchblade knife in [my] presence" (*Citizen,* Dec. 16, 1971). Rumors about "a firearms arsenal of undefined size in some of the male dormitories, and [that] there was an undercurrent of comment that white students and black were preparing for impending trouble" (*Citizen*, Dec. 16, 1971) circulated throughout the campus. A disturbance in a female dormitory resulted in a number of faculty and security officers having to restore order. On Monday, December 13, a number of Black students occupied the administration building. They brought with them eight demands which were presented to President Weatherford. These demands included: reversal of the decision about the termination of the counselor; a dismissal of specific members of the faculty and staff "because of their overt racist acts"; a search for weapons; and refuge in the administration building for protection and security until the situation was rectified (*Citizen*, Dec. 16, 1971).

The immediate reaction of the administration was to close school early for the Christmas vacation. All students were urged to leave campus by 5 p.m. on Tuesday, December 14. Dr. Weatherford felt that "it [had] become evident that an academically profitable examination week, [was] not feasible." He hoped that "closing one week earlier [would] allow passions to cool over vacation...and the ideal of brotherhood [would] be reasserted in the new year in this college" (*Citizen*, Dec. 16, 1971).

When classes resumed in January, there was outward calm. During the break, the counselor had reached an agreement with the college to go on terminal leave until June 30, 1972. He and his family left Berea. On campus, the faculty created a project called Operation Zebra. Its purpose was to "welcome the students back to campus in an atmosphere of friendship and reconciliation" (*Citizen*, Jan. 6, 1972). The restoration of this outward calm brought to a close the fifth and shortest period of the history of Berea College.

Even though the fifth stage may have been the shortest period of the college's history, it was one of the most traumatic for those affiliated with Berea. During this period, Black students were no longer satisfied with the status quo. They wanted more Black students enrolled at the school. They wanted Black Studies courses. And, they wanted these courses to be taught by Black faculty. Of course, these demands were being made at other institutions of higher learning in the United States, so what occurred at Berea was not unique. However, this offered little comfort to Bereans; many thought that the school's history would insulate it from the Black Revolution.

As has been stated earlier, this history included opening the doors of Berea to all races despite personal attacks against individuals like John G. Fee. It included having a Black person on the Board of Trustees until 1914, ten years after the Day Law was ruled to be constitutional. It included re-opening the doors of Berea College to Black students before the rest of the nation had to experience the marches and demonstrations of the Civil Rights Movement. It included having Black speakers and students from historically Black schools at Berea before the Day Law was amended so that White Berea students could have an opportunity to interact with their darker skinned brothers and sisters. All of these actions were initiated because Bereans believed that this was their Christian duty. Thus, why was this period so chaotic?

The answer can be found in the Berea College Self-Study, 1973-74. A questionnaire was sent to students and staff members. They were asked to respond to the following question:

> To what degree do you think that special programs and acitvities such as the Black Students Union, the Black

Ensemble, convocations, Black Studies courses, and certain aspects of Issues and Values, of Religious and Historical Perspectives, and of other courses fulfill our [interracial] commitment?

The responses are summarized below:

	excellent or good	fair	poor or unsatisfactory
Staff	31.3%	42.8%	25.9%
Students	19.3%	31.7%	46.0%

Comments to this question fell into two categories: "those which recognize the need for self-identity among blacks, and those which recognize the shortcomings of attempts to program such identity" (Self-Study, 1973-74. p. 302). Both groups, students and staff, supported the interracial commitment, but the issue was whether or not Black-oriented activities were "divisive" and "aggressive." Added to this scenario was "a decided dislike for Appalachia and for white Appalachians" by Black students. As a result, although Berea College was a Christian college, it was a divided community. There were two major schools of thoughts. "One school emphasize[d] frank discussions in which racism may be confronted and either eradicated or ameliorated. The other school--placing a high value on toleration, decency, and courtesy--believe[d] the less said about racial problems the better." The fifth stage had been so chaotic because it was a transitional era from the fourth stage in which the latter school of thought controlled to the sixth and present stage, in which the former school of thought has probably gained the advantage in a difficult and continuing struggle.

The Sixth Stage: A New Direction

In the Fall Term of the 1970-71 academic year, a new curriculum was implemented at Berea. Two areas dealt specifically with the interracial commitment. First, a new course entitled Issues and Values was added to the General Education curriculum. This course was,

> ...designed to bring all freshmen in contact with current issues, the Christian commitment and the role of values; to encourage freedom of expression and to work toward ease and competence in oral and written communication; to provide close contact with a faculty member. Black America and Appalachia will be two of the continuing issues. (Folder of Curriculum Committee, 1969, p. 5).

By incorporating this course into the curriculum, the leaders of Berea College were insuring that all graduates of the institution were exposed to the Christian, Appalachian, and interracial commitments from an academic perspective. Unfortunately, for a variety of reasons, this course was replaced in the curriculum by a course known as Freshman Seminar in the Fall of 1982. This course is designed to: "involve [all freshmen] in a critical study of the topic Freedom and Justice as it relates to the commitments of Berea College, to Appalachia, the Christian faith, the kinship of all people, or the dignity of labor [Berea College Catalog, 1987-1989]. This is viewed as an unfortunate change by this observer because no longer are all students exposed to knowledge about the Black experience. Each section of the course deals with only two of the Great Commitments; a decision made by the specific faculty member. Presently, less than fifty percent of the sections deal with the interracial commitment.

Another change implemented in 1970 was, the creation of a cultural area requirement. It is "a requirement structured to acknowledge the plurality of cultures and our need to understand them, and to help us meet our commitment to the brotherhood of man" (Folder of Curriculum Committee, 1969). This requirement could be fulfilled by successfully completing three levels of foreign language or two cultural area courses in either Black or Appalachian culture and one in non-Western culture. In the summer of 1987 a study was initiated to determine how students were fulfilling the requirement, especially the option dealing with either Black or Appalachian culture. The study revealed that the overwhelming majority of the students were choosing to avoid the Black Studies course and enrolling in an Appalachian Studies course. (Racism was probably one of the reasons, but it was not the only reason that students, both Black and White, were avoiding Black Studies courses; the perceived difficulty of certain teachers was also a factor). In 1988 the faculty approved a change, effective in the Fall of 1988, that students not choosing the foreign language option would have to complete a Black studies course, an Appalachian Studies course, and a non-Western course. One result of this change will be to increase the number of students exposed to information about the Black experience. Another result should be to decrease the tension between the commitments to Appalachia and to interracial education. In the 1983-84 Self-Study, the faculty and staff respondents to a questionnaire mentioned this tension the most often when they noted a conflict among the Great Commitments. This change will not cause the tension to disappear, but it will reduce the competition for students among the faculty that teach Appalachian or Black Studies courses.

The number of Black Americans enrolled at Berea College has fluctuated from a high of 152 in 1973 to a low of 88 in 1974. On a percentage basis, the low was in 1982 when there were 89 Black American students who composed only 5.6% of the student body. The total college enrollment was 1,403 in 1974 and 1,588 in 1982. In 1985 the seventh president of the institution, Dr. John Stephenson, appointed a committee composed of all segments of the college community to evaluate Berea College and to offer suggestions to him in order to prepare Berea for the 21th century. One area that was examined was the student of the future. One suggestion offered by the committee, and accepted by the president, concerned the number of Black American students enrolled at Berea College. Now, the institution is committed to enrolling and retaining a number of qualified Black American students by 1992 which is between 15 to 25% of the college's total enrollment. (Long Range Planning Document, 1987). Without a doubt, if this goal is achieved, many will argue that it will result in some traumatic changes at Berea; however, some would argue that the most traumatic change occurred in 1983 when the Black Cultural Center and Interracial Education Program came into existence.

The process which led to the creation of this office began in September 1979 when Department of Health, Education and Welfare (HEW) audit team visited the campus. Despite the positive news from HEW that "In terms of providing the spirit, financing, facilities, etc., equally and supportively," the institution was making great strides, the leaders of Berea College were aware that even though "Berea attracts people who generally share the College's stated objectives it is still a microcosm of American society. Prejudice and misunderstanding probably exist in proportions not too different from those which would be found in most other communities" (Report on Interracial Education, p. 14). As a result the Board of Trustees Educational Policies Committee requested that the administration report "on the health and development of interracial education program and resources needed for program enrichment and for recruitment of Black faculty, administrators, and students." The first step taken by the administration was to write a report based upon information gathered "by a limited number of College administrators". This report mentioned and discussed the curriculum, the efforts to recruit more Black American students, efforts to recruit Black faculty and staff, and extracurricular activities. It was in this last area that the administrators believed that presented "some of our greatest challenges to our commitment to interracial education", possibly because it was the area of the greatest choice. As stated in the report: "Here, we become aware that while one can schedule, program, and promote interracial experiences one neither can (nor really desires to) command that individuals share in these experiences. Indeed at some point we must recognize and respect each group's desire (and need) to share the familiar with those who are most comfortable." (Report on Interracial Education, p. 10). In spite of the validity of the last statement, the task was clear--what programs should exist at Berea College in order to attempt to reduce the amount of prejudice and misunderstanding and respond to the challenge?

In November 1979, President Weatherford appointed a committee of eleven individuals, which included all five Black members of the faculty and staff, to develop answers for this question. The mandate of this committee was "to develop a recommendation on steps the college should take in its interracial program to more effectively carry out the commitment to equality and brotherhood (Weatherford, Nov. 30, 1979). The committee's final report was presented to the Board of

Trustees in April 1980. Many of its recommendations were similar to those offered by other committees which had studied the issue. However, there seems to have been one major difference–its definition of interracial education.

Throughout its deliberations, the committee drew a distinction between interracial education as opposed to multi-cultural education. To the majority of the committee, "the goal of multi-cultural education with special emphasis on Black and Appalachian cultures should replace that which is often perceived to be the more limited emphasis on interracial education" (Report of the Committee on Interracial Education, p. 1). To these members of the committee,

> ...the goal of multi-cultural education is intended to emphasize the importance of all people developing an understanding and respect for diversity. An emphasis on culture should replace the limited concentration at Berea on racial issues...Most importantly, the recognition of cultural diversities can lead people to understand that the objective of education is not to assimilate Blacks and Appalachians into the dominant values of American society, but to permit all persons to grow and develop through an enhanced understanding of both their own heritage and the heritage of others (Report of the Committee on Interracial Education, p. 9).

Based on this rationale, the committee recommended the college "establish a Black Studies Center with staffing and responsibilities comparable to the Appalachian Studies Center (created in 1970). The purpose of this Center would be "to stimulate and coordinate course offerings on Afro-American culture in various departments, to encourage off-campus programs and experience for students which will serve to enhance the understanding of Black culture, and to develop institutional relationships with other organizations which share the Berea commitment to racial equality and multi-cultural understanding." (Report of the Committee on Interracial Education, p. 9).

As previously stated, this recommendation led to the creation of the Black Cultural Center and Interracial Education Program in July 1983. To ascertain why there was a four year time period between the creation of the position and the recommendation, one need look no further than the title for the answer, an issue which has constantly plagued the Berea College community and was mentioned earlier in this essay. Does self-identity for Blacks divide the races? The two schools of thought gave two different answers. One school placed emphasis on frank discussions about racism while the other school felt the less said about racism, the better. Eventually, they decided to compromise. This explains the long, "cumbersome and confusing" title of the Black Cultural Center and Interracial Education Program.

While the center does serve as a source of renewal and cultural affirmation for Blacks, its larger purpose is to build common bonds among the races and focus attention on the issues of integration and equality in the college community and the world at large. It has the following objectives:

> To promote interracial and multicultural understanding on campus and in our area with special emphasis on black/white relationships;
> To emphasize the equality of all persons and to stress our common bonds;
> To stimulate academic departments to include an Afro-American studies emphasis in their programs, and;
> To provide or to stimulate through other departments programs and cultural events on various ethnic perspectives with emphasis on the black experience. (Black Cultural Center and Interracial Education Program Brochure).

Lofty goals, but the institution was founded by individuals who had lofty goals. In many ways, the Black Cultural Center and Interracial Education Program is only a continuation of their efforts.

Conclusion

As the preceding review indicates, since its founding, the members of Berea College have been involved in a struggle for control of the soul of the institution. This struggle revolves around not whether there should be certain commitments, but instead the controversy involves what specific actions are necessary to achieve or implement the commitments. As stated by the respondents for the 1983-1984 Self-Study, usually when a conflict is perceived to exist, it centers around the commitments to serve Appalachians and to interracial education (p. 11). This conflict existed in the nineteenth century. It exists in the twentieth century. And unfortunately, it will probably exist in the twentieth-first century. The rationale for this opinion is tragic, but simple.

Although they are members of the same community, like all human beings, all Bereans do not have the same perspective. Few have been able to do as former President Weatherford did. That is, they have not been able to focus upon the unity of the Great Commitments. In the 1983-84 Self-Study, he stated:

> The Appalachian and interracial commitments both represent service to groups of special need. The interracial commitment grows out of Christ's view of all persons as children of God. Liberal learning and learning through work experience are complementary avenues of educating the whole person. Liberal learning affirms the importance of values for noble living and Christian education gives direction to the search for values but, as practiced at Berea, leaves freedom for rational inquiry. (p. 15).

Even though they may disagree about implementation and see only the tension between the Great Commitments instead of the unity mentioned by Weatherford, Bereans know that their institution and its history are unique. As stated in the 1983-1984 Self-Study,

> The College's past stands as a moral assignment to the present, and no generation of Bereans has ignored it. The Great Commitments unite past objectives into a whole and establish goals for the future. (p. 5-6).

This moral assignment means during the sixth stage of the College's history that there will be Black oriented courses and activities and efforts to recruit and retain, at a minimum, a specific number of Black students and faculty. The task is to insure that this emphasis on diversity does not deter from efforts to learn about our similarities as human beings. Maybe the members of the Berea College community will be able to accomplish this task. For those who doubt that this goal can be achieved, they should remember the history of the institution, especially the first stage when John G. Fee could not be dissuaded. Thus, in the opinion of this observer, based upon the history of Berea College, it is possible to balance a commitment to Appalachia with a commitment to interracial education within a Christian context. However, the history also reveals that there must be committed dedicated leadership in order to accomplish this lofty goal. This leadership will determine the future direction of the institution. This is the lesson individuals affiliated with other insitutions that are beginning to incorporate sensitivities and mission statements towards cultural and ethnic diversity and integration should learn from the Berea story. Not only must the administration and faculty be committed to their particular disciplines, but they also must be committed to the mission of the institution. Without this commitment, the efforts to achieve cultural and ethnic diversity and integration will be doomed to failure.

References

Secondary Sources

Burnside, J., (1986). Suspicion versus faith: Negro criticisms of Berea College in the Nineteenth Century. In L. Jones (ed.) *Reshaping the image of Appalachia*. Berea, KY: Berea College Appalachian Center.

Ellis, W., Everman, H. & Sears, R., (1985). *Madison County: 200 years in retrospect*. Madison County Historical Society.

Hall, B. & Heckman, R., (1980). Berea's First Decade. *The Filson Club History Quarterly*, 42.

Nelson, D., (1974). Experiment in interracial education at Berea College. *Journal of Negro History, 59,* (1).

Peck, E. & Smith, E., (1982). *Berea's first 125 Years, 1855-1980*. Lexington, KY: The University Press of Kentucky.

Primary Sources

A *Berea Citizen*. Hutchins Library, Berea College. Microfilm. School Records available in the Berea College Archives

B. Berea College Catalog 1987-1989
Berea College Self-Study Report, 1973-1974
Berea College Self-Study Report, 1983-1984
Folder of Curriculum Committee, 1969
Long Range Planning Document, 1987
Report of the Negro Studies Committee
Blacks 1924-1970
Black Consultants Folder
Brochure of the Black Cultural Center and Interracial Education Program
Report on Interracial Education
Report of the Committee on Interracial Education
History and Political Sciences Department - Afro-American
Afro-American Studies Program

C. Personal Collections of Dr. and Mrs. Cleo Charles

D. Unpublished manuscript by Florence Brown, (1989).

About the Contributors

Henry L. Allen (Calvin College, Grand Rapids, MI 49546)

Henry Allen is currently Associate Professor of Sociology at Calvin College. He has degrees from Wheaton College (IL) and the University of Chicago. Dr. Allen's professional interests are in studying race relations, the sociology of work, and the sociology of education. He has pursued these interests by analyzing churches, Christian colleges, and other social institutions both theoretically and empirically.

Deborah Bainer (Ohio State University, Dept. of Education, Mansfield, OH 44906)

Deborah Bainer teachers professional teacher education at the Ohio State University Mansfield campus with an emphasis on multicultural instruction. She conducts student teacher seminars, develops field experience programs with public schools and supervises elementary and secondary student teachers in multicultural settings. Prior to teaching at Ohio state, Dr. Bainer chaired the Biola University Department of Education where she received a Faculty Research Grant for her work related to multicultural instruction.

Andrew Baskin (Berea College, Berea, KY 40404)

A native of Alcoa, Tennessee, Andrew Baskin has been the Director of the Black Cultural Center and Interracial Education Program at Berea College since 1983. He earned a B.A. degree in history from Berea and a M.A. degree in American history from Virginia Tech.

Michael J. Boivin (Spring Arbor College, Spring Arbor, MI 49283)

Michael J. Boivin is a Professor of Psychology at Spring Arbor College and Adjunct Research Investigator in Psychiatry at the University of Michigan. He has a M.A. and Ph.D. degree in Experimental Analysis of Behavior from the Psychology Department of Western Michigan University. Dr. Boivin has taught psychology courses in the Spring Arbor College program for inmates at the State Prison of Southern Michigan since 1979. His present research interests are in neuropsychology and the evaluation of brain/behavior relationships. He resides in Jackson, Michigan, along with his wife, Grace, and four children.

Harold W. Darling (Spring Arbor College, Spring Arbor, MI 49283)

Harold Darling has completed thirty-five years of teaching at Spring Arbor. His Ph.D. is in Educational Guidance and Counseling from Purdue University, earned in 1958. Dr. Darling's special areas of interest are counseling and the integration of psychology and Christianity.

Abraham Davis Jr. (713 North 8th Street, Philadelphia, PA 19123)

A Christian African-American, Dr. Davis is a practicing rhetorician and dramatic oral interpreter of prose and poetry, with special interest in that of African-Americans and American Indians. He has taught college courses in classic and modern rhetoric, English composition, cross-cultural communication, and oral interpretation. Dr. Davis commenced at South Carolina State College for "Negroes" in 1956 and retired in 1988 after teaching at Indiana University and in several Christian liberal arts colleges including Houghton, Asbury, Messiah, Eastern Mennonite, and Calvin.

Carol Jenkins (Biola University, La Mirada, CA 90639)

Carol Jenkins teaches sociology at Biola University. Although most of her research is in the area of rural ethnicity and family farm issues, she has a long-standing interest in mentoring Anglo faculty in understanding the dynamics of the multicultural classroom. She has served Biola as Chair of the University Ethnic Concerns Committee, Chair of the University Task Force on Faculty Development, and presented professional papers concerning issues confronting the multicultural classroom. Dr. Jenkins recently received a Faculty Research Grant to continue her work concerning issues related to minorities in American society.

Donald N. Larson (Route 2, Box 134S, Osceola, WI 54020)

Donald N. Larson is currently senior consultant for cross-cultural learning at Link Care Center, Fresno, CA, consultant on language and cultural learning for the Foreign Mission Board of the Southern Baptist Convention, and scholar-in-residence, Bethel College, St. Paul, MN. He is author of *Guidelines for Barefoot Language Learning* and co-author with Dr. William A. Smalley, of *Becoming Bilingual: A Guide to Language Learning*. He is editor of *Barefootnotes* and author of a variety of other publications. He was the first director of the Interchurch Language School (now Christian Language Study Center) in Manila, Philippines, linguist-in-residence at the Union Language School, Bangkok, Thailand, and has played a variety of roles in the development of language schools in Indonesia and Bangladesh. Dr. Larson is a member of the Evangelical Free Church of America and taught Greek and linguistics at their college (Trinity College, Deerfield, IL) for twelve years, after graduation from Wheaton in 1949. His M.A. and Ph.D. are in linguistics from the University of Chicago.

D. John Lee (Calvin College, Grand Rapids, MI 49546)

D. John Lee was born in Vancouver, British Columbia, a third generation Chinese-Canadian. He attended a Swedish-Canadian Evangelical Free Church and received an A.A. degree from its Canadian college, Trinity Western. After completing his B.A. at the University of British Columbia, he did a M.S. degree in Counseling Psychology at Western Washington University. His Ph.D. is in cognitive psychology from Kansas State University. Dr. Lee taught psychology and social work at Tabor College, a German-Russian-American Mennonite Brethren college and is currently working among the Dutch-American Christian Reformed at Calvin College.

Alvaro L. Nieves (Wheaton College, Wheaton, IL 60187)

Alvaro Nieves is currently chairman of the Department of Sociology and Anthropology at Wheaton College (IL). He is active in teaching in the areas of statistics and race and ethnic relations. As an organizational social psychologist, he has been particularly interested in the issues of racial and ethnic diversity in higher education, church, and para-church organizations. As such Dr. Nieves has served as a consultant and frequent speaker to such groups. In addition, he has broadly addressed social justice issues and continues to speak out in appropriate forums.

Kenneth Polite (Biola University, La Mirada, CA 90639)

Kenneth Polite is an Associate Professor and Director of Clinical Training at the Rosemead School of Psychology. A licensed psychologist, Dr. Polite has been active in issues dealing with psychology as a profession.

Rodger R. Rice (Calvin College, Grand Rapids, MI 49546)
After eight years in academic administration at Calvin College, Rodger Rice returns to the Sociology and Social Work department where he will serve as Director of the Social Research Center. He chaired the task force that wrote the master plan for Calvin College's becoming genuinely multicultural and has administered its implementation for five years. Dr. Rice earned the Ph.D. is sociology from Michigan State University and has taught and conducted research in sociology and demography at Calvin and the University of Southern California.

Tony M. Wong (Biola University, La Mirada, CA 90639)
Tony M. Wong is an Associate Professor at the Rosemead School of Psychology, Biola University. A second-generation Chinese-American, he is also a licensed psychologist and has a part-time practice in clinical neuropsychology.

Author Index